AF575219

Hagiography
and Modern Russian
Literature

MARGARET ZIOLKOWSKI

Hagiography and Modern Russian Literature

PRINCETON UNIVERSITY PRESS

Published by Princeton University Press, 41 William Street,
Princeton, New Jersey 08540
In the United Kingdom: Princeton University Press, Guildford, Surrey

Library of Congress Cataloging in Publication Data will be
found on the last printed page of this book

ISBN 0-691-06737-6

Publication of this book has been aided by a grant
from The Andrew W. Mellon Foundation

Acknowledgment is made to the American Association of Teachers of Slavic and East European Languages for permission to reproduce Chapter Two, "Hagiography and History: The Saintly Prince in the Poetry of the Decembrists," which appeared in a shorter form in *Slavic and East European Journal* 30, no. 1 (1986): 29-44; and for permission to reproduce Chapter Six, "Anti-Hagiography: Tolstoy's Assault on Orthodoxy," acknowledgment is made to *South Atlantic Review (SAR)*, where portions originally appeared as "Hagiographical Motifs in Tolstoy's 'Father Sergius,' " *SAR* 47, no. 2 (1982): 63-80

This book has been composed in Linotron Garamond

Clothbound editions of Princeton University Press books
are printed on acid-free paper, and binding materials are
chosen for strength and durability. Paperbacks, although satisfactory
for personal collections, are not usually suitable for library rebinding

Printed in the United States of America by Princeton University Press,
Princeton, New Jersey

Designed by Laury A. Egan

FOR MY PARENTS

CONTENTS

PREFACE

No one contemplating the embalmed body of Vladimir Lenin lying in state in its tomb on Red Square can doubt the lasting importance of the figure of the saint for Russian culture. Yet in the course of my reading of nineteenth- and twentieth-century Russian novels, stories, and poetry, I became convinced that the impact of hagiography, of the multifarious literature devoted to saints, on modern Russian literature has been both greatly underestimated and tremendously neglected by literary scholars. Examples of the influence of hagiographic writings on individual authors and works are often cited, but the vast extent of this literary phenomenon is nowhere adequately described. In part this reflects lingering prejudices regarding the quality and significance of medieval Slavic literature.

In writing the following pages, I have attempted to produce a discussion suitable for a general audience. However, my work assumes some familiarity with the broad outlines of Russian literature of the past two centuries. Its major aim is the identification and analysis of the most common types of usage of hagiographical material by Russian writers, as well as the variety of purposes that inspired this exploitation of their cultural past. In pursuing this aim, I did not attempt to produce a definitive, comprehensive structural analysis of the genre of hagiography; this would be the task of another, very different book. Rather, my focus is on the perception of hagiography by modern Russian writers themselves. What they regarded as worthy of imitation, or attack, and why—these are the questions I have tried to answer.

In doing the research for this book, I was greatly aided by summer grants from the American Council of Learned Societies, the National Endowment for the Humanities, the American Philosophical Society, and the Kennan Institute for Advanced Russian Studies. My study of hagiography in particular was facilitated by postdoctoral fellowships from the International Research and Exchanges Board and the Andrew W. Mellon Faculty Fellowships in the Humanities at Emory University. As a graduate student, I was supported during the writing of my dissertation on the Life of a medieval saintly prince by a fellowship from the American Association for University Women.

Since I first began to study Russian literary works, several scholars, all former teachers, have had an impact on the development of my interests. My undergraduate adviser, Richard Burgi, first fostered my curiosity about the use of ancient and medieval literature by modern Russian writers. My dissertation director, Riccardo Picchio, helped me gain an appreciation of hagiography as a flexible and often sophisticated mode of expression. Victor Erlich provided a constant example of the merits of considering literary developments from a broad cultural perspective. More recently, at Princeton University Press I received sympathetic readings for my work and many useful comments.

While I have been engaged in the actual research and writing of this book, I have often turned to members of my family for advice and criticism. My parents, Theodore and Yetta Ziolkowski, and my husband, Robert Thurston, read drafts and made many helpful observations of both a specific and a general nature. My father's typological acuteness, my mother's emphasis on readability, and my husband's knowledge of Russian history were all greatly appreciated. Nor should I overlook the willingness of my brothers, Jan and Eric, to supply me with much needed library materials. My husband, my parents, and my brothers were all unfailingly encouraging during the various stages of this project, and for that I thank them. I also thank my husband for simply listening . . . and listening.

NOTE ON TRANSLITERATION AND DATES

THE SYSTEM of transliteration employed in this work is the one used by the Library of Congress, with a few exceptions. Some proper names are given in their more familiar English forms (Leo Tolstoy rather than Lev Tolstoi, for example).

Transliteration in the notes makes no exceptions for familiar English forms of proper names. Tolstoy appears as Tolstoi, Herzen as Gertsen, for example. With works written in languages other than Russian, the names of authors appear exactly as spelled. Chyzhevs'kyi may thus appear as Čiževskij or Tschižewskij, for example.

All dates are given according to the Julian calendar, in use in Russia until 1918. In the nineteenth century this calendar was twelve days behind the Gregorian calendar of the West, in the twentieth century thirteen days.

ABBREVIATIONS USED IN THE NOTES

Pss	*Polnoe sobranie sochinenii (Complete Works)*
Psst	*Polnoe sobranie stikhotvorenii (Complete Poems)*
Ss	*Sobranie sochinenii (Collected Works)*
SEEJ	*Slavic and East European Journal*
TOdl	*Trudy Otdela drevnerusskoi literatury (Proceedings of the Department of Old Russian Literature)*

Hagiography and Modern Russian Literature

CHAPTER ONE

Introduction

Everyone of us has met people sitting reverently lost in thought over some Life of Eustathius and Placidas or Feodosii of the Caves,—and everyone must admit that they could ponder over this more deeply and fruitfully than over much of our contemporary literature.

Vasilii Kliuchevskii

The hem of our Russian caftan shows below the European frockcoat; we have shaved our beards, but have not washed our faces.

Ivan Kireevskii

IN 1880 a flood made attendance at Easter services impossible for people in the vicinity of Abramtsevo, then the estate of Savva Mamontov, a wealthy Moscow industrialist and enthusiastic patron of the arts. This incident gave rise to the idea of building a church on the estate itself. Those involved in the project, members of Mamontov's artists' colony, decided to construct the church in medieval Novgorodian style. Before finishing the designs, they visited Iaroslavl' and Rostov-the-Great, which were considered to possess some of the finest examples of Old Russian art and architecture. By the time the church was completed in 1882, several of the most prominent artists of the latter part of the nineteenth century had participated in its planning and construction.[1] The result was a building which, though representative of a highly stylized interpretation of Old Russian architecture, pays eloquent tribute to an enthusiasm for medieval art.

[1] The church itself was designed primarily by Apollinarii Vasnetsov and Vasilii Polenov, the iconostasis and wall paintings were done by Il'ia Repin, Mikhail Nesterov, Apollinarii Vasnetsov, and Polenov, while the mosaic floor of the church was designed and partially laid by Viktor Vasnetsov. The group concerned itself with every detail; Polenov even applied himself to designing the embroidered vestment and covers. For discussion of the project, see Camilla Gray, *The Great Experiment: Russian Art 1863–1922* (New York, 1962), 14–15.

Far from being an isolated episode in the history of Russian culture, the church at Abramtsevo is only one illustration of the growing interest throughout the eighteenth and especially the nineteenth centuries in pre-Petrine Russia, its art, architecture, music, religion, and literature. This interest expressed itself in part in an effort to recognize and preserve native cultural artifacts. This was the impetus for many scholarly expeditions throughout Russia which sought to record ancient artistic and architectural monuments.[2] Medieval icons were eventually the beneficiaries of such enthusiastic rediscovery and restoration. This kind of antiquarian approach to medieval culture was evident as well in numerous attempts, like the one at Abramtsevo, to adapt medieval subjects and techniques to contemporary architectural and artistic projects. Buildings constructed in the so-called "Russian style," the Moscow Historical Museum (1873–1883) and city duma building (1890–1892), for example, and paintings like Vasilii Surikov's "Boiarynia Morozova" (1881–1887) and Viktor Vasnetsov's "After the Battle of Igor' Sviatoslavich with the Polovtsy" (1880) all owe their genesis at least in part to the revival of interest in and appreciation of medieval Russia.[3] Many artists turned increasingly to subjects characteristic or evocative of medieval Russia. Apollinarii Vasnetsov devoted himself to pictorial representations of medieval Moscow, while his brother specialized in icons and fairytale scenes.[4] At the end of the century several artists produced paintings of scenes of isolated monastic life.[5] The paintings by Mikhail Nesterov devoted to the life of one of Russia's greatest saints, Sergii of Radonezh (1314–1392), provide an excellent example. Such endeavors often involved an interrelationship between different spheres of cultural activity. Thus the ethnographic novels of Pavel Mel'nikov-Pecherskii to some extent inspired Nesterov, while Il'ia Repin agreed to produce illustrations for Nikolai Leskov's adaptations of medieval hagiographical legends.[6]

[2] For more details, see Tamara Talbot Rice, *A Concise History of Russian Art* (New York, 1963), 234.

[3] For a more extensive list of buildings constructed in the "Russian style," see M. A. Il'in and E. A. Borisova, "Arkhitektura," in *Istoriia russkogo iskusstva*, vol. 9, pt. 2 (Moscow, 1965), 265, 268.

[4] Gray, *Great Experiment*, 16.

[5] For a list of such paintings, see I. I. Nikonova, "M. V. Nesterov," in *Istoriia russkogo iskusstva*, vol. 10, pt. 1 (Moscow, 1968), 298–99.

[6] On Nesterov, see Nikonova, "M. V. Nesterov," 297. On the collaboration between

In the music world, the Balakirev circle, which included the composers Milii Balakirev, César Cui, Modest Musorgsky, Aleksandr Borodin, and Nikolai Rimsky-Korsakov, revealed an enthusiasm for native folk, historical, and religious motifs that helped to introduce a renaissance in Russian music.[7] Here as well their activities included both preservation and adaptation. Balakirev, who is remembered for his collection of folk songs that appeared in 1866, later also transcribed ancient liturgical chants.[8] As in art, in music historical and legendary themes became popular. Examples include operas like Musorgsky's *Boris Godunov* (1872), which was based on Alexander Pushkin's drama of the same name, Borodin's *Prince Igor'* (1890), and Rimsky-Korsakov's *The Legend of the Invisible City of Kitezh* (1903–1904).

In literature, the second half of the nineteenth century also witnessed a rash of efforts to locate and collect medieval and folk monuments of various kinds, both oral and written. While the ethnographer Aleksandr Afanas'ev sought out popular tales and legends, scholarly and religious groups published new editions of saints' Lives and other types of religious literature. The novels of Mel'nikov-Pecherskii, which described the peculiarities of isolated communities of schismatics, attracted attention, as did historical fiction like Aleksei K. Tolstoy's dramatic trilogy devoted to the Time of Troubles, the violent interregnum at the turn of the seventeenth century. A particular area of interest was literature concerned with saints. In the 1870s and 1880s the adaptation of hagiographical legends and tales from the Middle Ages enjoyed a certain vogue, while throughout the latter half of the century several writers, most notably Fedor Dostoevsky, applied hagiographical techniques to contemporary characters and situations. The variety of ways in which writers throughout the nineteenth and early twentieth centuries exploited hagiographical literature and its conventions in their own writings is the subject of this study.

The background to the exploration of hagiography as an area of literary endeavor is of paramount importance in appreciating its cultural significance. It would be a mistake to regard the widespread enthusiasm for pre-Petrine culture that manifested itself in the late nineteenth century as a spontaneous development. The roots of this minor renaissance

Repin and Leskov, see Leonid Grossman, *N. S. Leskov: Zhizn'—tvorchestvo—poetika* (Moscow, 1945), 225.

[7] Richard Anthony Leonard, *A History of Russian Music* (New York, 1968), 65.

[8] Leonard, *History of Russian Music*, 75–76.

can be traced at least to the beginning of that century and involve a variety of complex historical, religious, and ideological considerations. When viewed in this light, the accomplishments at Abramtsevo appear less a beginning than a logical culmination of established trends.

The developing curiosity about medieval Russian literary and artistic productions was to a large extent preceded by an heightened interest in Russian history. As early as the eighteenth century, a gnawing sense of cultural inferiority vis-à-vis the West drove some members of the educated elite to seek inspiration in the past, "to show that Russia, no less than other countries, had produced great men, and that she was no Johnny-come-lately in the family of nations."[9] This purposeful search through the past was in part encouraged by a growing recognition by some upper-class Russians that the reforms introduced by Peter the Great had not been an unmitigated blessing.[10] Increased public demand for a lively, colorful, and suitably flattering account of Russian history was eventually met by the popular author Nikolai Karamzin, whose *History of the Russian State* (*Istoriia gosudarstva Rossiiskogo*, 1818–1829) enjoyed an unprecedented success. Karamzin and some of his contemporaries, the publisher Nikolai Novikov, for example, recognized that history could serve a propagandistic function by instilling patriotism.[11] Karamzin's magnum opus contributed to the fulfillment of this end, not only for the early nineteenth-century reading public, but for subsequent generations as well. "I grew up on Karamzin," Dostoevsky wrote to the publicist and literary critic Nikolai Strakhov, who himself had as an adolescent greatly admired the historian's writings.[12] Throughout the century, Karamzin's tendentious views were eagerly embraced by many conservatives.

Karamzin's *History* did not win the complete approval of all segments of the literate population. Its avowedly pro-autocratic ideological stance provoked the scorn of many liberals. Yet even as it irritated or enraged,

[9] Hans Rogger, *National Consciousness in Eighteenth-Century Russia* (Cambridge, Mass., 1960), 188.

[10] Cf. J. L. Black, *Nicholas Karamzin and Russian Society in the Nineteenth Century: A Study in Russian Political and Historical Thought* (Toronto, 1975), 7, 26, 29.

[11] Cf. Rogger, *National Consciousness*, 244.

[12] Dostoevsky's comment occurs in a letter of 2 December 1870. See F. M. Dostoevskii, *Pis'ma*, vol. 2 (Moscow, 1930), 300. On Strakhov, see Linda Gerstein, *Nikolai Strakhov* (Cambridge, Mass., 1971), 6.

it often awakened or intensified an interest in Russian history.[13] The case of Karamzin and his supporters and detractors amply demonstrates that from very early in the century, adherents of political perspectives ranging from the most conservative to the most radical exhibited a desire to analyze the Russian past. One way in which this desire expressed itself was in attempts to amass information and locate ancient literary monuments, like chronicles, tales, or saints' Lives.

Some of these efforts preceded the appearance of Karamzin's *History*. The activities of the members of the Rumiantsev circle in the second and third decades of the nineteenth century are especially significant.[14] The nobleman Nikolai Rumiantsev (1754–1826) used his vast wealth both to acquire manuscripts, books, and other antiquities and to support the work of several scholars on a variety of topics, many of which related to the Slavic Middle Ages. His collection eventually became an important part of the Lenin Library holdings. From the late eighteenth century on, various other societies, circles, and enterprising individuals also collected and studied chronicles and other literary works, as well as folklore and Old Russian verse.[15] Karamzin himself made use of some previously unexploited sources, including certain saints' Lives.[16] As the century progressed, efforts aimed at locating and examining the literature of the past continued to increase.

It was not only an uneasy sense of inferiority that contributed to the growth of concern for the Russian past, but also a nationalistic spirit fueled by contemporary political events. Like many Europeans, conservative Russians were tremendously worried by the French Revolution and its aftermath. As hostility developed in the early years of the nineteenth century between Napoleon's France and Alexander I's Russia, nationalism found increasing expression in artistic renditions of glorious episodes from Russian history.[17] For example, Vladislav Ozerov's

[13] Cf. Anatole G. Mazour, *Modern Russian Historiography* (Princeton, 1958), 69.

[14] For more details on the activities of the Rumiantsev circle, see Peter K. Christoff, *The Third Heart: Some Intellectual-Ideological Currents and Cross Currents in Russia, 1800–1830* (The Hague, 1970), 40–41.

[15] On the collection of folklore in particular, see Christoff, *Third Heart*, 20, 31.

[16] J. L. Black, "The Primečanija: Karamzin as a 'Scientific' Historian of Russia," in J. L. Black, ed., *Essays on Karamzin: Russian Man-of-Letters, Political Thinker, Historian, 1766–1826* (The Hague, 1975), 131, 143.

[17] Edward C. Thaden, "The Beginning of Romantic Nationalism in Russia," *American Slavic and East European Review* 13 (1954): 513.

play *Dmitrii Donskoi* (1807), which deals with the Russian victory over the Mongols in 1380, had a highly successful response when it premiered shortly after the battle of Preussisch-Eylau.[18] Such patriotic literature, which often descended into bathos and crude jingoism, became a regular component of the Russian literary scene. The Russian defeat of Napoleon, the Polish uprising of 1831, and later the Crimean War, as well as periodic outbursts of nationalistic exhortations by the tsarist government, contributed to an atmosphere that fostered this tendency.

In addition to nationalistic sentiments, another factor that stimulated a fascination with the past in the early nineteenth century was the influx of romantic literature, particularly the historical novels of Sir Walter Scott. While a knowledge of English was not common among upper-class Russians, in the 1820s many were exposed to the writer's works through French or Russian translation.[19] Some of the latter were produced by foremost Russian poets, like Vasilii Zhukovskii. These works did much to remedy the low opinion many Russians had of the Middle Ages in general. Moreover, as Peter K. Christoff points out in his discussion of the impact of romanticism on Russian intellectuals, "from thoughts of England, it was but a step to the medieval Slavic world."[20] Scott's captivating descriptions of the medieval period did much to dispel any lingering doubts some liberal Russians may have had about its suitability as an object of admiration.[21] In addition, in the following decades the vogue for native "Waverley" novels, which began with Mikhail Zagoskin's enormously popular *Iurii Miloslavskii, or the Russians in 1612* (1829), further enhanced the popularity of the Russian Middle Ages. The enthusiasm for such novels continued for many years; as late as 1862, Aleksei K. Tolstoy produced *Prince Serebriannyi*, which reflected Scott's strong influence. Not everyone shared the reservations expressed by the critic Vissarion Belinskii, whose attitude towards medieval Russian culture is cuttingly expressed in his comments on Old Russian literature:

> Without any doubt, our literature began in 1739 when Lomonosov sent his first ode from abroad . . . Is it necessary to try to

[18] Thaden, "Beginning of Romantic Nationalism," 513; and D. S. Mirsky, *A History of Russian Literature From Its Beginnings to 1900* (New York, 1958), 68.

[19] Christoff, *Third Heart*, 60.

[20] Christoff, *Third Heart*, 62.

[21] Cf. Christoff, *Third Heart*, 62.

> prove that the "Lay of Igor"s Campaign," "The Legend of the Don Battle," the eloquent "Epistle of Vassian to Ivan III," and other historical monuments, folk songs, and scholastic spiritual oratory have exactly the same relation to our literature as the monuments of antediluvian literature, if they were discovered, to Sanskrit, Greek, or Latin literature?[22]

Throughout the early and mid-nineteenth century, many Russians succumbed to a greater or lesser extent to the lure of the past. As a group, none fell so fully under its sway as the Slavophiles, a circle of thinkers who found inspiration in the cultural legacy of Old Russia and the Orthodox Church. They played an important role in bringing various aspects of medieval and traditional Russian culture to the attention of their contemporaries.

The Slavophile conception of medieval Russia was a highly idealized and romanticized one.[23] One of the most astute observations about their attitude was enunciated by the writer Sergei Aksakov regarding his son Konstantin, a Slavophile historian, when he commented that it would be desirable for the latter to "remain his entire life in his pleasant state of error, for enlightenment [would be] impossible without grave and bitter disappointment; so let him go on living and believing in the perfection of Rus'."[24] There was indeed something touchingly naive about the Slavophile devotion to Old Russia and rejection of the westernizing tendencies introduced by Peter the Great. Konstantin Aksakov's fellow Slavophile, the eminent folklorist Petr Kireevskii, is said to have expressed regret that he bore the same name as Peter, while the philosopher and wit Petr Chaadaev observed with tongue in cheek that Aksakov himself wore 'native' clothing, including a sheepskin hat, only to be mistaken on the streets for a Persian.[25] Their personal foibles

[22] V. G. Belinskii, *Pss*, vol. 1 (Moscow, 1952), 65 (footnote).

[23] For more discussion of this point, see Nicholas V. Riasanovsky, *Russia and the West in the Teaching of the Slavophiles: A Study of Romantic Ideology* (Cambridge, Mass., 1952), 172.

[24] Cited in V. D. Smirnov, *Aksakovy, ikh zhizn' i literaturnaia deiatel'nost'* (St. Petersburg, 1895), 67.

[25] On Petr Kireevskii's regrets, see Andrzej Walicki, *The Slavophile Controversy: History of a Conservative Utopia in Nineteenth-Century Russian Thought*, trans. Hilda Andrews-Rusiecka (Oxford, 1975), 123. Chaadaev's witty observation is mentioned by Herzen in his memoirs. See Aleksandr Gertsen, *Ss*, vol. 9 (Moscow, 1956), 148.

aside, however, the Slavophiles did much to bring medieval and traditional Russian culture to the attention of the educated public:

> They were vociferous and consistent advocates of the need for returning to the original and native sources of Russian life. To effect this goal, many of them took action: Peter Kireevskii collected folk songs, Ivan Kireevskii helped the monks at Optina Pustyn' to edit the works of fathers and monastic reformers of the Eastern Church, Constantine Aksakov and Alexis Khomiakov wrote books or articles concerning Russian history and Orthodox Church theology, Constantine Aksakov studied Russian peasant customs and traditions, and Iurii Samarin participated in the preparatory committees whose work paved the way for the emancipation of the Russian serfs.[26]

In spite of their efforts, the influence of the Slavophiles nonetheless remained limited, and at times their attitudes encountered opposition not only from their more European-oriented contemporaries, the so-called Westernizers, like Alexander Herzen and Belinskii, but from the conservative tsarist government as well. But with the development of the Russian Panslavist movement, which has been called the "ideological heir of Russian Slavophilism," an often chauvinistic attitude towards Slavic culture attracted a widespread following.[27] Stimulated to some extent by the Crimean War, the movement later gained impetus from the events leading up to the Russo-Turkish War of 1877–1878. In Panslavism, which in Russia more often assumed the form of a thinly veiled Panrussianism, nationalism and a romanticized conception of Slavdom coalesced with the expansionist political aims of many conservatives. Given some official recognition, in the late 1850s and 1860s the Panslavists established Slavonic Benevolent Committees, organizations interested in strengthening ties among the Slavs, which sought to promote their efforts largely through various educative efforts.[28] The membership of these organizations drew on university,

[26] Edward C. Thaden, *Conservative Nationalism in Nineteenth-Century Russia* (Seattle, 1964), 32.

[27] Michael Boro Petrovich, *The Emergence of Russian Panslavism, 1856–1870* (New York, 1956), 32.

[28] On the aims of the Slavonic Benevolent Committees, see Michael T. Florinsky, *Russia: A History and An Interpretation*, 2 vols. (New York, 1953), 2: 990; and Frank

ecclesiastical, and political circles, as well as on conservative intellectuals like Dostoevsky.[29]

There is no doubt that many Russians remained firmly convinced of the need to emulate European models to achieve progress at home. At the same time, however, the combination of nationalism with a romantic idealization of the past helped create an atmosphere conducive to the examination of Old Russian culture. For many, this culture was inseparable from Russian Orthodoxy. In this regard, a comment made by the Slavophile Ivan Kireevskii on the benign role of the Church in pre-Petrine Russia is illuminating: "fathoming all the intellectual and moral convictions of people, it [the Church] invisibly guided the state to the realization of the highest Christian principles, while never interfering with its national development." In the same context, he also observed that "Russian society developed independently and naturally, under the influence of a single internal conviction fostered by the Church and everyday tradition."[30] Such an idealized conception of the role played by Orthodoxy in Russian historical development was by no means limited to the Slavophiles. In a review of a new edition of saints' Lives that began to appear in 1868, the historian Vasilii Kliuchevskii observed:

> Perhaps nothing better than a saint's Life allows us to sense that this immense field was not cleared and ploughed up by an axe or wooden plough alone, and that not only the notorious Moscow Ivans gave the state such vitality, but that their material creation was also served by the best moral forces of the people, in the form of [the Moscow metropolitans] Petr and Aleksii, Sergii [of Radonezh], and many others. Perhaps we would look more seriously at ourselves and at our future, if we knew and appreciated better these moral forces that labored for us in the past.[31]

The equation here of the best of medieval Orthodoxy with the best of popular impulses is typical of a romantic attitude embraced by many pre-revolutionary Russian intellectuals. In *The Brothers Karamazov*

Fadner, *Seventy Years of Pan-Slavism in Russia: Karazin to Danilevskii 1800–1870* (Washington, D.C., 1962), 241.

[29] Florinsky, *Russia*, 2: 990.

[30] I. V. Kireevskii, *Pss*, vol. 1 (Moscow, 1911), 205–206.

[31] "Velikie minei chetii, sobrannye vserossiiskim Mitropolitom Makariem," *Sbornik statei*, vol. 3, *Otzyvy i otvety* (Petrograd, 1918), 10.

(1880), Dostoevsky's Father Zosima expresses sentiments about the national significance of Russian holy men very similar to those of Kliuchevskii.

The attraction to medieval Russian culture that intensified in the course of the nineteenth century did indeed include a large component of interest in Russian Orthodoxy in general and religious literature in particular. Of the various types of religious literature, saints' Lives easily came to exert the most broadly based appeal, largely because of the dramatic excitement their often fanciful narratives had to offer.[32] Understanding the type of exposure to hagiographical literature experienced by the Russian reading (and listening) public is critical to an appreciation of its cultural role. Before turning to this question, however, one should consider briefly some additional factors that facilitated an interest in religion and, more specifically, in hagiography.

In his history of the Orthodox Church, Timothy Ware comments on the unfairness of considering the synodical period of Russian Orthodoxy, which began with Peter the Great (1682–1725), "simply as a time of decline."[33] This criticism of a popular conception regarding the condition of the Church in the nineteenth century will bear close scrutiny. While a common view of the Church both then and now centers on a drunken and debauched priesthood and monkhood of the type depicted by radical painters like Vasilii Perov, known for his satirical portrayals of rural Russian life, and while certainly elements of the clergy were subject to the kind of corruption described by the provincial priest Ioann Belliustin in his anonymous exposé, *Description of the Rural Clergy* (*Opisanie sel'skogo dukhovenstva*, Leipzig, 1858), this is by no means the entire story. Rather, within the limits of its circumscribed position in relation to the state, from the late eighteenth century on the Church enjoyed a revival in several spheres of its existence.

One of the areas of ecclesiastical life in which a very noticeable spiritual renaissance occurred was in the monasteries. Towards the end of the sixteenth century the state had begun to curb both the accumulation of monastic wealth and the number of monks.[34] In the eighteenth century these efforts reached a peak when the number of monks was

[32] On the interest in saints' Lives in Russia through the centuries, see A. Iakhontov, "Zhitiia sviatykh v ikh znachenii dlia domashnego chteniia," *Strannik* 3 (1892): 682–704.

[33] Timothy Ware, *The Orthodox Church* (Baltimore, Md., 1963), 137.

[34] Sergius Bolshakoff, *Russian Mystics* (Kalamazoo, Mich., 1977), 52.

severely curtailed and Peter the Great abolished the office of patriarch, replacing the latter with the Holy Synod, which consisted of a number of clerics headed by a lay official, the ober-procurator. Later in the century Catherine the Great continued the campaign against the monasteries, closing many of them and confiscating much monastic property.[35] It was only under Paul I (1796–1801) and his successors, Alexander I (1801–1825) and Nicholas I (1825–1855), that the Church was able to regain some of its influence and monasticism was again permitted to flourish.[36] Yet even as early as the end of the eighteenth century, there were indications of an Orthodox monastic revival both inside and outside Russia.

Two of Russia's greatest mystics, Tikhon of Zadonsk (1724–1783) and Serafim of Sarov (1759–1833), were active at the end of the eighteenth and the beginning of the nineteenth century. While both monks were greatly venerated and eventually canonized, Tikhon in particular commanded the respect of many educated Russians. In the early part of the century his writings were read by some members of Masonic circles.[37] Later he met with a positive reaction from writers as diverse as Nikolai Gogol, Leo Tolstoy, and Maxim Gorky.[38] Perhaps the most famous instance of an admiration for Tikhon by a Russian writer is that of Dostoevsky, who used the holy monk at least to some extent as a model in creating the characters of both Father Zosima and the retired bishop Tikhon in *The Possessed* (1872).

An equally influential, if less well-known, contemporary of Tikhon of Zadonsk was Paisii Velichkovskii (1722–1794), a dedicated monastic reformer who left the Russian empire at an early age, partially because of the official persecution of monks, and spent the rest of his life on Mount Athos and in Rumania.[39] Paisii was instrumental in reinstilling a high degree of spiritual commitment among many Slavic Orthodox

[35] For more discussion of these actions, see Bolshakoff, *Russian Mystics*, 56–57; and Igor Smolitsch, *Russisches Mönchtum: Entstehung, Entwicklung und Wesen 988–1917* (Würzburg, 1953), 406–13, especially.

[36] On this period, see Bolshakoff, *Russian Mystics*, 99–101.

[37] Nadejda Gorodetzky, *Saint Tikhon of Zadonsk: Inspirer of Dostoevsky* (Crestwood, N.Y., 1976), 216.

[38] See Gorodetzky, *Saint Tikhon*, 217; M. Gor'kii, *Lev Tolstoi, A. P. Chekhov, V. G. Korolenko* (Moscow, 1928), 52; L. N. Tolstoi, *Pss*, vol. 28 (Moscow, 1957), 56.

[39] On Paisii and his disciples, see Bolshakoff, *Russian Mystics*, 79–98; and Smolitsch, *Russisches Mönchtum*, 482–95.

monks of his own and subsequent generations. One of his most important achievements was the translation into Slavonic of the *Philokalia*, an anthology of Eastern Orthodox mystical and ascetical writings published in Venice in 1782.[40] This translation was published in Russia in the late eighteenth century. Regarding the impact of the *Philokalia*, the theologian Georges Florovsky has written: "Publication of the Slavonic-Russian *Philokalia* was an event not only in the history of Russian monasticism but generally in the history of Russian culture. It was both an accomplishment and a stimulus."[41]

Together with the proselytizing activities of Paisii's disciples, the *Philokalia* did much to revive the institution of the elder (*starets*), the type of spiritual director immortalized in Dostoevsky's Zosima. Ivan Kireevskii summarized the crucial role the elder played for many Russians, both lay and ecclesiastical: "More essential than all possible books and thoughts is to find an Orthodox starets to whom you can reveal each of your thoughts, and from whom you can hear not your own more or less reasonable opinion, but the judgment of the Holy Father."[42] In the nineteenth century the major center for the implementation of theories of eldership (*starchestvo*) was the monastery of Optina Pustyn' near Moscow. The increasingly well-known elders in residence there attracted the attention and visits of lay believers, and even sceptics, from all classes of society. In addition, by the 1870s readers could read the thoughts of the Optina elders in brochures and religious magazines.[43] And the publication of *The Brothers Karamazov* contributed indirectly to the popularization of the institution of eldership.

The ecclesiastical revival in the nineteenth century was not, however, limited to the development of the spiritual talents of individual monks.The Church evinced a desire for reform in other ways as well. One area in particular need of improvement was the ecclesiastical

[40] For more specific details on the contents of the *Philokalia*, see *Encyclopedic Dictionary of Religion* (Washington, D.C., 1979). Some excerpts from the *Philokalia* have been translated into English. See E. Kadloubovsky and G.E.H. Palmer, eds., *Early Fathers from the Philokalia, together with some writings of St. Abba Dorotheus, St. Isaac of Syria, and St. Gregory Palamas* (London, 1954).

[41] Georgii Florovskii, *Puti russkogo bogosloviia* (Paris, 1937), 127.

[42] Cited by Metropolitan Seraphim (of Berlin and Germany) in his *Die Ostkirche* (Stuttgart, 1950), 306.

[43] Dmitry F. Grigorieff, "Dostoevsky's Elder Zosima and the Real Life Father Amvrosy," *St. Vladimir's Seminary Quarterly* 11 (1967): 26.

schools, whose Orthodox foundations had been undermined by excessive and badly integrated Western influence.[44] The intellectually sophisticated monk Filaret (Drozdov) (1782–1867), who subsequently became the metropolitan of Moscow and author of the emancipation proclamation freeing the serfs in 1861, greatly encouraged reforming the schools in accordance with Orthodox traditions.[45] While Filaret's own orientation was much influenced by Western writers, he was keenly aware of the need to develop an independent Orthodox theology and philosophy. Under his direction, the ecclesiastical schools began to explore theological and philosophical questions in a serious fashion well before such interests manifested themselves in the secular sphere.[46] In fact, Florovsky claims that the network of ecclesiastical schools served as "the real social basis for the entire development and expansion of Russian culture and enlightenment in the nineteenth century."[47]

As the century progressed, the philosophical and theological enthusiasm generated in ecclesiastical circles contributed to the initiation of ambitious publishing enterprises. At Optina the elders Makarii and Amvrosii directed the editing and publishing of (among other works) writings of the Byzantine ascetics Isaac the Syrian (d. circa 460), John Climacus (d. 649), Maximus the Confessor (d. 662), and Simeon the New Theologian (d. 1032); the Russians Nil Sorskii (d. 1508) and Paisii Velichkovskii; and the Lives of Gregory Sinaite (d. 1310), Paisii, and, after his death, Makarii himself.[48] Makarii was greatly aided by the editorial assistance of Ivan Kireevskii and his wife Natal'ia. Nor was Optina the only site of such activities. At the Academy of Kazan', for example, under the general rubric of *Monuments of Ancient Russian Ecclesiastical Literature* (*Pamiatniki drevnerusskoi dukhovnoi pis'mennosti*), var-

[44] Robert L. Nichols, "Orthodoxy and Russia's Enlightenment, 1762–1825," in Robert L. Nichols and Theofanis George Stavrou, eds., *Russian Orthodoxy under the Old Regime* (Minneapolis, 1978), 82.

[45] For discussion of Filaret's character and activities, see Nichols, "Orthodoxy and Russia's Enlightenment," 79–84.

[46] Nichols, "Orthodoxy and Russia's Enlightenment," 84.

[47] Florovskii, *Puti russkogo bogosloviia*, 231.

[48] For lists of the works published under the direction of the Optina elders, see Nicholas Arseniev, *Holy Moscow: Chapters in the Religious and Spiritual Life of Russia in the Nineteenth Century* (London, 1940), 90–91; Sergii Chetverikov, *Optina Pustyn': Istoricheskii ocherk i lichnye vospominaniia* (Paris, 1926), 49, 65; Grigorieff, "Dostoevsky's Elder Zosima," 29.

ious saints' Lives and other religious works were published.[49] By the end of the pre-revolutionary period there were forty-four publishing houses, some church-affiliated, some private, almost exclusively devoted to do the publication of religious materials ranging from Gospels to Lives.[50] It has been claimed that the publication of such materials was second only to popular and children's literature.[51]

In considering the general impact of Orthodoxy on nineteenth-century Russian culture, the absence of a strict division between the religious and secular worlds should be recognized. The area of university education provides a good example of the overlap between the two. The role of the Church in education in general has often been underestimated.[52] In his work on Orthodoxy and Russia's enlightenment, Robert Nichols attempts to combat this prejudice, to demonstrate that "the Russian church played a profoundly important role in Russia's educational and professional growth" and "to stress the very close relationship between these schools and their students on the one hand and the broad intellectual and cultural currents on the other."[53] One of the most telling bits of evidence Nichols adduces to support his arguments involves the sometime seminarians who later became university professors. A noteworthy case is that of Kliuchevskii, who came from a rural priestly background and studied at the Penza Seminary before going to Moscow University.[54] In this context, it is significant that Kliuchevskii's first major piece of historical research dealt with the use of Old Russian saints' Lives as historical sources.[55] Kliuchevskii's Moscow University mentor, the historian Sergei Solov'ev, was also the son of a priest.[56] Members of the clergy, professors at ecclesiastical academies,

[49] George A. Maloney, *A History of Orthodox Theology Since 1453* (Belmont, Mass., 1976), 66.

[50] Edward Kasinec, "A Bibliographical Essay on the Documentation of Russian Orthodoxy during the Imperial Era," in *Russian Orthodoxy under the Old Regime*, 206.

[51] Kasinec, "Bibliographical Essay," 206.

[52] For a discussion of this point, see Nichols, "Orthodoxy and Russia's Enlightenment," 65–66. See also Nicholas Rzhevsky, *Russian Literature and Ideology: Herzen, Dostoevsky, Leontiev, Tolstoy, Fadeyev* (Urbana, Ill. 1983), 15–16.

[53] Nichols, "Orthodoxy and Russia's Enlightenment," 67.

[54] On Kliuchevskii, see Anatole G. Mazour, *Modern Russian Historiography*, 112–13; and Nichols, "Orthodoxy and Russia's Enlightenment," 69.

[55] *Zhitiia sviatykh kak istoricheskii istochnik* (Moscow, 1871). This work was Kliuchevskii's masters thesis.

[56] On Solov'ev's background, see Mazour, *Modern Russian Historiography*, 98–100.

and professors educated in ecclesiastical schools also belonged to various learned societies, like the Society of History and Russian Antiquities founded at Moscow University.[57]

A clerical background was not uncommon among other members of the intelligentsia and the educated elite. For example, Nikolai Strakhov was both son and nephew of members of the "white," or married, priestly clergy (as opposed to the "black," or celibate, monastic clergy). He attended the seminary in provincial Kostroma before entering the University of St. Petersburg.[58] Konstantin Pobedonostsev, who gained widespread notoriety as the reactionary ober-procurator of the Holy Synod in the latter part of the century, was the grandson of a priest and the son of a professor of rhetoric and Russian literature who had studied at the Moscow Ecclesiastical Academy.[59] It has been observed that "the appearance of two descendants of the academically trained clergy among the defenders of established order in Russia suggests the importance of the church in Russian society during the nineteenth century."[60] Other well-known Russians who were decidedly non-establishment in their inclinations, but whose family background had a clerical connection, include the writer Leskov, whose paternal grandfather was a priest, and the radicals Nikolai Chernyshevskii and Nikolai Dobroliubov, both of whom were the sons of priests and had some exposure to seminary education.[61] This type of background was not uncommon among the so-called *raznochintsy* (literally, men of various ranks) prominent in the radical movements of the second half of the nineteenth century.[62] In short, the infiltration of those exposed most directly and extensively to religion into the mainstream of Russian society was an important factor in the dissemination of Orthodox culture.

[57] For more details, see Nichols, "Orthodoxy and Russian Enlightenment," 73.

[58] On Strakhov's background, see Thaden, *Conservative Nationalism*, 12; and Gerstein, *Nikolai Strakhov*, 1–7.

[59] On Pobedonostsev's background, see Thaden, *Conservative Nationalism*, 12.

[60] Thaden, *Conservative Nationalism*, 12.

[61] On Leskov's background, see Hugh McLean, *Nikolai Leskov: The Man and His Art* (Cambridge, Mass., 1977), 4–5. On Chernyshevskii and Dobroliubov, see the entries on them in *Russkie pisateli: biobibliograficheskii slovar'* (Moscow, 1971). On early religious influences on certain other nineteenth-century writers, see also Rzhevsky, *Russian Literature and Ideology*, 20.

[62] For detailed discussion of the term *raznochintsy* and the role played by the raznochintsy in Russian history, see the entry on them in Joseph L. Wieczynski, ed., *The Modern Encyclopedia of Russian and Soviet History* (Gulf Breeze, Fla., 1982), vol. 30.

Another factor which should be stressed in considering the interest in medieval Orthodox culture among educated Russians is the exposure to religious literature and monastic life they often received as children. In Dostoevsky's *The Idiot* (1868), Rogozhin mentions that his mother is a devotee of the *Reading Menaea* (*Chet'i minei*), a famous collection of saints' Lives that will be described in more detail below. As a child, Dostoevsky himself was enchanted by these stories, and in prison in 1849 he returned to them.[63] Later in life his library included a wide range of hagiographic and other religious literature.[64] In his childhood, Dostoevsky also made yearly pilgrimages with his family to the Holy Trinity Monastery founded by Sergii of Radonezh where the modern town of Zagorsk now stands, and when he returned from exile in 1859 one of the first places he visited was this same monastery.[65] Similarly, in his youth the poet Aleksei Apukhtin went every year with his mother to Optina Pustyn', where he was much impressed by the elder Makarii.[66] The prominent liberal lawyer and politician Vasilii Maklakov mentions in his memoirs that his mother constantly read her children a collection of saints' Lives.[67] Maxim Gorky also grew up hearing and reading the Lives of the saints and remained enthusiastic about some of them even as a politically radical adult.[68] And in the late 1890s his contemporary Leon Trotsky turned like Dostoevsky to the Lives of the saints while in prison.[69]

Not everyone exposed to such influences retained a positive impression. The anarchist Mikhail Bakunin, who as an adolescent was forced by his uncle to read the *Menaea* aloud and exhorted to accept it unques-

[63] On Dostoevsky's childhood attraction to the *Reading Manaea*, see Dmitry F. Grigorieff, "Dostoevsky and the Russian Orthodox Church" (Ph.D. diss., University of Pennsylvania, 1958), 11. On the writer's prison reading of the *Menaea*, see L. P. Grossman, "Biblioteka Dostoevskogo," in his *Seminarii po Dostoevskomu. Materialy, bibliografii i kommentarii* (Moscow, 1922), 8. For detailed discussion of Dostoevsky's religious background, see Joseph Frank, *Dostoevsky: The Seeds of Revolt, 1821–1849* (Princeton, N.J., 1976), 42–53.

[64] For a list of the contents of Dostoevsky's library, see Grossman, "Biblioteka Dostoevskogo," 42–45, especially.

[65] On Dostoevsky's childhood visits to the monastery, see Frank, *Dostoevsky*, 46.

[66] D. P. Bogdanov, "Optina Pustyn' i palomnichestvo v nee russkikh pisatelei," *Istoricheskii vestnik* 122 (1910): 338.

[67] Vasilii Alekseevich Maklakov, *Iz vospominanii* (New York, 1954), 18.

[68] On the specific Lives with which Gorky was familiar, see M. Gor'kii, *Ss*, vol. 13 (Moscow, 1951), 54, 138, 180.

[69] Bertram D. Wolfe, *Three Who Made a Revolution: A Biographical History* (New York, 1964), 207.

tioningly, later claimed that this experience made the first inroads on his faith.[70] But even in the cases of more westward-oriented Russian intellectuals, it would be a mistake to assume an absence of some familiarity with, and even enthusiasm for, Orthodox religious literature. It should come as no great surprise, then, to find Alexander Pushkin recommending the *Menaea* to his contemporaries or to discover that one of Alexander Herzen's earliest literary efforts was a reworking of a legend from the same collection.[71] Even in the cases of those who purportedly rejected the Orthodoxy of their childhood, its impact often resurfaced in transmuted fashion.

The present study is specifically concerned with the impact of hagiographical literature on nineteenth and early twentieth-century writers. The nineteenth century was characterized by a host of developments that facilitated an interest in medieval culture. As regards hagiography in particular, the century witnessed the increasingly widespread availability of such literature in a number of forms. A brief overview of this material is essential to an examination of its exploitation by Russian writers.

The major collections of saints' Lives available to the nineteenth-century writer were the *Prolog* and the *Reading Menaea*; the former is the Slavic equivalent of the Greek Orthodox synaxarion, a collection of abbreviated Lives. The *Reading Menaea* takes its name from the Greek word for months (μηναῖα); the title of the *Prolog* is a translating error—the Greek word referring to the introduction was erroneously interpreted as the title of the work. In both the *Prolog* and the *Menaea* the entries are arranged according to the calendar. The major difference between the two is that the *Menaea* accounts are much longer; the *Menaea* was originally intended to be read, the *Prolog* to be heard. Both were translated from the Greek relatively early: their oldest extant copies can be dated to the twelfth century.[72] Although accounts of Russian saints were added to them over the centuries, most of their material remains early Christian in subject. For example, of the 120-odd saints

[70] E. H. Carr, *Michael Bakunin* (New York, 1961), 10.

[71] Pushkin's recommendation occurs in a letter to P. A. Pletnev written in April 1831. See Aleksandr Pushkin, *Pss*, vol. 14 (Leningrad, 1941), 163. For discussion of Herzen's story "The Legend of St. Theodora" ("Legenda," 1836), see Chapter 3.

[72] N. K. Gudzy, *History of Early Russian Literature*, trans. Susan Wilbur Jones (1949; reprint, New York, 1970), 27. For detailed discussion of the composition and translation from the Greek of the *Prolog* and the *Menaea*, see, for example, M. N. Speranskii, *Istoriia drevnei russkoi literatury*, 3d ed., vol. 1 (Moscow, 1921), 205–13.

whose stories are recounted in the July volume of one particular version of the *Menaea*, fewer than ten are Russian.[73] In some later editions of the *Menaea* this inequity was somewhat remedied by the addition of supplements containing only Lives of Russian saints.

Both the *Menaea* and the *Prolog* underwent numerous redactions. The most ambitious revision of the former was directed in the sixteenth century by Metropolitan Makarii of Moscow, whose intention was to produce a vast synthetic compilation of all the sacred writings to be found in the Russian lands.[74] The basis for this *Menaea* was the old translated Greek *Menaea*, to which were added some Lives that had circulated independently, as well as some material from the *Prolog*. The contents were subjected to extensive revision in accordance with contemporary literary tastes and Makarii's own notions of piety. This version of the *Menaea* was published in part between 1868 and 1915.[75]

The *Menaea* compiled by Makarii never acquired the popularity of a later version produced by St. Dmitrii, the metropolitan of Rostov (1651–1709). Dmitrii's *Menaea* was primarily based on a sixteenth-century Latin reworking of a tenth-century Byzantine work.[76] It also included Lives of Russian saints. This version of the collection became the most popular among Russians into the nineteenth and even the twentieth century.[77] It was, for example, Dmitrii of Rostov's *Menaea* that Dostoevsky read in the Peter and Paul Fortress.[78] In addition to the full-length Church Slavonic versions of the *Menaea*, others were also available. For example, there were abridgments that included the most famous Lives and were narrated in contemporary Russian. Dostoevsky's library included a copy of such a version. A full-length Russian *Menaea* appeared early in this century.[79]

[73] See *Zhitiia sviatykh na russkom iazyke, izlozhennye po rukovodstvu Chet'ikh-Minei sv. Dmitriia Rostovskogo, s dopolneniiami iz Prologa* 12 vols. (Moscow, 1902–1911), vol. 11.

[74] On Makarii's intentions, see Florovskii, *Puti russkogo bogosloviia*, 25.

[75] *Velikie minei-chetii, sobrannye vserossiiskim mitropolitom Makariem* 8 vols., 16 pts. (St. Petersburg, 1868–1915). On Makarii's revisions, see Florovskii, *Puti russkogo bogosloviia*, 25; and Gudzy, *History*, 343.

[76] For details on Dmitrii of Rostov's sources, see Florovskii, *Puti russkogo bogosloviia*, 54.

[77] Ivan Kologrivof, *Essai sur la sainteté en Russie* (Bruges, 1953), 295, 392.

[78] Cf. Grossman, "Biblioteka Dostoevskogo," 8.

[79] See n. 73 above. Other collections of saints' Lives that appeared in the second half of the nineteenth century were *Zhitiia sviatykh: vybrannye i sokrashchenno izlozhennye i prazdniki pravoslavnoi tserkvi* (St. Petersburg, 1886); and *Zhitiia sviatykh zhen v pustyniakh Vostoka* (Viatka, 1871).

The *Menaea* consists largely of works typically designated as Lives, that is, biographical sketches of saints couched in reverential terms. When considering both the *Menaea* and especially the *Prolog*, however, it is important to beware of defining hagiography too narrowly, of mistakenly assuming that hagiographic works are limited to full biographies.[80] In fact, such biographies constitute only a subgenre. Regarding hagiography itself, Athanasius' fourth-century Life of St. Anthony has been said to have initiated "a genre of writing in the Christian tradition which was to grow over the centuries into an unwieldy mass, the dimensions of which still resist total comprehension."[81] In a similar vein, Alexandra Olsen, who has pursued a detailed examination of the genre of hagiography, argues that:

> The differences are so great that one cannot make generalizations about what a "typical" hagiographic work might be, although one can make broad statements about hagiography as a literary genre. The definition found in a standard modern dictionary, "biography of saints," is inadequate because not all hagiographic narratives are full biographies . . . Hagiography is a curiously amorphous genre which may be defined only by subject-matter, not by form or style.[82]

Such caveats are eminently applicable to the sphere of Orthodox Slavic hagiography. Of Russian hagiography in particular the medievalist Riccardo Picchio has stated: "Frequently transcending the limits of the *vita* genre, Old Russian hagiographic compositions may conform to the schemes of other literary modes of expression such as sermons and chronicle accounts."[83]

Far more flexible and satisfactory than the blinkered equation of hagiography with Lives is Olsen's own definition of a hagiographical work: "It is an account in either verse or prose which describes the lives, or incidents therefrom, deaths, or miracles of saints. The accounts . . . all have some underlying polemical purpose."[84] This definition is espe-

[80] Alexandra Hennessey Olsen, " 'De Historiis Sanctorum': A Generic Study of Hagiography," *Genre* 13 (1980): 410.

[81] Lawrence S. Cunningham, "Hagiography and Imagination," *Studies in the Literary Imagination* 18 (1985): 79.

[82] " 'De Historiis Sanctorum'," 424.

[83] *Handbook of Russian Literature*, ed. Victor Terras (New Haven, 1985), s. v. "hagiography."

[84] " 'De Historiis Sanctorum'," 424.

cially applicable to the *Prolog*, where many entries are episodical rather than biographical. It should also be mentioned that the inclusion of many early Christian anecdotes in the Greek synaxarion, and hence the Russian *Prolog*, resulted from a shift in the meaning of the Latin *sanctus*, which in the early Christian era meant simply pious or revered and only later came to mean saint.[85] This is why the *Prolog* contains a number of stories about people who, though admittedly virtuous, would not have been considered saints if they had lived somewhat later. Yet because of their inclusion in the *Prolog*, accounts of their activities acquired the status of hagiography.

Like the *Menaea*, the *Prolog* quickly added other translated and original material, soon becoming three times longer than the Greek original.[86] Printed for the first time in 1640, it reappeared periodically during the eighteenth and nineteenth centuries under the auspices of both the Holy Synod and the Old Believers (the name given to a large group of schismatics whose quarrel with the official Russian Orthodox Church went back to the seventeenth century).[87] The writer who seemed most captivated by the *Prolog* was Leskov, who owned several copies of it (including one issued by the Old Believers) and reworked several of its stories.[88]

In addition to both full and abridged versions of the *Menaea* and the *Prolog* that circulated in the nineteenth century, other hagiographical collections appeared that were devoted to specific groups of saints. For example, Andrei Murav'ev published a work devoted to the saints of the Russsian North.[89] Archbishop Filaret of Chernigov produced a compendium of Lives of female saints.[90] Paterika devoted to the monks of particular monasteries, like the Holy Trinity Lavra mentioned earlier and Solovki Monastery in the White Sea, were also published.[91]

Hagiography took more popular forms as well. Especially in the later

[85] Lawrence Walter Montford, "Civilization in Seventh Century Gaul as Reflected in Saints' Vitae Composed in the Period" (Ph.D. diss., St. Louis University, 1973), 32.

[86] Dmitrij Čiževskij, *History of Russian Literature from the Eleventh Century to the End of the Baroque* ('s-Gravenhage, 1962), 21.

[87] On the publication of the *Prolog*, see McLean, *Leskov*, 562.

[88] Cf. McLean, *Leskov*, 562.

[89] *Russkaia fivaida na severe* (St. Petersburg, 1855).

[90] *Zhitiia sviatykh podvizhnits vostochnoi tserkvi*, 2nd ed. (St. Petersburg, 1885). I have been unable to discover when the first edition appeared.

[91] The paterikon of the Holy Trinity Monastery was published in Moscow in 1896, the paterikon of the Solovki Monastery in St. Petersburg in 1873.

nineteenth century cheap and accessible versions of saints' Lives published by both ecclesiastical and private publishers were distributed in the countryside and sold at markets and fairs with great success.[92] Much of this kind of hagiography can be classified as *lubok* literature, cheap editions of literature that drew on subjects popularized in the *lubki*, mass-produced popular engravings. It catered to a fondness for the more sensational saints, like the early Christian martyr George (of dragon fame), Bishop Nicholas the Wonderworker of Myra (fourth century), Alexis, the Man of God (fifth century), and the holy fool Vasilii the Blessed of Moscow (d. 1521).[93] For the illiterate, public readings often included saints' Lives.[94]

Yet another conduit for the dissemination of hagiographical literature was the primary schools, both church and government-sponsored.[95] Russian law required that an obligatory component of the curriculum in these schoools be instruction in what was traditionally designated as *Zakon Bozhii* (literally, the Law of God), a potpourri of biblical and ecclesiastical history, prayers, and catechistical passages. Textbooks devoted to this subject often included some hagiography. A textbook by Platon Afinskii that appeared in numerous editions contains, among other things, accounts of the early Byzantine saints Emperor Constantine and his mother Helen, along with Lives of Prince Vladimir of Kiev (the first Christian ruler of Russia), his grandmother Ol'ga, and the monastic saints Feodosii of the Kievan Cave Monastery and Sergii of Radonezh.[96] This textbook was still in use in the province of Moscow as late as 1911.[97]

[92] Jeffrey Brooks, "Readers and Reading at the End of the Tsarist Era," in William Mills Todd III, ed., *Literature and Society in Imperial Russia, 1800–1914* (Stanford, Cal., 1978), 127; and Arthur Benoit Eklof, "Spreading the Word: Primary Education and the Zemstvo in Moscow Province" (Ph.D. diss., Princeton University, 1976), 267.

[93] Brooks, "Readers and Reading," 121. Other popular editions of saints' Lives included, among others, those of the Russian holy fool Prokopii; the martyrs Prince Mikhail of Chernigov and his boyar Fedor; Vladimir and Ol'ga, the first Christian rulers in the Russian lands; the saintly monk Sergii of Radonezh; and the Byzantine saint Philaretus the Merciful. These were all published separately between 1862 and 1870.

[94] Brooks, "Readers and Reading," 125.

[95] Even as late as 1905, church schools made up 46 percent of the primary schools. See Robert L. Nichols and Theofanis George Stavrou, "Introduction," in *Russian Orthodoxy Under the Old Regime*, 6–7.

[96] See, for example, Platon Afinskii, *Kniga dlia dukhovno-nravstvennogo chteniia i pervonachal'nogo nastavleniia v Zakone Bozhiem sostavlennaia dlia nachal'nykh narodnykh uchi-*

Hagiographical legends often served as the basis of folk tales and legends, and this in turn suggests another fruitful source of hagiographical material. In the later nineteenth century an interest in pre-Petrine culture was more than matched by an interest in folk culture. From the 1850s on in particular, much effort was devoted to the collection of folk literature. Many of the pieces published had a pronounced hagiographical slant.

An important bridge between oral and written hagiographical literature was provided by the so-called "spiritual verses" (*dukhovnye stikhi*).[98] Originally based on written, largely ecclesiastical sources, the "spiritual verses" often acquired a great popularity. One of the most widely known of such compositions was devoted to Alexis, the Man of God, and was published for the first time in 1848 by Petr Kireevskii, whose other efforts in this area were mentioned above.[99] In his poetic adaptation of the legend of Alexis, Boris Almazov made use of this work, as well as the *Menaea* account.[100] Later in the century the scholar Aleksandr Veselovskii produced the important multivolume collection, *Researches into Russian Spiritual Verse* (*Razyskaniia v. oblasti russkogo dukhovnogo stikha*) (St. Petersburg, 1880–1891), subsequently used extensively by the twentieth-century writer Aleksei Remizov as the basis for some of his short pieces.[101]

Folk literature marked by a hagiographical tendency was also represented by the highly popular collection compiled by Afanas'ev, *Russian Folk Legends* (*Narodnye russkie legendy*) (1859). Afanas'ev's book was an immense success with the reading public although it was quickly suppressed by the authorities and remained suppressed until 1914 because of ecclesiastical objections.[102] It appeared in London, however, and was

lishch i sel'skikh shkol, 10th ed. (Moscow, 1874). On instruction in *Zakon Bozhii* and various textbooks, see D. P. Sokolov, "Prepodovanie Zakona Bozhiia," in N. Kh. Vessel', ed., *Rukovodstvo k prepodovaniiu obshcheobrazovatel'nykh predmetov*, (St. Petersburg, 1874), 199–355.

[97] Eklof, "Spreading the Word," 355.

[98] Cf. Iuliia Sazonova, *Istoriia russkoi literatury: Drevnii period* 2 vols. (New York, 1955), 2: 215.

[99] Cf. V. P. Adrianova, *Zhitie Alekseia Cheloveka Bozhiia v drevnei russkoi literature i narodnoi slovesnosti* (Petrograd, 1917; The Hague, 1969), 63.

[100] Adrianova, *Zhitie Alekseia*, 436.

[101] See, for example, Remizov's stories "O bezumii Irodianom" (1906), "Mariia Egipetskaia" (1906), and "Gnev Ilii Proroka" (1906).

[102] For more details on the reception of Afanas'ev's book, see V. Ia. Propp, "Legenda,"

familiar to and used by a number of writers, including Leskov, Tolstoy, and Vsevolod Garshin; Leskov counted it among his treasured volumes.[103]

An equally important source for hagiographical representations was medieval chronicles and contemporary histories. The chronicles were usually compiled by monks whose approach to historical material was unabashedly religious. Russian history was viewed as the continuation of biblical history, and the actions and activities of Russia's numerous princes were interpreted accordingly. Moreover, many of these princes were either officially canonized or unofficially venerated, and this affected the accounts of their careers. Much chronicle-writing thus falls quite easily into the category of hagiography.

A number of Russian writers turned directly to the chronicles in researching the background of their own literary works. Pushkin was familiar with certain chronicles, for example, as was Aleksei K. Tolstoy.[104] In fact, Tolstoy's depiction of the seventeenth-century Tsar Fedor in *Tsar Fedor* (1868) so impressed Kliuchevskii by its fidelity to the historian's conception of the tsar that he used excerpts from Tolstoy's play as illustrations of the character of the saintly ruler.[105] Some Russian intellectuals who showed a great interest in the chronicles were the Decembrists, early nineteenth-century revolutionary conspirators, who sometimes turned to the chronicles in reaction against Karamzin's presentation of this material in his *History*. Initially available only in manuscript form, the chronicles soon benefited from the same enthusiasm that led to the publication of other Old Russian literary monuments. In 1813, for example, Rumiantsev sponsored the production of a scholarly edition of the so-called *Primary Chronicle* (*Povest' vremennykh let*), Russia's earliest annalistic composition. In 1846, the Archaeographical Commission began to publish an extensive series of Old Russian chronicles.[106]

in *Russkoe narodnoe poeticheskoe tvorchestvo*, vol. 3, pt. 1, *Ocherki po istorii russkogo narodnogo tvorchestva serediny XVIII—pervoi poloviny XIX veka* (Moscow, 1955), 379.

103 See M. P. Cherednikova, "Ob istochnikakh legendy N. S. Leskova 'Skomorokh Pamfalon'," *Russkii fol'klor* 13 (1972): 115.

104 For more details on this point, see Ervin C. Brody, *The Demetrius Legend and its Literary Treatment in the Age of the Baroque* (Cranbury, N.J., 1972), 210, 262.

105 Cf. Brody, *Demetrius Legend*, 205; and V. O. Kliuchevskii, *Sochineniia*, vol. 3 (Moscow, 1957), 20.

106 *Polnoe sobranie russkikh letopisei*. By 1921 twenty-four volumes had been published.

In some instances histories and textbooks drawing on the old chronicles preserved the hagiographical orientation of their sources. The most important example of this tendency was Karamzin's *History*, which borrowed wholesale from the chronicles. Karamzin's narrative often betrays the inclination to generalization in black and white terms so typical of hagiography. Through Karamzin's *History*, the hagiographical approach to the Russian past gained a large audience. Some of the ramifications of this development will be discussed in greater detail in the following chapter.

Later in the century hagiography continued to exert an influence on the writing of history. One example of this is the historian Nikolai Kostomarov's series of brief biographies of eminent Russians of the Middle Ages, a number of whom were in fact canonized or considered saints.[107] The narrative style employed by this historian has been called "severely hagiographical."[108]

It is not always easy to identify the source of a given writer's knowledge of hagiography. Where a reworking of a specific legend or tale is involved, the exact source may often be pinpointed. When hagiographical motifs or themes are used in a more contemporary context, biographical information about what the writer read may be helpful. When that is lacking, one must resort to probabilities. That the matter of recognizing sources was seen as problematical even at the time is illustrated by Leskov's excitement on learning that someone had seen a copy of the *Prolog* in Tolstoy's study.[109] Yet all the evidence points to widespread knowledge of saints' Lives. Certainly many writers were familiar with the *Reading Menaea* or the *Prolog*. Many others were exposed to historical literature with a hagiographical slant. Still others had some type of childhood exposure to religious works or religious life. Most importantly, perhaps, the spirit of the times encouraged a reexamination of Russia's cultural past, an important component of which was hagiography.

The work of the Archaeographical Commission was continued after 1917 by the Soviet Academy of Sciences (Akademiia Nauk).

[107] *Russkaia istoriia v zhizneopisaniiakh ee glavneishikh deiatelei*, 3 vols. (St. Petersburg, 1874). Some of those to whom chapters were devoted included the Russian monks Feodosii of the Kievan Cave Monastery, Sergii of Radonezh, and Nil Sorskii; and the medieval princes Vladimir, Iaroslav, Vladimir Monomakh, Alexander Nevskii, and Dmitrii Donskoi.

[108] Sazonova, *Istoriia russkoi literatury*, 2: 153.

[109] Cf. N. S. Leskov, *Ss*, vol. 11 (Moscow, 1958), 102.

Just as no easy generalizations can be made about the ways in which Russian writers acquired knowledge of hagiography, it is impossible neatly to pigeonhole those who used hagiography in their own writings. Such writers were not limited to the devoutly Orthodox; the kinds of writers who exploited hagiography for literary purposes were as diverse as the works they produced. There were unquestioning believers among those who turned to hagiography; the nun and poet Elisaveta Shakhova is an extreme example. Others, like Dostoevsky, were ostensibly, if not consistently, Orthodox in their attitudes. Yet many other writers—Leskov, for example—transformed hagiography into a vehicle for the expression of their own religious beliefs, which might deviate to a significant degree from mainstream Orthodox thinking. Tolstoy used hagiography with specifically anti-Orthodox intentions.

In Olsen's definition of hagiography, she refers to the "underlying polemical purpose" of this kind of literature. Such a purpose, though often apparent in modern Russian works that use hagiography, is not necessarily religious in nature. Many of the works discussed in subsequent chapters employ hagiographical techniques to make a political or social statement. In general, the writers who were inclined to take such an approach to hagiographical literature were more politically radical than their religiously-minded contemporaries. Both Chernyshevskii and Gorky, for example, applied motifs borrowed from saints' Lives to the depiction of the ideal human being, an ideal that has little to do, formally speaking, with Orthodoxy. Finally, hagiography could be exploited to make a purely artistic point, as Aleksei K. Tolstoy does in his adaptation of the legend of John Damascene. In short, in the nineteenth and early twentieth century hagiography was made to serve a wide variety of purposes by writers with a broad range of concerns.

In adapting hagiography to the expression of their own thematic interests, Russian writers took several approaches: they reworked specific legends, they exploited hagiographical devices to create new hagiography, and they adapted hagiographical themes and devices to wholly different purposes that may even be antithetical to the spirit of saints' Lives. Generally speaking, in the first instance an old story is given new meaning, in the second a new story is invested with an old meaning, and in the third a new story acquires its meaning through the idiosyncratic use of old devices. Writings of all three kinds will be considered in the course of this study.

The organization adopted in subsequent chapters, while roughly chronological, also reflects structural considerations. Chapter Two considers the way in which hagiography reached the poetry of the Decembrists largely through the medium of written history, specifically Karamzin's multivolume composition and various primary chronicle sources. Of central importance here is the figure of the saintly ruler, a type that gained much popularity on Russian soil. (This popularity has persisted to the present day and is exemplified by the recent canonization of Nicholas II [1894–1917] by the Russian Orthodox Church Outside Russia.) The Decembrist poems that treat specific medieval saintly princes often use accounts of the princes as a point of departure for portraying the ideal ruler. Their works are excellent examples of the adaptation of tradition to contemporary political ideology.

Chapter Three treats reworkings of specific hagiographical legends and tales, some found in the *Menaea*, others in the *Prolog* or collections like Afanas'ev's *Russian Folk Legends*. The saints and holy persons who figure in these works are generally early Christian, rather than Russian, in background. The authors who produced such adaptations, many of which appeared in the 1870s and 1880s, exhibit a great diversity of religious and ethical concerns. This is also true of a number of the works discussed in Chapters Four and Five, which examine examples of what may be termed neo-hagiography, the application of hagiographical conventions and features to contemporary characters and situations. In analyzing this usage of hagiography, Chapter Four focuses on two types of saintly personalities that consistently met with an enthusiastic response from Russian believers from the earliest times on, the holy fool (*iurodivyi*) and the saintly monk. The background for the development of these modes of sanctity will be discussed in detail at the beginning of Chapter Four. Much of this chapter is devoted to examination of some of the characters who appear in the later novels of Dostoevsky, the most prolific exponent of neo-hagiography in the nineteenth century.

Over the centuries, the type of the saintly monk manifested itself in two essentially incompatible kinds of spirituality, one emphasizing humility and a commitment to the interior life, the other giving greater prominence to external demonstrations of piety. Chapter Five is concerned with some neo-hagiographical embodiments of the latter in the writings of radical writers like Chernyshevskii and Gorky. This chapter also treats the impact of the autobiography of Archpriest Avvakum, the seventeeth-century religious leader who was an outstanding representative of the tradition of external piety, on literature produced both before and after the Revolution of 1917.

It is ironic that among the many uses of hagiography by Russian writers, not the least important has been as a weapon in the battle against Orthodoxy. Chapter Six focuses on Tolstoy's assault on Orthodoxy in his later life. It deals in particular with his critical examination of the figure of the saintly prince turned itinerant holy man in the unfinished work, "The Posthumous Notes of the Elder Fedor Kuzmich" ("Posmertnye zapiski startsa Fedora Kuzmicha," 1905), and with his attack on monasticism in the story "Father Sergii" ("Otets Sergii," 1890–1898). In the latter, Tolstoy attempts to expose some of the psychological weaknesses of a conventional hagiographical approach.

Throughout the following chapters, reference will frequently be made to the role played by topoi, that is, *loci communes* or commonplaces, which characterize virtually every stage of a saint's life and every aspect of his personality. Topoi supply idealized guidelines for behavior, and it may be argued that an author will employ topoi in order to accommodate his or her work to a general preconception about the probable actions and demeanor of a saint. As Kliuchevskii expressed it, the correct hagiographer strove to depict a type free from "all the trivial, concrete fortuities of personal existence."[110] Elsewhere he commented:

> For a Life what is of value is not the living wholeness of the character with its individual peculiarities and everyday surroundings, but only that side of it which fits a certain norm, which reflects a certain ideal . . . it [a Life] depicts not the life of a separate person, but on [the basis of] his destinies develops this abstract ideal.[111]

The scholar Nikolai Serebrianskii characterized this process as one of "hagiographical depersonalization."[112]

In the case of devout witnesses to the life of a saint, it seems plausible that such conventionalization, realized through topoi, might take place at the level of perception itself. What is often singled out for comment in the accounts of holy men are those features they share with their predecessors, for it is this communality of behavior that to a large extent endows them with status and authority. There is evidence that

[110] V. O. Kliuchevskii, *Sochineniia* (Moscow, 1957), 2: 255.

[111] Kliuchevskii, *Zhitiia sviatykh*, 436.

[112] N. Serebrianskii, *Drevne-russkie kniazheskie zhitiia (Obzor redaktsii i teksty)* (Moscow, 1915), 286.

eyewitnesses and later observers either search, consciously or unconsciously, for similiarities in the lives of saints or simply create them with varying degrees of calculation. It was common for medieval Russian hagiographers to borrow flattering material about a Byzantine saint in composing the Life of a Russian saint.[113] The continued prevalence of this kind of practice is illustrated by an episode in Joseph Kallinikov's novel *Women and Monks* (1930), which is set at the turn of the century. When an enthusiastic monastic artist tells his novice assistant a story about the founder of their monastery, attributing to him "all that he had ever read in the life of any saint" (586), the novice objects in bewilderment, recognizing the original sources for the descriptions.[114] The older monk dismisses his reservations, however: "away with all petty doubts and carping! The lives of all monks are the same everywhere. Our Staretz [elder] lived just as did the other saints, of whom history and tradition have given us the lives" (586). Salient here is the insistence on the homogeneity of monks' Lives. Such an insistence is echoed in the flippant comment of a modern scholar of hagiography: "When you've read one saint's Life, you've read them all."[115] These comments eloquently testify to the predominance of topoi in hagiographical literature.

An appreciation of the significance of topoi for hagiographical works is essential to an analysis of the impact of hagiography on later literature, for otherwise one risks perceiving the conventional as novel. It is also important to bear in mind that topoi should not be confused with formulae. While topoi may be expressed through formulae and indeed sometimes are, topoi themselves possess only a generalized thematic content and lack a fixed and precise articulation; this makes them extremely flexible narrative components.[116]

In his work on topoi in Old Russian literature, Dmitrii Chizhevskii found that possible topoi were not to be "deduced from general princi-

[113] Cf. Gudzy, *History of Early Russian Literature*, 25.

[114] Joseph Kallinikov, *Women and Monks*, trans. Patrick Kirwan (New York, 1930). First (incomplete) Russian edition published under the title *The Sacred Relics* (*Moshchi*). First complete authorized edition published under the title *Frauen und Mönche* (Leipzig, 1928).

[115] James Whitby Earl, "Literary Problems in Early Medieval Hagiography" (Ph.D. diss., Cornell University, 1971), 7. Cited in Olsen, " 'De Historiis Sanctorum'," 410.

[116] Cf. Dmytro Čyževs'kyj, "Zur Stilistik der altrussischen Literatur. Topik," in *Festschrift für Max Vasmer, Slavische Veröffentlichungen* 9 (1956): 107.

ples, but gathered inductively and discussed on [the basis of] examples."[117] Bearing this in mind, I shall not attempt here to enumerate all the topoi that occur in hagiographical works known to the Russians, but only to indicate certain broad narrative spheres frequently affected by this method of characterization. For example, the description of the childhood and youth of saints often lends itself to the accumulation of topoi. Whether a monastic or a princely figure, a saint is often portrayed as the child of noble and pious parents and demonstrates a precocious spirituality. This may express itself in a reluctance to engage in normal children's games and in a lack of interest in material things. Sometimes the child saint is distinguished by an extraordinary gift for learning (*puer senex*). In other instances, he or she may betray a lack of aptitude until divine intervention accomplishes a startling transformation.

Where future monastic saints are concerned, youthful piety soon gives rise to a desire to become a monk which is often discouraged by the parents of the saint. The mothers of Russian saints are especially notorious for attempting to prevent their sons from entering monasteries. Eventually the aspiring monk is able to pursue his ambition, however. At this point his relinquishing of his property is often emphasized and may be linked to a desire to fulfill the instructions of Matthew 19:21: "If you wish to be perfect, go and sell what you own and give the money to the poor and you will have treasure in heaven; then come, follow me."[118]

Traditional topoi common in the discussion of the monastic existence itself often involve ascetic feats and the successful struggle with various temptations, including lust. In the case of princely saints, the struggle against lust may manifest itself in the topos of the chaste marriage. Other topoi peculiar to the depiction of rulers include the expression of piety through charity, the building of churches, and a fondness for clerics. Some princes are characterized by an inspired military courage, while princely martyrs typically evince courage of another sort by calmly accepting their fates. In general the demeanor of saints at the moment of their deaths is marked by a remarkable peacefulness.

The divisions among Russian monks mentioned above will be dis-

[117] Čyževs'kyj, "Zur Stilistik," 107.

[118] Here and elsewhere, the edition of the Bible cited is *The Jerusalem Bible*, ed. Alexander Jones (Garden City, N.Y., 1968).

cussed in greater detail at the beginning of Chapter Four. Suffice it to say here that the keynote of the existence of many saintly monks portrayed in hagiographical literature is an all-encompassing humility that expresses itself in a conventionalized manner. The behavior of the holy fool also follows a stereotyped pattern, as does that of monks of more obdurate convictions. The specific topoi of these types will be considered at a later point.

The interest of Russian writers in hagiographical literature as a source of inspiration has been widespread and prolonged. Dostoevsky, Tolstoy, Pushkin, Gogol, Leskov, Chernyshevskii, Gorky, Boris Pasternak, and Alexander Solzhenitsyn—these are only a few of the Russian writers who have echoed, directly or indirectly, the hagiographical tradition. As this brief list suggests, the writers who turned to saints' Lives included both conservatives and radicals, believers and atheists, aristocrats and *raznochintsy*. But while scholars have frequently recognized the efforts in this area by individual authors like Dostoevsky and Leskov, the broader pervasiveness of the phenomenon has generally been overlooked.[119] This is a significant omission: an isolated consideration of such writers' use of hagiography may lead to misinterpretation or to an exaggerated sense of their originality in this regard.

In recent years, however, literary scholars in the United States and abroad have exhibited a pronounced and increasing curiosity about the literary adaptation of religious forms ranging from the biblical to the liturgical. This has resulted in a number of comprehensive typological studies.[120] Because of the central position often occupied by hagiography in Russian culture, a similarly wide-ranging discussion of the

[119] Al'bert Opul'skii, *Zhitiia sviatykh v tvorchestve russkikh pisatelei XIX veka* (East Lansing, Mich., 1986), discusses adaptations of specific hagiographical works by several writers. The extensive critical literature on the use of hagiography by Dostoevsky and Leskov will be discussed in more detail in subsequent chapters.

[120] See, for example, Earl Miner, ed., *Literary Uses of Typology: From the Late Middle Ages to the Present* (Princeton, N.J., 1977). In this collection of articles, see especially Theodore Ziolkowski, "Some Features of Religious Figuralism in Twentieth-Century Literature," 345–69. See also Albrecht Schöne, *Säkularisation als Sprachbildende Kraft* (Göttingen, 1958); Birgit H. Lermen, *Moderne Legendendichtung* (Bonn, 1968); Theodore Ziolkowski, *Fictional Transfigurations of Jesus* (Princeton, N.J., 1972); Dorothee Sölle, *Realisation: Studien zum Verhältnis von Theologie und Dichtung nach der Aufklärung* (Darmstadt, 1973); Karl-Josef Kuschel, *Jesus in der deutschsprachigen Gegenwartsliteratur* (Zurich, 1978); Paul J. Korshin, *Typologies in England, 1650–1820* (Princeton, N.J., 1982).

literary utilization of hagiography on Russian soil will contribute not only to the history of Russian belles-lettres, but also to Russian intellectual and religious history. Although the present discussion does not pretend to exhaustiveness—certain authors, like Gogol, have been deliberately omitted—, it does attempt to provide a thorough analysis of the major types of usage of hagiographical material by modern Russian writers.[121] Konstantin Aksakov once claimed that Russian history could be viewed as a saint's Life.[122] His belief is indicative of the pertinence of the hagiographical approach to the nineteenth- and early twentieth-century intellectual world. Modern Russian writers have extensively mined their medieval literary past. The major intention of this study is to demonstrate the richness and importance of their efforts.

[121] Gogol's exploitation of the Life of St. Acacius of Sinai has been treated in detail in the following articles: John Schillinger, "Gogol's 'Overcoat' as a Travesty of Hagiography," *Slavic and East European Journal* 16 (1972): 36–41; and K. D. Seeman, "Eine Heiligenlegende als Vorbild von Gogol's 'Mantel'," *Zeitschrift für slavische Philologie* 33 (1966): 7–21.

[122] K. S. Aksakov, *Sochineniia*, vol. 1 (St. Petersburg, 1915), 625. Cited in Peter K. Christoff, *K. S. Aksakov: A Study in Ideas* (Princeton, N.J., 1982), 323.

CHAPTER TWO

Hagiography and History: The Saintly Prince in the Poetry of the Decembrists

Karamzin is our first historian and our last chronicler.
Alexander Pushkin

He applied himself to spiritual matters, did not make idle conversation, did not like shameful words, avoided people of evil behavior, and always conversed with blessed people, always observed the divine Scriptures with deep tenderness, cared greatly about God's churches, and kept guard over the Russian land with courage.

The Discourse on Dmitrii Donskoi

AFTER the death of Nikolai Karamzin (1766–1826), the reputation of the belletrist and historian was kept alive partially by the salon-based efforts of his widow and his daughter Sof'ia.[1] Yet Sof'ia's filial devotion did not extend to reading her father's popular multivolume *History of the Russian State* (*Istoriia gosudarstva Rossiiskogo*, 1818–1829), because of her distaste for "the history of Russia, with all those Iaropolks and Sviatopolks."[2] In a similar spirit, Alexander Herzen's father, the capricious and irritable Ivan Iakovlev, glanced at the *History* because he had heard that Alexander I had read it, but put it aside in disgust: "It's all Iziaslavichi and Ol'govichi: to whom can this be of interest?"[3] Indeed, the life and times of Russia's numerous princes were sometimes only a source of tedium for Karamzin's potential audience. Among those contemporaries whose imaginations were captivated, however, were the future Decembrists, the upper-class instigators of an abortive uprising

[1] A briefer version of this chapter appeared in *SEEJ* 30 (1986): 29–44.

[2] Cited in J. L. Black, *Nicholas Karamzin and Russian Society in the Nineteenth Century: A Study in Russian Political and Historical Thought* (Toronto, 1975), 147.

[3] A. I. Gertsen, *Ss*, vol. 8 (Moscow, 1956), 88.

against Nicholas I in December 1825. In the 1820s and 1830s the literary output of these disenchanted young men included several poems devoted to various early Russian rulers. In these poems the characterization of the princes reveals traces of a hagiographical orientation.[4] The origin, nature, and impact of this particular hagiographical approach are the subject of this chapter.

The Saintly Prince in History and Legend

Sof'ia's and Iakovlev's narrow-minded sentiments about the *History* are curiously apposite, for it is distinguished by an exaggeratedly dynastic orientation. In Karamzin's view, Russia's history was the product of the actions of its rulers. Such is the gist of the conclusion of his dedication to Alexander I:

> History bequeathes the actions of magnanimous Tsars and inspires a love for their sacred memory in the most remote posterity. Graciously accept this book, which serves as a proof of this. The history of the people belongs to the Tsar (1: xvi).[5]

Karamzin had been making such pronouncements on the magnitude of the role of the tsar for over a decade.[6] He was also firmly convinced of the logical corollary to this notion, that an autocratic form of government was most appropriate for Russia.[7] At the end of the foreword to his *History*, he expressed the hope that "the firm foundations of our greatness will never change; that the principles of wise Autocracy and the Holy Faith may strengthen the union of the parts more and more" (1: xxviii). As the outgrowth of such convictions, the *History* was to a large extent a saga of the activities of a multitude of princes and a heavy-handed demonstration of the benefits of autocracy.

[4] Several of these poems are discussed by M. Raab in her wide-ranging article, "Obraz drevnerusskogo cheloveka v poezii pushkinskogo vremeni," *TOdl* 26 (1971): 13–32. In a section entitled "Drevnerusskii kniaz' kak ideal'nyi obraz sviazannogo s narodom pravitelia," Raab acknowledges the presence of hagiographical elements in the Decembrist portrayal of medieval rulers. See especially 24–25.

[5] The text of *The History of the Russian State* (*Istoriia gosudarstva Rossiiskogo*) referred to here and elsewhere is the edition published in St. Petersburg in 1892 (reprint, The Hague, 1969).

[6] For more details on Karamzin's earlier statements, see Black, *Nicholas Karamzin*, 40–41, 49.

[7] These views were outlined by Karamzin in his well-known *Memoir on Ancient and Modern Russia* (*Zapiska o drevnei i novoi Rossii*, 1811), which was not published in its entirety until 1870.

In his insistence on the essentially dynastic nature of history, Karamzin's perspective did not differ substantially from that of his eighteenth-century predecessors.[8] Where his *History* did stand alone was in its immense popularity, which persisted throughout the first half of the nineteenth century.[9] Even before the first eight volumes appeared in print in February 1818, interest in its contents had been stimulated by Karamzin's regular readings to select groups in both Moscow and St. Petersburg.[10] In addition, Karamzin's established reputation as the author of such sentimental favorites as "Poor Liza" ("Bednaia Liza," 1792) and his forays into the past in stories like "Natal'ia the Boyar's Daughter" ("Natal'ia, boiarskaia doch'," 1792) and "Marfa the Mayoress" ("Marfa Posadnitsa," 1803) could only enhance the attention given his venture into a less familiar sphere.[11] Even so, the initial excitement surrounding the appearance of the *History* was without precedent. Its publication has been called the greatest literary event of the epoch.[12] Alexander Pushkin reports that the first edition of 3,000 copies was sold out within a month and, with tongue in cheek, compares Karamzin's discovery of ancient Russia with Columbus' discovery of America.[13] When the controversial ninth volume appeared in 1821, one observer wittily claimed that "there's such an emptiness in the streets of Petersburg because everyone is absorbed in the reign of Ivan the Terrible."[14] This interest lasted long after the poet-historian's death. While numerous writers and scholars made direct use of the *History*, others imbibed its philosophy through the medium of a series of textbook adaptations.[15]

[8] P. Miliukov, *Glavnye techeniia russkoi istoricheskoi mysli*, 3d ed. (St. Petersburg, 1913), 167. On the importance of the princes in the *History*, see also R. E. McGrew, "Notes on the Princely Role in Karamzin's *Istorija gosudarstva Rossijskago*," *American Slavic and East European Review* 18 (1959): 12–24.

[9] Cf. Hans Rogger, *National Consciousness in Eighteenth-Century Russia* (Cambridge, Mass., 1960), 19; and Edward C. Thaden, "The Beginning of Romantic Nationalism in Russia," *American Slavic and East European Review* 13 (1954): 511.

[10] Black, *Nicholas Karamzin*, 168.

[11] Cf. Miliukov, *Glavnye techeniia*, 215.

[12] Alexandre Koyré, *La philosophie et le problème national en Russie au début du XIXe siècle* (Paris, 1929), 29.

[13] A. A. Pushkin, *Pss*, vol. 12 (Moscow, 1949), 305.

[14] N. I. Lorer, *Zapiski dekabrista* (Moscow, 1931), 67. Cited in S. S. Volk, *Istoricheskie vzgliady dekabristov* (Moscow, 1958), 385.

[15] See Black, *Nicholas Karamzin*, 130–32; and A. M. Davidovich, *Samoderzhavie v epokhu imperialisma* (Moscow, 1975), 174.

The success of Karamzin's work was not wholly unexpected. Since the eighteenth century there had been a demand for an "artistic" history, for an entertaining and flattering account of the Russian past.[16] In the early nineteenth century, as the patriotic sentiments evoked by the Napoleonic Wars fueled the wish to discover a noble past to match a heroic present, this desire became especially urgent.[17] Karamzin's novelistic approach, his handling of historical material as a "noble literary theme," corresponded precisely to the mood and desire of the times.[18] While there were previous multivolume histories of Russia, like those of Vasilii Tatishchev and Mikhail Shcherbatov, their infelicitous style did not endear them to the reading public.[19] Karamzin's *History*, which was deliberately intended to describe the past in a captivating manner, filled a conspicuous gap in Russian historiography.[20]

Not all the reactions to the *History* were unqualifiedly enthusiastic. While the pro-autocratic tendency of Karamzin's thinking appealed to conservatives, liberals were less entranced. Their reaction is most succinctly expressed by Pushkin's sarcastic epigram penned in 1819:

> В его "Истории" изящность, простота
> Доказывают нам, без всякого пристрастья,
> Необходимость самовластья
> И прелести кнута.

(In his *History*, refinement and simplicity try to prove to us, without any bias, the necessity for autocracy and the charms of the knout).[21]

Pushkin subsequently modified his opinion. The most consistently negative reaction to the *History* was found among the budding revolution-

[16] Cf. Rogger, *National Consciousness*, 188–89.

[17] Cf. N. A. Kotliarevskii, *Dekabristy: Kn. A. I. Odoevskii i A. A. Bestuzhev-Marlinskii: ikh zhizn' i literaturnaia deiatel'nost'* (St. Petersburg, 1907), 221.

[18] Cf. Miliukov, *Glavnye techeniia*, 214.

[19] Tatishchev's five-volume *Istoriia rossiiskaia s samykh drevneishikh vremen* first appeared in Moscow, 1768–1848. Shcherbatov's seven-volume *Istoriia Rossiiskaia ot drevneishikh vremen* first appeared in St. Petersburg, 1770–1791.

[20] Cf. Miliukov, *Glavnye techeniia*, 214. The most explicit formulation of his intentions by the author himself is cited by M. Pogodin, *N. M. Karamzin, po ego sochineniiam, pis'mam i otzyvam sovremennikov* (Moscow, 1866), 2: 2. See Anatole G. Mazour, *Modern Russian Historiography*, revised edition (Westport, Conn., 1975), 81. On the popularity of the *History*, cf. also Rogger, *National Consciousness*, 19.

[21] Vl. Orlov, ed., *Dekabristy: Poeziia, dramaturgiia, proza, publitsistika, literaturnaia kritika* (Moscow, 1951), 207.

aries, the Decembrists, many of whom had been exposed to the more liberal spirit of Western Europe while serving as officers in the campaigns against Napoleon and were now interested in abolishing serfdom and transforming Russia into a constitutional monarchy or, in the case of the more radical conspirators, a republic.[22] While often impressed by his command of the sources and his use of many heretofore unexploited materials, they found the political tenor of Karamzin's *History* offensive.[23] Above all, they objected to his pro-autocratic stance as well as what they perceived as his exaggerated appraisal of the role of the princes in Russian history.[24] In direct opposition to Karamzin, Nikita Murav'ev (1794–1843), one of the foremost members of the secret Petersburg-centered Northern Society of the Decembrists, insisted that "history belongs to the people."[25] Another conspirator, Mikhail Orlov (1788–1842), wrote to the poet Prince Petr Viazemskii that he had "awaited Karamzin's *History* as the Jews await the Messiah," but he objected to what he and many others considered a Normanist bias in discussing the origins of the Kievan state; the suggestion that the major role in the formation of early Kiev was played by Scandinavian princes was insulting to the patriotic feelings of many Decembrists.[26] On the other hand, the ninth volume of the *History*, devoted to an exposé of the tyranny of Ivan the Terrible, found favor with the Decembrists.[27] It was this volume that both Kondratii Ryleev (1795–1826) and

[22] On the impact of the Napoleonic campaigns on the Decembrists and other young liberals, see Koyré, *La philosophie et le problème national*, 27–28.

[23] On the grudging respect of the Decembrists for the *History*, see Volk, *Istoricheskie vzgliady*, 290, 293.

[24] On the admiration of various Decembrists for Karamzin's style, see Black, *Nicholas Karamzin*, 141; and Lauren G. Leighton, *Alexander Bestuzhev-Marlinsky* (Boston, 1975), 52. On the reaction of liberals in general, Allen McConnell has written: "Liberals, who resisted its fundamental theses—an all-competent autocracy and the necessity of serfdom—surrendered to its captivating style" (*Tsar Alexander I: Paternalistic Reformer* [New York, 1970], 193).

[25] A. M. Egolin, ed., *Dekabristy-literatory*, *Literaturnoe nasledstvo*, vol. 59 (Moscow, 1954), 582. It is worth noting here that when Nikolai Polevoi subsequently produced a history of Russia intended as a refutation of Karamzin's views, he entitled it the *History of the Russian People* (*Istoriia russkogo naroda*, 1829–1833).

[26] Orlov's comment is found in Egolin, *Dekabristy-literatory*, 566. On Decembrist attitudes to the founding of the Kievan state, cf. Peter K. Christoff, *The Third Heart: Some Intellectual-Ideological Currents and Cross Currents in Russia 1800–1830* (The Hague, 1970), 89.

[27] Volk, *Istoricheskie vzgliady*, 385–86.

Mikhail Bestuzhev (1800–1871), the younger brother of the popular Decembrist writer Aleksandr Bestuzhev (1797–1837), read in prison while awaiting interrogation and sentencing (and, in Ryleev's case, execution). Mikhail Bestuzhev later described his feeling that through his reading, fate had wished to acquaint him in advance with the "subtle caprices of despotism."[28]

The Decembrist attitude toward Karamzin's *History* was more complex than simply a distaste for the earlier volumes and an enthusiasm for the ninth. In the first place, the political views of the individual Decembrists were sufficiently diverse to preclude any but the most general statements concerning their attitude as a group towards Karamzin. Moreover and perhaps more importantly, a distinction must be made between the Decembrist reaction to Karamzin's intentions and their response to his actual narrative. In other words, while his ultimate theme may have been anathema to them, Karamzin, whose writings were often compared to those of Sir Walter Scott, possessed a widely acknowledged ability to tell a good story.[29] Kondratii Ryleev, who eventually owned two editions of the *History*, exclaimed after reading Karamzin's account of the reign of Ivan the Terrible: "I don't know at what to be more surprised, the tyranny of Ivan or the talent of our Tacitus."[30] Despite their manifold reservations concerning what they considered its reactionary tenor, many Decembrists fell under the sway of the *History*, adopting in the process, to a certain extent, Karamzin's bias concerning the role of the princes. The *History* stimulated a general interest in the past among the Decembrists, as it did among their contemporaries in general.[31] Some Decembrists felt that the only way to combat Karamzin's pernicious influence was on his own terms. As the Soviet scholar S. S. Volk points out, they would doubtless have agreed with the injunction of the poet Ivan Dmitriev (1760–1837): "It's necessary to beat Karamzin not with epigrams, but with chronicles."[32] A large number of Decembrists did in fact turn to the original chronicle

[28] M. K. Azadovskii, ed., *Vospominaniia Bestuzhevykh* (Moscow, 1951), 114.

[29] On Karamzin and Scott, see Mazour, *Modern Russian Historiography*, 82–83.

[30] Ryleev's comment is cited in A. G. Tseitlin, "O biblioteke Ryleeva," *Dekabristy-literatory*, 318. Tseitlin provides detailed information on the editions of the *History* and published chronicles found in Ryleev's library (318–19).

[31] Cf. Mazour, *Modern Russian Historiography*, 83.

[32] Letter from I. I. Dmitriev to A. I. Turgenev at the beginning of the 1820s. Cited in Volk, *Istoricheskie vzgliady*, 291.

sources, among them two poets who later wrote fictionalized accounts of various Russian princes, Prince Aleksandr Odoevskii (1802–1839) and Aleksandr Bestuzhev.[33]

In order to appreciate the impression made on Karamzin's readers, one must recall the medieval Russian perception of the prince's status expressed in the chronicles and other written sources: to a great extent it was precisely this view which Karamzin transmitted in his *History*. As is well known, medieval Russia, in contrast to Byzantium, often assumed the sanctity of its princes and canonized a large number of them. More than an eighth of pre-eighteenth century Russian saints, and more than a third of the 180 canonized from the Kievan period, were princes and princesses; with one exception, the only laic saints of the Kievan period were princes.[34] There is evidence to suggest, moreover, that often little distinction was made between princes formally recognized as saints and those never canonized.[35] It has been observed that "the myth of the saintly princes and princely saints was sufficiently comprehensive so that one would expect to find virtually all Russian princes sheltered under its wings. And, in fact, when we turn to all the available lists of saints, canonized or not, we find that our expectations come very close to being fulfilled."[36] The lure of the idealized saintly prince was sufficiently compelling to draw into its orbit even those who in other cultural contexts might not have attracted the least suspicion of sainthood.

The sacred identity often imputed to Russian princes was inevitably reflected in medieval Russian literature. The significance and development of the large body of Old Russian princes' Lives (*kniazheskie zhitiia*) within the context of hagiography still await full elucidation. As a group, the works traditionally designated as princes' Lives include not only *zhitiia*, that is, Lives in the strict sense of the word, but also *povesti* (stories), *slova* (discourses), *chteniia* (readings), and *skazaniia* (narratives). Many of these works found their way into the chronicles. While some cannot properly be termed life-writing because they focus not on the prince's character and activities, but on the events in which he par-

[33] On reading of the chronicles by the Decembrists, see Volk, *Istoricheskie vzgliady*, 291–94.

[34] Michael Cherniavsky, *Tsar and People: Studies in Russian Myths* (New Haven, 1961), 6, 10.

[35] Cf. Cherniavsky, *Tsar and People*, 30; and George P. Fedotov, *The Russian Religious Mind*, 2 vols. (Belmont, Mass., 1975), 2: 152.

[36] Cherniavsky, *Tsar and People*, 30–31.

ticipates, their tone is unquestionably hagiographical.[37] Where works written or revised under the impact of the so-called "Second South Slavic Influence" of the fourteenth and fifteenth centuries are involved, a pronounced tendency towards abstraction becomes noticeable. Elaborate concluding eulogies became an extremely important and well-defined component of Lives in general at this time, and in many instances the diminished role of biographical organization resulted in the virtual disappearance of the difference between Lives and ecclesiastical panegyrics and hymns.[38] At the other extreme, it is sometimes difficult to determine whether some princes' Lives should be distinguished from saints' Lives in general.

The precise definition of princes' Lives in relation to other hagiographical literature is not at issue here. Germane to the present discussion is the fact that the hagiographical approach characteristic of medieval treatments of princes frequently manifested itself in the chronicles.[39] As mentioned above, the various types of works called princes' Lives were often transmitted through the chronicles. In addition, even brief annalistic entries were sometimes subject to hagiographical interpretation. It may be argued that there was little literature produced in medieval Russia which can be termed secular in the strict sense of the word.[40] The monk-chroniclers saw Russian history as the continuation of biblical history.[41] The result was often a stereotyped characterization of events and people which relied greatly on topoi. In

[37] For discussion of the genre of princes' Lives, see especially Norman Ingham, "The Limits of Secular Biography in Medieval Slavic Literature, Particularly Old Russian," in *American Contributions to the Sixth International Congress of Slavists, Prague, 1968*, vol. 2 (The Hague, 1968), 181–99; and "Genre Characteristics of the Kievan Lives of Princes in Slavic and European Perspective," in *American Contributions to the Ninth International Congress of Slavists, Kiev, September 1983*, vol. 2 (Columbus, Ohio, 1983), 223–37. See also N. Serebrianskii, *Drevne-russkie kniazheskie zhitiia (Obzor redaktsii i teksty)* (Moscow, 1915), 284–95; and V. A. Grikhin, "Drevne-russkie kniazheskie zhitiia," *Russkaia rech'*, 1980, no. 2: 106–10.

[38] Cf. D. S. Likhachev, *Kul'tura Rusi vremeni Andreia Rubleva i Epifaniia Premudrogo* (Leningrad, 1962), 47; and V. O. Kliuchevskii, *Drevnerusskie zhitiia sviatykh kak istoricheskii istochnik* (Moscow, 1871), 365, 427.

[39] Cf. Raab, "Obraz drevnerusskogo cheloveka," 25.

[40] On the predominantly religious character of medieval Orthodox Slavic literature, see especially Riccardo Picchio, "Models and Patterns in the Literary Tradition of Medieval Orthodox Slavdom," in *American Contributions to the Seventh International Congress of Slavists, Warsaw, 1973*, vol. 2 (The Hague, 1973), 442–466.

[41] On the conception of literature as an open book, in imitation of the Bible, see Picchio, "Models and Patterns," 447.

chronicle accounts of princes this is particularly apparent in their eulogies.[42]

A characteristic eulogy is that of Konstantin, the son of Vsevolod III, found under the year 1218 in the *Laurentian Chronicle*, one of the annalistic compilations used by Karamzin:[43]

> That winter . . . the Christ-loving grand prince Konstantin . . . died. This blessed prince was exceedingly adorned with all good moral habits; he loved God with all his soul and all his desire, and he had an absolute fear of God in his heart and in his soul. He did not darken his mind with the vainglory of this perfidious world . . . [He] was upright, generous, meek, and humble. He showed mercy to all, took care of all, and even more loved wondrous and glorious charity and the building of churches, and he was concerned about this day and night; for he cared greatly about the building of God's beautiful churches, and he built many churches during his reign . . . He honored beyond measure the priestly and monastic orders . . . and the blessed man thought about the beggarly and the wretched . . . Thus he did not spare his estate, and he distributed to those in need. For in truth he was, in accordance with Job, an eye to the blind, a foot to the lame, and a hand to those deprived of comfort. And he artlessly loved all, clothed the naked, soothed the suffering, warmed those who would die in winter, comforted the sad, and did not grieve anyone in any way, but instilled wisdom in everyone with his words on corporeal and spiritual matters; for often he read books assiduously, and he did everything according to what is written. God justly endowed him with the meekness of David and with the wisdom of Solomon and he was filled with apostolic orthodoxy.[44]

This eulogy contains a series of topoi and sedulously avoids virtually all information which might distinguish Konstantin from other devout Christian princes. It presents an idealized portrait, a verbal icon, and is

[42] Cf. M. F. Antonova, " 'Slovo o zhitii i o prestavlenii velikogo kniazia Dmitriia Ivanovicha, tsaria Rus'skago' (Voprosy atributsii i zhanra)," *TOdl* 28 (1974): 151–52.

[43] On Karamzin's use of the chronicles, see J. L. Black, "The Primečanija: Karamzin as a 'Scientific' Historian of Russia," in J. L. Black, ed., *Essays on Karamzin: Russian Man-of-Letters, Political Thinker, Historian, 1766–1826* (The Hague, 1975), 133.

[44] *Polnoe sobranie russkikh letopisei*, vol. 1, 2d ed., vypusk 2 (Leningrad, 1927), cols. 442–43.

an extreme example of the tendency towards abstraction in medieval Slavic literature. It incorporates many of the most common topoi. The assertions of complete piety unmarred by excessively worldly concerns and the expression of this piety through charity and the building of churches are especially characteristic. These and other topoi recur, one might add, not only in the Lives of other Russian princes, but also in accounts of other nations' saintly rulers. Edward the Confessor (1004–1066), for example, is described as peaceable, charitable, a supporter of monasteries, and a supposed participant in a chaste marriage; Ladislas of Hungary (1040–1095) and Louis of France (1214–1270), among others, are credited with equal virtue. Where Russian saintly rulers differ most significantly from their European confreres is in their numbers.

Karamzin's *History* contains appraisals of certain princes which are as enthusiastic and hackneyed as any in the chronicles. In some instances his observations differ little from those of the monastic chroniclers. A good example is his commentary on Prince Mstislav of Tmutorokan' (?–1036), the son of the saintly Prince Vladimir, the Christianizer of Russia, and the brother of the revered martyrs Boris and Gleb:

> This prince, surnamed the Bold, did not experience the vicissitudes of military fortune: when he fought, he always won; terrible to his enemies, he was famed for his charity to the people and his love for his faithful retinue . . . He raised his sword against his brother, but he atoned for this cruelty, characteristic of that time, by his magnanimous peace with the defeated . . . The stone temple of the Mother of God in Tmutorokan', built by him as a sign of gratitude for the victory gained over the Kosogian giant, and the Church of the Savior in Chernigov remained as monuments to Mstislav's piety (2: 18).

As in numerous chronicle eulogies, Karamzin here emphasizes Mstislav's piety, charity, and courage, as well as his church-building activities.

Soviet scholars are often critical of what they see as Karamzin's prejudice in favor of the medieval Russian princes; in the opinion of Volk, for example, "in his idealization of the princes Karamzin knew no limit."[45] Western scholars as well have pointed to Karamzin's tendency

[45] Volk, *Istoricheskie vzgliady*, 336.

to exaggerate regarding the early princes in particular, to the extent of exceeding even the chronicle sources in emphasizing the positive or negative qualities of a given prince.[46] The partisan character of Karamzin's narrative is heightened by the fact that at times the border between his summary of chronicle accounts and his own appraisal becomes decidedly hazy.[47]

As a consequence, the *History* served, on one level, as a conduit for an essentially hagiographical portrayal of many Russian princes, particularly those of the Kievan period. This may have resulted both from an attempt by the historian to remain faithful to his chronicle sources and from the desire to support his pro-autocratic sentiments with numerous examples of virtuous rulers. Whatever the reasons, Karamzin did not break with the traditions embodied in the chronicles, but merely presented them to the nineteenth-century reading public in an updated garb.[48]

The Decembrists were thus exposed to the princely variety of hagiography not only through their own reading of various chronicles, but also through the mediated form exemplified by Karamzin. In addition to these historical expressions of princely sanctity, contemporary political life was also marked by a renewed emphasis on the rhetoric of the saintly prince, as evidenced, for example, by the granting in 1814 to Alexander I of the title "the Blessed" (*Blagoslovennyi*).[49] A variety of factors may have encouraged the Decembrists to accept partially, in spite of their democratic aspirations, a glorified image of certain princes. The military successes achieved by the Russians during the Napoleonic wars fostered the growth of nationalistic sentiments among educated Russians of various political tendencies.[50] "We were the chil-

[46] Black, "The Primečanija," 139–40.

[47] Cf. Black, "The Primečanija," 139; and L. N. Luzianina, "*Istoriia gosudarstva rossiiskogo* N. M. Karamzina i tragediia Pushkina *Boris Godunov* (K probleme kharaktera letopistsa)," *Russkaia literatura*, 1971, no. 1: 50.

[48] Iu. M. Lotman notes that "from [his] numerous documentary sources, Karamzin drew not only the 'plot' ['*siuzhet*'] of his narrative—the events and their order—, but also the point of view, the interpretation." See Iu. M. Lotman, "Puti razvitiia russkoi prozy 1800-x–1810-x godov," *Uchenye zapiski Tartuskogo gosudarstvennogo universiteta*, 1961, vypusk 104: 42. Cited in Luzianina, "*Istoriia gosudarstva rossiiskogo*," 49.

[49] Cherniavsky, *Tsar and People*, 139–40, 135.

[50] See n. 21 above. See also Volk, *Istoricheskie vzgliady*, 31, 439. The French Revolution as well had a massive impact on the development of nationalism throughout

dren of 1812," declared the Decembrists.[51] Like many of their conservative contemporaries, the Decembrists revealed a tendency to idealize medieval Russian history, particularly the Kievan period.[52] Where they most clearly parted company with the conservatives was in their avowed admiration for medieval Novgorod. For many Decembrists, that proud city-state, which had fallen victim in the fifteenth century to the centralizing tendencies of the Muscovite princes, symbolized "local freedom and communal social virtue."[53] This sentiment found especially clear expression in the poem "Novgorod" (1826) written by a young sympathizer of the Decembrists, Dmitrii Venevitinov (1805–1827), who referred to the city as "drevnii grad / Svobody, slavy i torgovli!" ("ancient city of freedom, glory, and trade!").[54] The Decembrist enthusiasm for Novgorod took many forms. In their drafts of constitutions they incorporated terminology for political institutions borrowed from that of the medieval city, the term *veche*, or town assembly, being perhaps the most well-known.[55] Their captivation was also expressed in other, more adolescent forms. In his room in St. Petersburg, for example, Nikita Murav'ev kept a "veche bell" which was used to summon his compatriots to meetings.[56]

An idealization of early Russian rulers from the time preceding the centralized autocracy seems a logical corollary to the idealization of an independent Novgorod. Just as the city was admired for the democratic spirit of its population and institutions, so many of the early princes were praised for their resistance to despotism in a variety of forms and for their laudable concern for their subjects. As will be seen, the civic virtues referred to by the chroniclers assume an especial prominence in Decembrist literature.

In choosing medieval personalities and themes as subjects for literary treatment, the Decembrists were responding to broadly European cul-

---

Europe, including Russia. See, for example, Hans Kohn, *Nationalism: Its Meaning and History*, revised edition (Princeton, N.J., 1965), 32.

[51] V. E. Iakushkin and M. I. Murav'ev-Apostol, *Russkaia starina*, 1886, no. 7, 159. Cited in Volk, *Istoricheskie vzgliady*, 31.

[52] Cf. Leonard Shapiro, *Rationalism and Nationalism in Russian Nineteenth-Century Political Thought* (New Haven, 1967), 31.

[53] Christoff, *Third Heart*, 79.

[54] The text of "Novgorod" is found in D. V. Venevitinov, *Pss* (Moscow, 1934), 82.

[55] Cf. Christoff, *Third Heart*, 147; and Marc Raeff, *The Decembrist Movement* (Englewood Cliffs, N.J., 1966), 12.

[56] Volk, *Istoricheskie vzgliady*, 326.

tural influences as well. The tremendous vogue enjoyed by the novels of Walter Scott had stirred the interest of many nineteenth-century Russians in the medieval period. Regarding the impact of Scott on the Decembrists, it has been suggested that "in Scott there was a blend of romantic and medieval that inevitably attracted a generation which saw as its mission the salvation of Russia—a mission which involved the discovery, if possible, of neglected values in Russia's own medieval past."[57] In addition, Ossianism, with its romanticized view of the medieval past, had had a distinct impact on contemporary literary tastes since the late eighteenth century.[58] The discovery in 1795 of the medieval classic "The Lay of Igor''s Campaign" ("Slovo o polku Igoreve") fanned the flames of this particular enthusiasm.[59] The bard Baian mentioned in this poem, a worthy competitor for the Gaelic Ossian, reappeared in poems by Decembrists, singing the glories of Russia's past.

At the center of "The Lay of Igor''s Campaign" stands a prince, the unfortunate Igor'. Even before the discovery of this work, medieval Russian princes had been considered suitable subjects for historical dramas in particular since the early eighteenth century. One of Russia's earliest classical dramas was Feofan Prokopovich's *Vladimir* (1705). Later in the century Mikhail Kheraskov made the saint's Christianizing activities the subject of the narrative poem *Vladimir* (1785). Aleksandr Sumarokov produced the drama *Mstislav* (1774), while even Catherine II employed her talents in writing Shakespearean imitations devoted to the earliest, legendary rulers of Russia.

Around the turn of the century Karamzin himself expressed the belief that medieval Russian heroes, by whom he seems to have meant primarily the princes, represented highly suitable subjects for artistic treatment.[60] In 1802 his interest in the artistic potential of Russia's dynastic past found theoretical expression in an article entitled "On Events and Characters in Russian History That Are Possible Subjects of the Arts" ("O sluchaiakh i kharakterakh v Rossiiskoi Istorii, kotorye mogut byt' predmetom khudozhestv"). In his article he describes in detail several possible scenes for paintings, including episodes involving Prince Vladimir, his grandmother St. Ol'ga, his sons Iaroslav the Wise and the aforementioned Mstislav of Tmutorokan', as well as

57 Christoff, *Third Heart*, 62.

58 Cf. Rogger, *National Consciousness*, 154.

59 Cf. D. S. Mirsky, *A History of Russian Literature: From Its Beginnings to 1900* (New York, 1958), 14.

60 Cf. Black, *Nicholas Karamzin*, 29.

several other princes and princesses. The purpose of such paintings, in Karamzin's view, would be to give life to major characters and events of Russian history, with the desirable consequence that "if a historical character is depicted strikingly on canvas or in marble, then he becomes more interesting for us even in the chronicles themselves: we are curious to discover the source from which the artist took his idea, and with great attention we read the description of the man's deeds, remembering what a lively impression his image made on us."[61] The artist thus becomes what Karamzin calls an "organ of patriotism."[62]

Although their conception of the proper message was very different, the Decembrists shared Karamzin's belief in the preeminently didactic function of depicting historical figures. Among the young revolutionaries, history was regarded as a rich source of models of patriotism and courage.[63] In an article "On Teaching History to Children" ("O prepodavanii istorii detiam") Pavel Cherevin (1802–1825), a member of the Northern Society, affirmed the importance of native exemplars and added: "A teacher of history is more than a teacher: he is a preacher, edifying a malleable young age with examples of the past."[64] The explicitly religious thrust of this statement indicates the Decembrists' exalted approach to historical material. In a more stridently patriotic vein, Fedor Glinka (1786–1880) wrote in 1816 that "the great deeds scattered through the chronicles of the fatherland, if one were to collect them, would make for Russia a necklace of glory, the like of which Greece and Rome scarcely possessed."[65] The reference to Greece and Rome is far from casual; one of the books popular in Decembrist circles was Plutarch's *Lives*.[66]

The Idealized Ruler in Decembrist Poetry Before the Uprising

An extensive discussion of the function of the historical examples embodied in literary form is found in the introduction to Ryleev's series

[61] *Sochineniia Karamzina*, vol. 7 (Moscow, 1803), 354.

[62] *Sochineniia Karamzina*, 7: 354.

[63] Volk, *Istoricheskie vzgliady*, 49.

[64] Cited in Volk, *Istoricheskie vzgliady*, 53.

[65] F. N. Glinka, *Pis'ma k drugu*, pt. 2 (St. Petersburg, 1816), 7–8. Cited in Volk, *Istoricheskie vzgliady*, 286.

[66] S. I. Mashinskii, ed., *Pisateli-dekabristy v vospominaniiakh sovremennikov*, vol. 1 (Moscow, 1980), 16.

of poems on historical personages, the "Meditations" ("Dumy," 1821–1823). Ryleev refers here to the intention of Julian Niemcewicz (1758–1841), the Polish author of *Historical Songs* (*Spiewy historyczne*, 1816), a collection of poems that inspired the form of Ryleev's own work: " 'To remind youth of the exploits of its ancestors, to acquaint it with the brightest epochs of the people's history, to bring together love for the fatherland with the first impressions of memory—here is the true way to inculcate in the people a strong attachment to the homeland' " (105).[67] Ryleev expresses his complete assent with this approach, saying that in writing the "Meditations" he was guided by the same aim: like Niemcewicz, he hoped to provide models worthy of emulation, a program for civic virtue. In the process, absolute fidelity to the supposed historical facts was sometimes sacrificed.[68]

Ryleev worked on the twenty-odd "Meditations" between 1821 and 1823. Many of the poems were initially published separately in journals and were later included in a volume which appeared in March 1825. After the uprising in December and Ryleev's execution in the following year, his works were forbidden and had to be disseminated secretly.[69] It was only in London in 1860 that the collection was reissued by Herzen and his fellow expatriate Nikolai Ogarev as part of their policy of myth-making about the Decembrists.

The question of the definition of the genre employed by Ryleev in the "Meditations" was highly controversial at the time of the poems' composition. Ryleev himself distinguished "Meditations" from tales and historical songs, but provided no details by way of explanation, other than the assertion that the Poles borrowed the genre from the Russians and not vice versa (so much for any debt to Niemcewicz!).[70] Among his contemporaries, the sole point of consensus appeared to be that the "Meditations" represented a hybrid, but of what precisely no one could say with certainty.[71] Recent Soviet scholarship suggests that

[67] Ryleev quotes Niemcewicz's remarks in Russian translation. The text of the "Meditations" ("Dumy") is found in K. F. Ryleev, *Psst* (Leningrad, 1971), 105–82.

[68] P. J. O'Meara, "Medieval and Eighteenth-Century Themes in the Work of Ryleev," *Study Group in Eighteenth-Century Russia, Newsletter*, No. 8 (September, 1980), 19.

[69] M. V. Nechkina, *Dekabristy* (Moscow, 1975), 162.

[70] See Ryleev, *Psst*, 105–6.

[71] Ryleev, *Psst*, 421–22. An especially detailed account of the controversy is provided in K. F. Ryleev, *Dumy*, ed. L. G. Frizman (Moscow, 1975), 174–83.

the problem may lie in Ryleev's inconsistent observance of the genre requirements created by him. While the monologue of the hero was theoretically intended to constitute the structural center of a given poem, in practice a "generic transformation" often took place, and in some poems the monologue occupies an insignificant position.[72]

Given this structural disorder, it is more profitable to analyze how the "Meditations" fulfill the poet's express intention of providing a blueprint for virtuous citizenship. In this light, the precise definition of genre becomes less important than the isolation of those thematic motifs that occur in a variety of stylistic contexts and bear the main burden of Ryleev's message. Pushkin's initial response to the "Meditations" was somewhat contemptuous: "They're all in the same style; they're made up of commonplaces (*Loci topici*) . . . The description of the place of action, the speech of the hero and—the moral teaching. There is nothing national or Russian in them . . ."[73] In view of an increasing fondness among contemporary writers for local color and realistic detail, his criticism is not surprising; Ryleev's heroes are indeed remarkably lacking in individuality and overtly national characteristics. Yet his paragons do not lack domestic cultural precedents, for many of the topoi employed by Ryleev derive from an idealized image of the saintly prince familiar to Russian hagiography.[74]

As a group, the "Meditations" span nine hundred years of Russian history, beginning with the semi-legendary Oleg and extending to the great eighteenth-century poet Gavrila Derzhavin (1743–1816). More than half of the "Meditations"—and the great majority of those referring to the early period—are based on chapters in Karamzin's *History*. A measure of Ryleev's sometime concern for the exact historical background of the figures treated in the poems is revealed by his request to the young historian Pavel Stroev to write the prefatory notes to most of the "Meditations"; as in the case of his model Niemcewicz, these are often quite detailed.

While most of the "Meditations" concern admirable figures, a few of

[72] Cf. A. E. Khodorov, "Zachinatel' dekabristskogo eposa," in B. S. Meilakh, ed., *Dekabristy i russkaia kul'tura* (Leningrad, 1975), 146–49.

[73] A. A. Pushkin, *Pss*, vol. 13 (Moscow, 1949), 175.

[74] Patrick O'Meara observes that "Pushkin's reservations about their lack of 'Russianness' indicate that his understanding of the term 'national' was essentially an aesthetic one, while Ryleev's was evidently more political and historical." See O'Meara, *K. F. Ryleev: A Political Biography of the Decembrist Poet* (Princeton, N.J., 1984), 184.

the poems focus on historical personages whom Ryleev (and often Karamzin) criticized to a lesser or greater extent—outright villains like Sviatopolk, the fratricidal murderer of Boris and Gleb; usurpers like the False Dmitrii; and early pagan princes not yet cognizant of the correct principles of princely behavior (Vladimir in his pre-Christian period, for example). The "Meditations" devoted to such rulers provide an opportunity for Ryleev to point by contrast to a superior model of princely activity. For example, in "Ol'ga at the Grave of Igor' " ("Ol'ga pri mogile Igoria"), Ol'ga denounces Prince Igor' to their young son Sviatoslav for his insufficient devotion to the needs of his people:

Вот, Святослав, к чему ведет
  Несправедливость власти;
И князь несчастлив и народ,
  Где на престоле страсти.
. . . .

Отец будь подданным своим
  И боле князь, чем воин;
Будь друг своих, гроза чужим,
  И жить в веках достоин!

> (Here, Sviatoslav, is where injustice of power leads; both the prince and the people are unhappy, where there are passions on the throne. . . Be a father to your subjects and more a prince than a warrior; be a friend to your own, a threat to others, and worthy to live forever!) (112).

This theme is repeated throughout the "Meditations": devotion to the needs of one's people should exceed personal ambition. The most extensive formulation of this attitude is found in the poem devoted to Derzhavin, whom Ryleev esteemed as a poet concerned with the "common good."[75] Ryleev quotes from Derzhavin's famous poem "To Rulers and Judges" ("Vlastiteliam i sudiiam," 1780), which in turn is a paraphrase of Psalm 82:

«Ваш долг на сильных не взирать,
Без помощи, без обороны
Сирот и вдов не оставлять
И свято сохранять законы.

[75] O'Meara, *K. F. Ryleev*, 182.

Ваш долг несчастным дать покров,
Всегда спасать от бед невинных,
Исторгнуть бедных из оков,
От сильных защищать бессильных».

("Your duty is not to gaze at the strong, not to leave orphans and widows without help, without defense, and sacredly to preserve the laws.

Your duty is to give succor to the unfortunate, always to save the innocent from misfortunes, to wrest the poor from their fetters, and to defend the weak from the strong") (172–73).[76]

This image of the ruler as the altruistic protector and succorer of his subjects pervades the medieval hagiography devoted of saintly princes. Ryleev does not quote the pessimistic conclusions of Derzhavin's paraphrase regarding the impossibility of depending on rulers and the necessity for relying on God alone; the idealistic young radical was presumably more optimistic about the possibilities for actualizing the desirable set of characteristics listed above. Yet he does often echo Derzhavin in singling out passions as destructive of princely integrity, as in the passage from "Ol'ga at the Grave of Igor' " cited above and in the following conclusions drawn by an anonymous observer in "Sviatopolk":[77]

«Ужасно быть рабом страстей!
Кто раз их предался стремленью,
Тот с каждым днем летит быстрей
От преступленья к преступленью».

("It is terrible to be a slave of passions! Whoever has once abandoned himself to their urging, with every day flies more quickly from crime to crime") (116).

Within the family of medieval Russian saintly princes, a division is sometimes made between passive martyrs and active military heroes. Many of the topoi employed in the characterization of the two types coincide, however. Boris and Gleb, on the one hand, and Alexander Nevskii, on the other, are probably the best-known representatives of

[76] Ryleev's word order differs slightly from that of Derzhavin.

[77] Cf. Derzhavin, "But you, like me, are passion-ridden [*strastnyi*]." See G. P. Derzhavin, *Stikhotvoreniia* (Leningrad, 1957), 92.

their respective types.[78] Both kinds of princes appear in Ryleev's "Meditations": of the three early Christian princes treated by the poet, two, Mstislav of Tmutorokan' and Dmitrii Donskoi (1350–1389), made their mark in the military sphere, while the third, Mikhail of Tver' (1271–1318), was a martyr slain by the Mongols. Ryleev also treated the princely saint Vladimir in two "Meditations," but both poems refer to the prince's pre-Christian period and will not be discussed here.

The princedom of Mstislav of Tmutorakan' was located to the south of Kiev in the eastern Crimea, and he often remained aloof from the affairs of his brothers, the other sons of St. Vladimir. In 1022 Mstislav was drawn into a war with the Kosogians (Circassians). The war came to an abrupt end when the Russian prince killed the giant Rededia, the Kosogian leader, in single combat. According to Karamzin's account, when Mstislav's strength began to fail him, he called on the Mother of God for help and after that was able to cut down the giant (2: 16). In his concluding appraisal of Mstislav's life and reign Karamzin offered the laudatory comments quoted above.

Ryleev's "Meditation" about Mstislav concerns only the encounter between the Kosogians and the Russians and the exciting combat between Mstislav and Rededia. His account of the episode adheres fairly closely to that of Karamzin, even to the extent that his characters often speak when the historian's do. It was doubtless such literal coincidences that led Fedor Dostoevsky to declare the "Ryleev was only Karamzin in verse—and that's all."[79] The poem reflects the stylistic impact of "The Lay of Igor"s Campaign" as well. The attacking Kosogians are compared to clouds and Mstislav to a falcon, a traditional metaphor for bravery. This bravery is emphasized throughout the poem. References to his courage culminate in a comparison between the Russian prince and the biblical David: "Rvanulsia burei raz"iarennoi, / I novyi Goliaf upal!" ("[The prince] rushed like an infuriated storm, and the new

[78] Cf. Serebrianskii, *Drevnerusskie kniazheskie zhitiia*, 288; and Cherniavsky, *Tsar and People*, 22–23. According to Cherniavsky, "as the passion-sufferers were princely saints, saints who had suffered because they were princes, so the active warrior-princes were saintly princes, princes who ruled gloriously because they were saints" (22–23). I have not felt it necessary to insist upon this distinction.

[79] Cited in V. A. Arkhipov, "Dvorianskaia revoliutsionnost' v vospriatii F. M. Dostoevskogo," in V. G. Bazanov and V. E. Vatsuro, eds., *Literaturnoe nasledie dekabristov* (Leningrad, 1975), 245. On Ryleev's literal borrowings from Karamzin, see especially Ryleev *Dumy*, ed. Frizman, 192–93.

Goliath fell!") (129). Such references were a stock component of hagiographical treatments of princes.[80] They both emphasized the continuity between biblical and Russian history and enhanced the status of saintly Russian figures; the eulogy of Konstantin quoted above contains comparisons of the same type. How thoroughly Ryleev had absorbed the hagiographical topoi for princes is indicated by an addition he makes to Karamzin's account of Mstislav's prayer for help, which in itself represents a topos. While the historian simply refers to the request for aid, Ryleev adds, quoting from Mstislav's words in the chronicle sources: "Sviataia deva! . . . / Ia khram sooruzhu tebe!" ("Holy Virgin! . . . I will build a temple for you!") (129). Mstislav's quid pro quo notions may appear a little crass, but, as noted above, the construction of churches as a sign of piety was a topos specifically associated with princes; in his eulogy of Mstislav, Karamzin discusses the prince's church-building activities in detail.

The "Meditation" as a whole, then, develops a picture of Mstislav as simultaneously brave and pious, qualities both in keeping with the traditional image of the saintly prince. The poem is somewhat unusual among the "Meditations," however, in that no explicit reference is made to the virtue manifested in the prince's attitude towards his subjects. More typical in this respect is the "Meditation" concerned with Dmitrii Donskoi, the Muscovite leader of the Russian forces that defeated the Mongol troops under Khan Mamai at the pivotal battle of Kulikovo Field in 1380.

Karamzin devotes a large part of the fifth volume of the *History* to an account of the life and reign of Dmitrii. He consistently emphasizes the mutual love of Dmitrii and his subjects; his eulogy of the prince is an especially glowing one in which numerous topoi have been incorporated without qualification (5: 65–66).[81] As in the case of Mstislav's encounter with Rededia, the account of the battle of Kulikovo itself stresses Dmitrii's combination of piety and courage. The prince insists on being at the front, where he bravely attacks the enemy while simultaneously reciting psalms. His piety also asserts itself after the defeat of the Mongols, when the wounded prince expresses his gratitude to heaven; in keeping with the hagiographical tone of the account, Ka-

[80] It is interesting to note that in Book Nine of Leo Tolstoy's *War and Peace*, a synod prayer asks that Alexander I defeat Napoleon as Moses did Amalek, Gideon Midian, and David Goliath.

[81] On Dmitrii's relationship with his subjects, see, for example, *Istoriia* 5: 16.

ramzin observes that God had saved Dmitrii in "a wondrous way" (5: 45).

Ryleev's poem also underscores Dmitrii's reliance on divine aid. In his opening speech the prince refers to the prayers on their behalf by Sergii of Radonezh in order to exhort his men. Later he reminds them that God is their refuge and source of strength. As in Karamzin's account, when the battle is over Dmitrii offers a prayer of thanks, referring again to Sergii's prayers and according all credit for the victory to God: "Emu vsia slava groznoi bitvy; / On, On proslavil nas!" ("To Him goes all the glory of the terrible battle; He, He alone brought fame to us!") (136). Such repeated insistence on the piety of the prince helps to sustain the impression of his saintliness.

In this context, Dmitrii's personal bravery and devotion to his subjects appear to be inherent components of his Christianity. Unlike Mstislav, who reigned in the brighter days of the early Kievan state, Dmitrii is portrayed by Ryleev as struggling against the despotism of the Mongol overlords. Khan Mamai is described as a tyrant, and Dmitrii, who is concerned with the restoration of the rightful status of his people, speaks of his aims with crusading zeal:

Летим—и возвратим народу . . .
Святую праотцев свободу
И древние права граждан.

(Let us fly—and return to the people . . . the sacred freedom of our forefathers and the ancient rights of citizens) (133).

While Karamzin does emphasize to a remarkable degree Dmitrii's egalitarian sentiments and rapport with the people, he does not impute quite such liberal thinking to the Muscovite prince. What is significant here is that Ryleev couches potentially radical sentiments in the altruistic, self-sacrificing terms typical of a conventionalized image of a prince. Where he departs from a medieval hagiographer is not in attributing civic concerns to Dmitrii, but in the degree to which he emphasizes them.

The theme of Dmitrii Donskoi's role in the battle of Kulikovo Field also proved attractive to a young epigone of the Decembrists, a student at Kharkov University named Vladimir Rozal'on-Soshal'skii, the author of a poem entitled "Baian on Kulikovo Field" ("Baian na Kulikovom pole," 1825), which purports to be the medieval bard's observations of the famous battle.[82] Like Ryleev, in his poem Rozal'on-Soshal'skii condemns Mamai as a tyrant and speaks of the restoration of freedom. Baian seeks the admiration of Dmitrii's achievement on behalf of "Rus' sviataia" ("holy Rus' ") and describes the prince wielding the "zavetnyi mech ottsov" ("sacred sword of his fathers"), a sword later referred to as the "svobody strazh sviashchennoi" ("guardian of sacred freedom") (270).[83] In his cursory summary of Russian history, Baian mentions a number of renowned and saintly princes. A continuity is thus implicitly established between Dmitrii and his saintly predecessors. The poem concludes with an apostrophe to the prince in which Baian asserts that "v mire byl ottsom, i uzhasom sred' boia" ("in peacetime he was a father, and in the midst of battle a terror") (270), both conventional assessments of the correct role of a prince.

Rozal'on-Soshal'skii's poem differs from Ryleev's in that he does not attempt to enter into Dmitrii's inner psychology. Instead he confines himself to the grandiloquent generalizations about the prince's greatness supposedly appropriate for a medieval bard. The two treatments coincide, however, in their fidelity to the image of the saintly prince. In neither poem does the Muscovite prince step outside the realm of abstract virtue so dear to hagiography.

The third early Christian prince given a separate "Meditation" by Ryleev is Mikhail of Tver'. The latter was the victim of internecine rivalry on the part of Prince Iurii of Moscow, who disputed his right to the grand principality of Vladimir and eventually won the support of the Khan of the Golden Horde. When Iurii's wife, the Khan's sister, died in captivity in the course of the ensuing war between Tver' and Moscow, the Khan summoned Mikhail and had him tortured and killed. Strictly speaking, the prince was not a martyr for the faith in the same way as Mikhail of Chernigov (1179?–1246), for example, but, as in the case of Boris and Gleb, the fact of martyrdom overshadowed its predominantly political causes. (Such an extreme response to essentially political assassinations was not peculiar to Russian religious thought; Edward the Martyr of England [962–978], slain at the instigation of his stepmother Elfrida, achieved sainthood in a similar

[82] On Rozal'on-Soshal'skii, see M. Tsiavlovskii, "Epigony dekabristov (Delo o rasprostranenii 'zlovrednykh' sochinenii sredi studentov khar'kovskogo universiteta v 1827 g.)," *Golos minuvshego*, 1917, nos. 7–8: 95–104, especially.

[83] The text of "Baian on Kulikovo Field" ("Baian na Kulikovom pole") is found in Orlov, *Dekabristy*, 270.

manner, as did Wenceslas of Bohemia [907–929] and Oswin of Northumbria [d. 651].)

Karamzin's account of this episode stresses the prince's piety and close relationship with his subjects. Mikhail is not driven by ambition, but is instead "ready to sacrifice everything for the good of Russia" (4: 116). "I always loved the fatherland," he tells his confessor, "but could not stop our [the princes'] vicious discord; at least I will be content, if only my death calms him" (116). Mikhail passes the time before he is slain in prayer and psalm-singing. Even immediately before he is attacked, he stands calmly praying. He exemplifies to a remarkable extent the familiar combination of courage, piety, and concern for Russia rather than for himself.

Ryleev's poem begins with Mikhail's journey to the Golden Horde. Even at this point he is called "kniaz'-stradalets znamenityi" ("the renowned sufferer-prince") (130), his martyrdom thus being immediately anticipated. When the Mongols speak scornfully of his lost glory, Mikhail shows no concern for his own fate, but instead bewails conflict among its princes as the source of Russia's present misfortune. Ryleev makes this point even more strongly than Karamzin:

Я любил страну родную
И пылал разрушить в ней
Наших бед вину прямую:
Распри злобные князей.

(I loved my native country and burned to destroy in her the direct cause of our misfortunes: the wicked discord of the princes) (131).

As in the *History*, Mikhail's willingness to sacrifice himself for the general good of the country is also emphasized:

Не хочу своим спасеньем
На родимый край привлечь
Кавгадыя с лютым мщеньем,
И Узбека грозный меч!

(I do not want with my own salvation to attract to my native land Kavgadyi with fierce vengeance, and the terrible sword of Uzbek!) (131).

His altruism is thus implicitly contrasted with the partisan selfishness of other princes. As in Karamzin's account, the prince's goodness acquires an otherworldly aura as he awaits his fate calmly reading psalms. Ryleev ends the poem with a reminder that Mikhail is universally revered and regarded as a saint by the church.

Of the three "Meditations" devoted to early Christian princes, this is the most explicitly hagiographical. Mikhail's status as a martyr naturally facilitated this approach, and it should be noted that Ryleev gives meticulous attention to the gory details of the saint's death. Yet in none of the three poems does Ryleev eschew such traditionally hagiographical touches as psalm-reading and prayers for divine aid; instead he incorporates them as major components of his own portraits of the princes. The poet's paean to civic virtue is thus built on a hagiographical foundation.

None of the other "Meditations" is devoted to saintly princes properly speaking. Yet the characteristics associated with the saintly prince frequently recur in the portrayal of other historical figures and are often held up as worthy of emulation. Prince Iziaslav, the son of Vladimir and the pagan Rogneda, begs his mother to tell him of the deeds of his grandfather, the Varangian prince Rogvolod: "Kak on srazhalsia na voine, / I o liubvi k nemu naroda" ("How he fought in war, and about the people's love for him,") (118). Rogneda willingly responds with an inspired account of her father's bravery, popularity, and somewhat improbable meekness. Similarly, Prince Andrei Kurbskii, the Russian military hero who fled from Ivan the Terrible, is described in formulaic terms as "V sovete mudryi, strashnyi v brani, / Nadezhda skorbnykh rossiian" ("wise in council, terrible in battle, the hope of sorrowful Russians") (141). Nor is Ryleev reluctant to describe more recent historical figures in such fashion: Artemii Volynskii, the cabinet minister who resisted the influence of the Empress Anna's favorite Biron and was executed for treason in 1740, is said to have been "Dushoiu chist i prav v delakh" ("pure in soul and upright in deeds") (166). The poet refers to him explicitly as a martyr and describes his bravery and civic commitment in reverential tones: "Svershil, ispolnil dolg sviatoi, / Otkryl vinu narodnykh bedstvii" ("He performed and fulfilled his sacred duty, he uncovered the cause of the people's great misfortunes") (166). In the mythology of many Russian nationalists, Volynskii did in fact acquire the status of a holy martyr.[84]

One of the admirers of the "Meditations" was Ryleev's fellow con-

[84] Cf. Rogger, *National Consciousness*, 25.

spirator, the poet Aleksandr Bestuzhev, who wrote in 1823 that Ryleev had "opened a new path in Russian poetry, choosing as his aim to arouse the valor of his fellow-citizens with the exploits of their ancestors."[85] Bestuzhev himself had turned as early as 1821 to the theme of the saintly prince in a verse passage of "A Leaf from a Guard Officer's Diary" ("Listok iz dnevnika gvardeiskogo ofitsera") devoted to Alexander Nevskii (1219–1263). The passage concerns the so-called Battle on the Ice at Lake Peipus between the Russians and the Teutonic Knights in 1242 and reflects Bestuzhev's reading of the Novgorod chronicle, the *Sofiia Annals* (*Sofiiskii vremennik*), which had recently been published.[86] In an afterword to the account, Bestuzhev describes, in highly laudatory terms, Alexander's triumphant arrival in Pskov. A similarly uncritical spirit pervades the preceding account of the battle. Alexander himself is described as an avenging angel who energetically pursues and destroys the enemy. His piety is emphasized, and once again there is a pre-battle prayer, expressing not only the motif of reliance on divine aid but also the similarly stereotyped notion of the abnegation of glory for oneself: "Ne nam, o Gospodi, ne nam, / A Imeni Tvoemu dai slavu" ("Not to us, O Lord, not to us, but to Your Name give glory") (31).[87]

After the appearance of the "Meditations" Bestuzhev himself produced a poem about "Mikhail of Tver' " (1824). Like Ryleev's poem on the same subject, Bestuzhev's poem is based on Karamzin's account of the martyrdom of the prince. Bestuzhev, who had written darkly that "time will judge Karamzin as a historian," did find the *History* appealing from a purely literary point of view. In the same context he went on to say that "his contemporaries' debt of truth and gratitude crowns this eloquent writer, who with his charming, flowering style has made a decisive revolution for the better in the Russian language."[88] In its major thematic emphases, Bestuzhev's treatment of the subject of

[85] V. A. Arkhipov et al., ed., *Poliarnaia zvezda, izdannaia A. Bestuzhevym i K. Ryleevym* (Moscow, 1960), 23.

[86] *Sofiiskii Vremennik*, ed. Pavel Stroev (1820–1822).

[87] The passage under discussion is found in A. Bestuzhev, *Pss*, vol. 12 (St. Petersburg, 1839), 29–32.

[88] *Poliarnaia zvezda*, 17. On Bestuzhev's appreciation of the literary qualities of the *History*, cf. Black, *Nicholas Karamzin*, 141; and Leighton, *Alexander Bestuzhev-Marlinsky*, 52.

Mikhail evokes that of Ryleev. The prince exhibits a calm and pronounced spirit of civic self-sacrifice:

> Пора расстаться мне с тобою
> И Михаиловой главою
> Купить отечеству покой.

(It is time for me to part with you and with Mikhail's head to buy peace for the fatherland) (171).[89]

Mikhail begs his son Konstantin to refrain from seeking vengeance after his death, thus revealing in another way his meek Christian spirit. The only traditional element absent from the poem is a reference to the prince's popularity with his subjects. Nonetheless his courage and altruism reveal him as a saintly prince.

The major difference between Bestuzhev's and Ryleev's poems lies in Bestuzhev's much greater use of romantic tropes. The poem opens at night in a dark and gloomy prison, a favorite romantic setting. The identities of Mikhail and his son are not immediately revealed, which adds to the atmosphere of mystery. Most evocative of high romanticism is the obsession with revenge. In contradiction to his father's wishes, Konstantin calls on "the god of vengeance" ("bog mesti") (172) to punish the Mongols, and eventually his request is answered:

> Он внял ему, сей сильный бог,
> Россиянам восстать помог
> И снял с лица земли тиранов:

(He heeded him, this strong god, he helped the Russians to rise in rebellion and removed the tyrants from the face of the earth) (172).

Such fate-ridden thinking is alien to hagiography.[90] Yet the overlay of romanticism does not obscure the essentially traditional image of the prince.

Another poet with Decembrist sympathies who was attracted to the

[89] The text of "Mikhail of Tver' " ("Mikhail Tverskoi") is found in I. M. Semenko, ed., *Poety-dekabristy* (Leningrad, 1960), 171.

[90] Raab observes that at the end of the poem, the hagiographical point of view is overlaid by "revolutionary-romantic pathos." See "Obraz drevnerusskogo cheloveka," 29.

image of the saintly prince was Pavel Katenin (1792–1853).[91] His poem "Mstislav Mstislavich" (1820) concerns the bravery of another Prince Mstislav, in this case the Galician prince surnamed "the Bold" (*Udaloi*) (?–1228) who battled the Mongols on the River Kalka in 1223 when they first threatened the Russian lands. Mstislav was the son-in-law of Kotyan, the Polovtsian khan who convinced the prince that the Russians should take the offensive against the Mongols. But the Russian forces were poorly organized and suffered a massive defeat. Although Mstislav and his son-in-law Prince Daniil of Volynia escaped, many others perished, including several princes. These events are recounted in several chronicles, as well as in Karamzin's *History*. The medieval chroniclers and Karamzin concur in assigning part of the blame for the Russian failure to what Karamzin calls Mstislav's "excessive vanity" (3: 151), the *Laurentian* chronicler his "envy"—Mstislav appears to have attacked the Mongols on his own initiative without waiting for the forces of the Kievan and Chernigov princes.[92]

Katenin's Mstislav shows no trace of petty ambition, however. The poem opens when the battle on the Kalka is already raging. The prince is portrayed as wounded. Katenin knew that this detail was not in accordance with the historical facts, but explained that he had "willfully embellished" the story.[93] The addition of this unhistorical detail provides an opportunity to underscore Mstislav's noble courage: in spite of his wound, he struggles to lift himself from the ground. This pathetic scene inspires the narrator to call on God not to permit a Christian to die in this fashion. A rescuer, in the person of Mstislav's son-in-law, fortuitously appears; as in Bestuzhev's "Mikhail of Tver'," his identity is not immediately revealed. Ignoring his own wound, Daniil summons help, and the prince is carried to a boat and safety. On the trip to the other shore Mstislav regains consciousness, only to be confronted by the chilling sight of the Russian defeat. He gives way to paroxysms of self-reproach, largely for what he perceives as the long-term consequences of this defeat, which he fears has made possible the henceforth unhampered success of the Mongols. (In fact, the Mongols mysteriously

[91] Katenin had been a member of the Union of Salvation. However, in 1822 he was exiled from St. Petersburg and was not granted permission to return until August 1825. He did not participate in the uprising of December 14.

[92] *Polnoe sobranie russkikh letopisei*, vol. 1, 2d ed., vypusk 3 (Leningrad, 1928), col. 507.

[93] P. A. Katenin, *Izbrannye proizvedeniia* (Moscow, 1965), 672.

vanished back into the steppes for more than a dozen years.) "O gore, vechnoe mne gore, / Chto ia vinovnik pervyi zla" ("O woe, eternal woe to me, that I am the first perpetrator of evil") (112), laments Mstislav.[94] He concludes this orgy of self-castigation by expressing the hope that God will heed the prayers of the Russians. When the boat reaches the other shore, all fall to the ground and pray.

"Mstislav Mstislavich" portrays the saintly prince at fault. Like many other princes, Mstislav is courageous, pious, and concerned with the Russian people. Unlike them, however, he has committed a terrible error. Yet no allusions are made to his vanity or selfish ambition. The actual nature of his failing is left vague and hence does not contradict the overall impression of nobility. The effect is very similar to that produced by the portrayal of Prince Igor' in "The Lay of Igor"s Campaign," a work which exerted both a stylistic and a thematic influence on Katenin's poem; the poet makes extensive use of the negative comparisons so characteristic of "The Lay," for example.[95] The theme of a tragic defeat filled with fateful implications, central to "The Lay," is also key to Katenin's poem. In fact, Katenin, in contrast to Ryleev, seems less interested in analyzing the ideal ruler than in developing the notion that the battle on the Kalka was the beginning of the end for the Russians. While the image of the saintly prince occupies a certain place in the poem, it is therefore of much less importance than in many of the other poems discussed here.

At the end of 1825 the Decembrists attempted to put their varied theories into practice, rising in the north on December 14 and in the south about two weeks later. During their defiant occupation of the Senate Square in St. Petersburg, Karamzin joined the royal staff with Nicholas I on Admiralty Boulevard.[96] The supporter of autocracy considered the uprising the product of the baneful influence of Napoleon's lack of respect for law and order.[97] He would probably have been horrified to realize that some of the Decembrists viewed their actions as a justifiable reaction against the views epitomized by the *History*;

[94] The text of "Mstislav Mstislavich" is found in Katenin, *Izbrannye proizvedeniia*, 107–12.

[95] On the influence of "The Lay of Igor"s Campaign" on "Mstislav Mstislavich," see Vl. Orlov's introduction to P. A. Katenin, *Stikhotvoreniia* (Leningrad, 1954), 39.

[96] Anatole G. Mazour, *The First Russian Revolution, 1825; the Decembrist Movement, its Origins, Development and Significance* (Berkeley, Cal., 1937; Stanford, Cal., 1977), 176.

[97] Black, *Nicholas Karamzin*, 93.

Viazemskii later wrote that in a sense the uprising represented "a criticism, with armed force, of opinions professed by Karamzin, that is, by the *History of the Russian State*."[98]

Immediately before the uprising some of the Decembrists contemplated their intended actions in a highly romanticized light. Ryleev had to be dissuaded by Nikolai Bestuzhev, the brother of the poet, from dressing for rebellion in a combination of peasant and military costume "in order to link the soldier with the peasant in the first act of their mutual freedom."[99] Another of the conspirators, the poet Prince Aleksandr Odoevskii, scion of a noble family which traced its lineage to the saintly martyr Prince Mikhail of Chernigov, exclaimed on the eve of the St. Petersburg rebellion: "We will die, oh, how gloriously we will die!"[100] As is well known, many of the Decembrists, like Odoevskii, were members of some of Russia's oldest noble families, and it does not seem overly farfetched to imagine that the courage of the early Russian princes may have served as an inspirational model to some of these young men, in much the way that Ryleev had hoped. In this context, it is worth noting that popular opinion subsequently viewed the savage repression of the Decembrists as a systematic attack on the Slav nobility by the German contingent within the government.[101]

The Image of the Prince in Decembrist Poetry After 1825

The Decembrists did not abandon their interest in the Russian past as a subject for literary treatment after their abortive uprising. Wilhelm Kiukhel'beker (1797–1846) wrote "Iurii and Kseniia" (1832–1836) and "Prokofii Liapunov" (1834); Bestuzhev "The Raiders: A Tale of the Year 1613" ("Naezdy: Povest' 1613 goda," 1831); and Odoevskii "Zosima" (1829–1830?). As regards saintly princes in particular, Aleksandr Bestuzhev and Aleksandr Odoevskii wrote narrative poems devoted to Prince Andrei the Good of Pereiaslavl' (1102–1141) and Prince Vasil'ko of Terebovl' (1067?–1125), respectively. These two poems, "Andrei, Prince of Pereiaslavl' " ("Andrei, kniaz' pereiaslav-

98 P. A. Viazemskii, *Pss*, vol. 2 (St. Petersburg, 1879), 218.

99 *Vospominaniia Bestuzhevykh*, 36.

100 Cited in Kotliarevskii, *Dekabristy*, 17.

101 Mazour, *First Russian Revolution*, 196.

skii," 1827) and "Vasil'ko" (1829–1830), are the most interesting treatments of saintly princes produced by Decembrist poets.

For a variety of complex reasons, Bestuzhev cooperated readily and fully with the tsarist authorities during the investigation of the Decembrist conspiracy.[102] He was therefore treated much more mildly than many of the other conspirators, spending only two years in exile in Siberia and being allowed to continue his literary career even there. In the 1830s he achieved tremendous popularity writing numerous romantic tales under the pseudonym of Aleksandr Marlinskii. Many of these tales are set in the Caucasus, the field of Bestuzhev's own activities in the 1830s and the site of his death in 1837.

Bestuzhev began writing "Andrei, Prince of Pereiaslavl' " in prison in Finland, before his exile to Siberia in 1827. The work, published in segments (in some instances without the author's permission), was never completed. When he went into exile, Bestuzhev entrusted the manuscript of the first two chapters of the poem to an acquaintance and was nonplussed to see the first chapter appear in print anonymously in 1828. The second chapter appeared under similar circumstances two years later.[103] Bestuzhev reacted to these developments by firing off some authorial comments on the poem and two excerpts from an intended fifth chapter. These were published in the course of the next two years, and in 1832 it finally became generally known that the author of the poem was Aleksandr Marlinskii, then already immensely popular. The poem remained uncompleted.

In his statement, "A Few Words from the Composer of the Tale 'Andrei, Prince of Pereiaslavl',' " in which Bestuzhev discusses at length the writing and publication of the poem, he asserts his ignorance, due to circumstances, about the specific details of Andrei's reign: "Rummaging in the bag of memory . . . , I came across Andrei, prince of Pereiaslavl', called the Good: I chose him as my scapegoat [*grekhonosets*]; I burdened him with all the sins of my poetic Israel, all the mistakes of memory" (78).[104] At the same time, however, the supposed penitent cannot resist crowing over the critics who did not notice his geographical blooper in locating Andrei's princedom near the Danube,

[102] A detailed account of this episode is given in Leighton, *Alexander Bestuzhev-Marlinsky*, 19–28.

[103] For details, see A. Bestuzhev-Marlinskii, *Psst* (Leningrad, 1961), 276.

[104] The text of Bestuzhev's comments and of "Andrei, Prince of Pereiaslavl' " ("Andrei, kniaz' pereiaslavskii") are found in Bestuzhev-Marlinskii, *Psst*, 77–136.

not the Dnieper. Bestuzhev's claims of abysmal ignorance are somewhat disingenuous; his poem reveals a good grasp of the essentials of the conflicts in which Andrei was involved.

Prince Andrei the Good, the youngest son of Vladimir Monomakh (1053–1125), became prince of southern Pereiaslavl' after his father's death. During the internecine conflicts of subsequent years Andrei sided with his older brothers against the Ol'govichi, the sons of Prince Oleg Sviatoslavich of Chernigov (?–1115). This led to conflict with Prince Vsevolod of Chernigov, who had designs on the borderlands between the Pereiaslavl' and Chernigov principalities.[105] Karamzin devotes several pages to an account of these interprincely struggles, and Andrei emerges as a noble and saintly figure. When the Ol'govichi try to convince him to hand over Pereiaslavl', he refuses: "I will not leave here alive. Let Vsevolod steep his hands in my blood! He will not be the first: Sviatopolk, power-loving like him, also killed Boris and Gleb; but did he enjoy his power for long?" (2: 126). In comparing Andrei to the princely martyrs Boris and Gleb, Karamzin reinforces the impression of Andrei's saintliness. The marked accordance in tone between Karamzin's and Bestuzhev's appraisals of the prince suggests that Bestuzhev was familiar with the account given in the *History*, of which he had made extensive use in composing a number of other works.[106] He may also have acquired some knowledge of Andrei directly from a chronicle.[107]

Andrei does not appear in person until the second chapter of Bestuzhev's poem. In the first, a conversation between two Polovtsian bandits on the general political situation precedes the entrance of Roman, one of the major characters in the poem. The messenger of Prince Vsevolod of Chernigov, Roman happens to save Svetovid, the son of the boyar Liubomir, from drowning. The youthful and idealistic Svetovid adores Andrei, but his father is plotting the prince's downfall. Liubomir is despicable and driven by ambition; Roman is brave but misguided.

[105] Cf. George Vernadsky, *Kievan Russia* (New Haven, 1973), 98.

[106] Leighton lists the following works as influenced by Karamzin: "Gedeon" (1821), "Roman and Ol'ga: A Tale of Olden Times" ("Roman i Ol'ga: Starinnaia povest'," 1823), "The Traitor" ("Izmennik," 1825), and "The Raiders: A Tale of the Year 1613" ("Naezdy: Povest' 1613 goda," 1831). See Leighton, *Alexander Bestuzhev-Marlinsky*, 77.

[107] On Bestuzhev's extensive reading of the chronicles, see especially Volk, *Istoricheskie vzgliady*, 291–92.

The personality of Andrei looms large in the background throughout the chapter. Even Polovtsian chit-chat provides testimony of the prince's goodness, as when the two bandits complain of his efforts at protecting travellers and conclude: "Ne luchshe l' . . . / Katit' palatki boevye / Za Dnepr ili za tikhii Don?" ("Wouldn't it be better . . . to move our fighting tents beyond the Dnieper or the quiet Don?) (83)." Another positive stroke is added to Andrei's portrait when Liubomir and his groom discuss the reluctance of the boyar's nephew to join the conspiracy against Andrei. The groom observes that "Vsego sil'nei ego pugaet, / Chto kniaz' grazhdanami liubim" ("What frightens him most of all is that the prince is loved by the citizens" (99). Liubomir is untouched by this observation and dismisses with contempt both the love of the people and Andrei's peaceable disposition.

Andrei emerges in the first chapter of the poem as a strong but peaceful prince admired by his people. The second chapter further promotes this image. It opens with a description of Andrei's daily dispensing of justice. This description of the prince leaves no doubts as to his innate goodness. Calling him a father among the family of his people, the narrator emphasizes how highly regarded Andrei is and how modest and peaceful his demeanor. In conversation with Roman, Andrei reveals that, in addition to all his other virtues, he is wise as well. He questions the legitimacy of Vsevolod's intentions and stresses his own peace-loving nature. When Roman speaks of Vsevolod's desire to unify Rus', Andrei cannily observes that "vlastoliubie taitsia / Pod sim nameren'em sviatym" ("love of power hides beneath this sacred intention") (111). Peaceable though he may be, however, Andrei is as brave as he is good; he concludes his discussion of the current political situation by affirming his refusal to recognize the suzerainty of Vsevolod. Andrei's discourse and the people's demonstrations of love for the prince begin to sow doubts in Roman's mind as to the justice of Vsevolod's cause, doubts which Svetovid does his best to foster with fulsome praises of his hero. The decisive factor for Roman, however, is witnessing Andrei's bravery in fighting a bear during a hunt. He confesses to Andrei that he had wrongly interpreted his peacefulness as a sign of weakness and still wonders why Andrei avoids glory. The gist of Andrei's reply is that glory is vanity and he has instead dedicated his bravery to the public well-being. He tells his new convert of his hopes for a wonderful future filled with peace and brotherly love. From the brief fragments of Chapter Five, however, it is clear that these hopes are doomed to disappointment.

In his responsiveness to the people, his bravery, and his humility, Andrei is truly a model Christian prince. Only the external signs of piety, references to church-building, for example, are missing from his portrait. His inner virtues are powerfully evocative of the stereotypically Christian worldview often attributed to saintly princes. As in the earlier "Mikhail of Tver'," the introduction of many of the trappings of conventional romanticism—Roman's ominous dreams, for example—does not obscure the essentially traditional basis of his character.

Perhaps the most overtly hagiographical literary treatment of a prince by a Decembrist poet is Odoevskii's narrative poem "Vasil'ko." The impact of the hagiographical tradition on the features of this victim of internecine discord is so pronounced that it has been conceded even by Soviet scholarship.[108]

Like other writers discussed in this chapter, Odoevskii was a member of the Northern Society; he was also one of Ryleev's enrollees.[109] After the uprising he was incarcerated in the Peter and Paul Fortress in St. Petersburg, then sent for ten years to Siberia, where he wrote "Vasil'ko." Like "Andrei, Prince of Pereiaslavl'," this poem is fragmentary. Only the first, second, and fourth chapters are extant; a third chapter was lost by another Decembrist.[110]

The poem is based on the chronicle story of the blinding of Prince Vasil'ko of Terebovl' (1067?–1125). Karamzin's version appears in the second volume of the *History*. The chronicle accounts go back to one included in the earliest annalistic composition, the *Primary Chronicle* (*Povest' vremennykh let*), which found its way into numerous other compilations. Odoevskii's historical expertise and familiarity with the chronicles were extensive, and he may have been acquainted with Karamzin's account and/or one of the many versions of the *Primary Chronicle* account.[111]

[108] See A. A. Iliushin, "Poemy dekabristov na temy Drevnei Rusi (vtoraia polovina 20-x–30-e gody)," *Vestnik Moskovskogo universiteta*, Series 7 (*Filologiia, zhurnalistika*), 1965, no. 1: 49.

[109] Mazour, *First Russian Revolution*, 128.

[110] A. I. Odoevskii, *Psst* (Leningrad, 1958), 216. The poem was not published until 1882.

[111] On Odoevskii's historical knowledge, see Kotliarevskii, *Dekabristy*, 67; and M. A.

According to the chronicles, after the Union of Liubech in 1097, which was intended to maintain peace among Russia's numerous princes, Prince David of Vladimir-Volynia succeeded in convincing Prince Sviatopolk of Kiev that Vasil'ko had been involved in the murder of Sviatopolk's brother Iaropolk and was now conspiring with Vladimir Monomakh against David and Sviatopolk. Convinced by David's lies, Sviatopolk agreed to persuade Vasil'ko to come to Kiev while on a visit to a nearby monastery. When he arrived in Kiev, Sviatopolk and David imprisoned and later blinded the unfortunate prince, a method of dealing with one's political opponents long practiced by the Byzantines, but horrifying to the Russians.[112] Eventually Vasil'ko was avenged for this crime (even excessively so, in the eyes of the chroniclers).

The first part of Odoevskii's poem is set in Terebovl'. It begins with Vasil'ko's appearance to the people to inform them of the accord reached at Liubech and to suggest that they should take advantage of the current harmony among the Russians to wage war against their Polish enemies. This first "song" ends with Vasil'ko's conversation with his wife about her fears and forebodings, his departure, and her prayers and lament; laments in particular were a stock component of princes' Lives. Vasil'ko's virtues receive constant attention throughout the song. His paternal relationship to his subjects is emphasized from the very beginning. His speech to them is an "otecheskoe slovo" ("fatherly discourse"), and he addresses them as "syny moi" ("my sons") (88).[113] Later an old man tries to dissuade the prince from initiating a military campaign by listing the various benefits to the populace that derive from the prince's presence; he has in mind primarily Andrei's ability to administer justice in a manner satisfactory to all segments of the population. In addition to enviable juridical talents, concern for the people, and obvious bravery, the prince has another virtue: he is pious, most notably in his intention of paying his respects at the monastery of St. Michael and his reliance on divine aid: "Ia pomolius', i dast pobedu nam/ Zastupnik moi, nebesnyi voevoda" ("I will pray and my intercessor, the heavenly commander, will give us a victory") (92). Vasil'ko's relations with his wife are also characterized by an observance of the

Briskman, "Liricheskii geroi dekabristskoi poezii perioda katorgi i ssylki," in *Dekabristy i russkaia kul'tura*, 178.

[112] Cf. Vernadsky, *Kievan Russia*, 90.

[113] The text of "Vasil'ko" is found in Odoevskii, *Psst*, 89–123.

Christian proprieties; thus, rather than display excessive passion at his departure, he chastely kisses her brow and makes the sign of the cross over her.

To the bright image of Vasil'ko the following song juxtaposes the somber ones of Sviatopolk and David. At a feast given by Sviatopolk in Kiev an unknown itinerant minstrel sings of a bloodthirsty raven among the eagles. The reference is clearly to David, which the latter realizes, but Sviatopolk, encouraged in his suspicions by David, decides that Vasil'ko is meant. David cunningly incites the angry prince to violence, while himself hypocritically claiming that he does not wish to break the peace. The full extent of David's depravity becomes evident at the end of the song, when he pays a visit to the local pagan cultists. He witnesses various colorful rites, and receives a lecture on the importance of boldness and dependence on the proper, namely pagan, divinities in realizing one's ambitions. Though he appears to hesitate somewhat in committing himself to the gods of his ancestors, there is little mystery about the ultimate decision of this proud and unprincipled prince. Thus a tidy juxtaposition emerges between Christian virtue as personified by Vasil'ko and ruthless pagan ambition embodied in David; although Vasil'ko does not appear in the second song, his virtue acquires a greater luster by contrast.

The missing third song of the poem contained an account of how Vasil'ko was lured to Kiev and thrown into prison.[114] The fourth song opens in Kiev, where the love of the local people for Vasil'ko causes Sviatopolk to have second thoughts about his actions: "Kak on liubim, kak on liubim, David!" ("How he is loved, how he is loved, David!") (114). This sentiment is very similar to that expressed in regard to Andrei of Pereiaslavl' by Liubomir's nephew and, as in Bestuzhev's poem, it serves to reinforce the impression of the link forged by his virtue between the prince and the common people. Yet David insists that it is impossible to set Vasil'ko free and offers to take him away, to which Sviatopolk readily and cravenly agrees.

Vasil'ko's behavior when seized by David's men is highly conventionalized, like that ascribed to Mikhail of Tver' in both Ryleev's and Bestuzhev's poems. He remains calm, even serene, and expresses his faith through prayer. Only when the ruffians violently prevent his son from following him does he exclaim: "O Bozhe, Bozhe! . . . / Kak Iova

[114] Cf. Odoevskii, *Psst*, 216–17.

menia Ty iskushaesh'" ("O God, God, . . . You try me like Job") (118). Yet Vasil'ko maintains his faith and, even when he realizes that something dreadful is about to take place, throws himself into ardent prayer. After a graphically described blinding, the prince is taken to a priest's house, where he regains consciousness and, discovering that his bloodstained shirt is gone, laments: "Ee zachem vy sniali? Net, v sorochke, / Net, ia khotel, odetyi v krov' moiu, / Predstat' pered vsevyshnego Sud'iu" ("Why did you take it off? No, I wanted to appear before the Most High Judge in my shirt, dressed in my blood") (122). This detail is borrowed directly from the chronicle account (and is also repeated by Karamzin). It underscores the prince's status as a pitiful victim, as do the assertions of the priest attending the prince that his innocence will be upheld in heaven and in succeeding generations. The poem ends with Vasil'ko's imprisonment by David. The gloomy ending and the poem's pessimistic tendency in general have often been interpreted as a veiled allusion to the fate of the Decembrists in general and Odoevskii in particular.[115]

The hagiographical tenor of Odoevskii's poem thus reaches a climax virtually unmatched by the other works discussed. Not only is Vasil'ko's generous and longsuffering nature in keeping with the requirements of princes' Lives, but the emphasis on the inevitability of divine justice imparts a thoroughly Christian atmosphere not only to the character of the prince, but also to the entire world in which Vasil'ko moves. Moreover, as in the case of "Andrei, Prince of Pereiaslavl'," the touches of romanticism, such as the theatrical pagan rites and the mysterious figure of the prescient minstrel, do not undermine the characterization of Vasil'ko as a saintly prince.

THE RELATIONSHIP between the Decembrists and their princely heroes is a complex one. On the one hand, poets like Ryleev have been credited with imputing Decembrist sentiments to historical figures.[116] Yet, although the princes who figure in poems by Decembrists often sound suspiciously like nineteenth-century opponents of Russian autocracy, these works were much more than anachronistic presentations of Decembrist ideas in medieval trappings. Significant domestic cultural influences were at work on Ryleev, Bestuzhev, Odoevskii, and others in

[115] Cf. Kotliarevskii, *Dekabristy*, 69; and Iliushin, "Poemy dekabristov," 52.
[116] Cf. Volk, *Istoricheskie vzgliady*, 19.

the form of Karamzin's *History* and the medieval chronicles. The figure of the saintly prince may have proved appealing to the Decembrists because it already contained many of the ingredients of civic virtue cherished by them, including courage and self-abnegation in favor of a concern for the needs of the masses. That in comparison to Karamzin, for example, the Decembrists gave greater emphasis to, and even exaggerated, these elements is indubitable. It should be recognized, however, that they exploited their historical sources not only by borrowing plots, but also by adapting the conceptions of princely goodness found in these sources. The Decembrists thus made use of medieval hagiography in much the same way that they incorporated the terminology of medieval Novgorod in their drafts of constitutions. In both cases they wished to revive old, admired ideals that corresponded to their own beliefs. Moreover, it is apparent that in turning to domestic models for their political views the Decembrists by no means derived their inspiration solely from foreign sources.

For all their attention to virtuous exemplars from Russian history and the figure of the saintly prince in particular, the Decembrists did not leave behind them a fertile tradition of civic poetry devoted to medieval Russian princes.[117] Ironically, however, many of the Decembrists themselves subsequently underwent a process of political canonization in radical and liberal circles. Their own essays and memoirs contributed to this tendency, as did the concerted propagandistic efforts of Herzen and Ogarev. Some of the most unabashedly hagiographical treatment was reserved for Ryleev. Described in glowing terms by many of the survivors of the 1825 uprising, he was also the subject of a poem by Ogarev, "To the Memory of Ryleev" ("Pamiati Ryleeva"), that served as a dedication to the 1860 London edition of the "Meditations." In the final stanzas of the poem the character of Ryleev assumes a distinctly saintly aura:

> Рылеев мне был первым светом . . .
> Отец! по духу мне родной-
> Твое названье в мире этом
> Мне стало доблестным заветом

[117] One exception was a poem by Lev Mei (1822–1862), "Alexander Nevskii" ("Aleksandr Nevskii," 1861). The composer Nikolai Rimsky-Korsakov began, but did not complete a cantata based on this poem. See L. A. Mei, *Izbrannye proizvedeniia* (Moscow, 1962), 441.

И путеводною звездой.
Мы стих твой вырвем из забвенья, . . .
Восстановим для поклоненья
Твою страдальческую тень . . .
И будет подвиг твой свободный
Святыней в памяти народной
На все грядущие года.

(Ryleev was my first light . . . Father! my spiritual kinsman—in this world your name became for me a valorous precept and a guiding star. We will snatch your poetry from oblivion, . . . We will restore for worship your martyred shade . . . And your free exploit will be a sacred thing in the people's memory in all the years to come).[118]

The poet and political martyr here moves into the same realm of abstract, hagiographical virtue inhabited by his own princely heroes.[119]

[118] The text of "To the Memory of Ryleev" ("Pamiati Ryleeva") is found in N. P. Ogarev, *Stikhotvoreniia i poemy* (Leningrad, 1956), 291.

[119] Another poem glorifying the Decembrists is Adelbert von Chamisso's "Die Verbannten" (1831). The first part of the poem consists of a paraphrase of Ryleev's "Meditation" devoted to Andrei Voinarovskii, while the second is a romanticized account of Aleksandr Bestuzhev in exile based on the latter's meeting with the German scholar Adolf Ermann. Cf. I. G. Upokoeva, *Revoliutsionno-romanticheskaia poema pervoi poloviny XIX veka: Opyt tipologii zhanra* (Moscow, 1971), 91. Much more recently, the poet Evgenii Kushev produced a series of poems on the Decembrists subsumed under the general title "The Decembrists" ("Dekabristy," 1966). These poems are found in his book, *Ogryzkom karandasha: Stikhi i proza* (Frankfurt, 1971).

CHAPTER THREE

Hagiography Revised: Adaptations of Legends and Tales

And if you are looking for amusements and entertainments—read the stories, words and deeds, and passions of the saints.

Monk Georgius of the Zarub Cave

The characters of the figures about whom these hagiographical stories were composed constitute, in the felicitous phrase of St. Savva of Zvenigorod, "the spiritual beauty" of our people.

Nikolai Leskov

THE ADAPTATION of hagiographically inspired accounts of medieval princes was largely limited to the poetic efforts of Decembrist poets. Other kinds of reworkings of hagiographical literature enjoyed a more diverse authorship. These works, based on entries from collections of saints' Lives like the *Reading Menaea* (*Chet'i minei*) and the *Prolog* (*Prolog*), as well as hagiographical folk tales, were produced throughout the nineteenth century by a wide range of writers. Their composition acquired particular popularity later in the century. A variety of approaches to the adaptation of hagiography was exemplified by these reworkings, from the punctiliously conservative to the deliberately iconoclastic. The methodology employed in these reworkings and the types of saintly figures described in them are the subject of this chapter.[1]

The novels of Fedor Dostoevsky contain occasional discussions of the merits of religious literature. In the course of his autobiographical reminiscences in *The Brothers Karamazov* (*Brat'ia Karamazovy*, 1880), Father Zosima tells his listeners which biblical and hagiographical works are

[1] Many of the works treated in this chapter, like the stories and poems by Aleksei K. Tolstoi, Alexander Herzen, and Vsevolod Garshin, and Nikolai Leskov's and Leo Tolstoy's *Prolog* adaptations, are also discussed by Al'bert Opul'skii in his *Zhitiia sviatykh v tvorchestve russkikh pisatelei XIX veka* (East Lansing, Mich., 1986).

most likely to touch the heart of a peasant. The saints' Lives he singles out for praise include those of Alexis, the Man of God (fifth century), a Roman patrician who adopted the way of humble anonymity, and Mary of Egypt (fifth century?), who turned from a life of sin to one of penitence. At first glance, the monk's choice may appear overly recondite; neither of the saints he mentions is Russian or even Slavic. Yet Zosima was not alone in his admiration of the self-effacing holy beggar and the harlot turned desert solitary. Throughout the middle ages, both official ecclesiastical and folk accounts of the Lives of Alexis and Mary won a large audience among the Slavs, as well as among their Western European contemporaries. In Russia this popularity persisted into the nineteenth century and eventually found expression in poetic treatments by the little-known writers Elisaveta Shakhova (1822–1899) and Boris Almazov (1827–1876).

The Religious Narratives of Shakhova and Almazov

Shakhova was a nun and poet whose religious development, her nephew and editor said, claimed the interest of the great nineteenth-century Russian mystic Ignatii Brianchaninov. Shakhova spent much of her life in convents. Her collected works were not published until several years after her death.[2] Almazov's life was conducted in more secular surroundings. As a poet, he was best known for his humorous and satirical poems, like his parodies of Alexander Pushkin, Mikhail Lermontov, and Nikolai Nekrasov. He also produced a series of poetical retellings of medieval French and Spanish literary works, including *La chanson de Roland.* Until it ceased publication in 1856, Almazov was associated with the conservative journal *The Muscovite* (*Moskvitianin*).[3]

Despite their very different existences, Shakhova and Almazov apparently shared a similar philosophy regarding the reworking of hagiographical material. While their iambic form endows them with a superficial modernity, both Shakhova's and Almazov's poems are

[2] *Sobranie sochinenii v stikhakh Elisavety Shakhovoi*, ed. N. N. Shakhov (St. Petersburg, 1911).

[3] On Almazov, see the entries on him in *Russkii biograficheskii slovar'*, vol. 2 (St. Petersburg, 1910); and *Russkie pisateli: biobibliograficheskii slovar'* (Moscow, 1971). See also Anon., "B. N. Almazov," in B. N. Almazov, *Sochineniia*, vol. 1 (Moscow, 1892), iii–xxiv.

conservative compositionally as well as religiously. Precisely because of this, they provide an excellent point of departure for a discussion of more radical reworkings. Shakhova's and Almazov's narrative poems exemplify the process by which a medieval work could be updated to appeal to nineteenth-century tastes without destroying or drastically undermining its original significance. At the same time, the particular saints chosen by the two writers as subjects for their poems deserve consideration because, with some important qualifications, they represent in extreme form an ideal of sanctity that attracted numerous nineteenth-century Russian writers, whatever their own religious persuasions.

The *Menaea* Life of Mary of Egypt is a story of radical and unusual repentance.[4] It begins with a description of the chance encounter between Mary and the pious monk Zosima in the desert, the favorite domicile of the early Christian hermits. Impressed by Mary's obvious saintliness, Zosima begs to hear her story. Although constantly belaboring her own sinfulness, the saint finally consents. According to her account, Mary spent her youth in Alexandria wallowing in debauchery. A constant search for new thrills eventually led her to Jerusalem. Arriving in the city on a feast day, she noticed a large crowd gathered outside a church and attempted to join in the festivities, but was prevented from entering the church by an unseen force. In trying to understand why this occurred, Mary suddenly perceived with shocking clarity what a terrible life she had been leading. Prostrating herself before an icon of the Mother of God, she prayed for her intercession. Miraculously, the invisible barrier was lifted and she was able to cross the threshold of the church. Her gratitude inspired her to obey when a voice instructed her to enter the desert.

When Zosima meets Mary, she has been wandering in the desert for almost fifty years, fighting an arduous but ultimately victorious battle against a variety of temptations. The humble zealot has only one request for the monk, that he return the following year to celebrate the Eucharist for her. When Zosima returns yet again, he finds the saint's

[4] Tradition has it that the early Christian writer Sophronius heard the story of Mary from monks who had transmitted it orally for generations. See Derwas Chitty, *The Desert a City: An Introduction to the Study of Egyptian and Palestinian Monasticism under the Christian Empire* (Oxford, 1966), 153. The *Menaea* Life is found under April 1. Here and elsewhere the version of the *Menaea* referred to is that of Dmitrii of Rostov, which was the most widely read in the nineteenth century.

uncorrupted body lying with a message written in the sand beside it; only now does he learn Mary's name, which she had previously refused to reveal. The old monk despairs of being able to bury the body himself, but a lion appears to help him; this miraculous occurrence reflects a topos.[5] Afterwards he returns to his monastery to begin disseminating the tale of Mary's sanctity.

The story of Mary of Egypt illustrates two major notions. Most obviously, it points to the belief that despite one's sins, redemption is still possible. In this regard, Mary's story has much in common with the legends surrounding other early Christian penitent harlots, like Mary Magdalene, Pelagia of Antioch, and Thais of Egypt. It also illustrates the belief that sanctity does not necessitate conventional religious observances or a close affiliation with the official church. Instead, a steadfast commitment to an individualized vision of Christian morality is most important. This maverick and generally unintellectual spirituality gained the approval of many educated nineteenth-century Russians, and they often evoked it in reworking hagiographical legends and tales. Their taste reflected a historically well-established precedent. From the early medieval period on, Russians showed a greater enthusiasm for the less convention-bound among their own holy men and those bequeathed to them by Byzantium. In its most radical form, this predilection for idiosyncratic religiosity expressed itself in the cult of holy fools (*iurodivye*), which in Russia reached proportions unprecedented in Byzantium.[6]

Almazov's poetic rendering of Mary's Life, "Mary of Egypt" ("Mariia Egipetskaia"), adheres closely to the account given in the *Reading Menaea*.[7] As in the *Menaea*, the poem begins with Zosima's departure from his Palestinian monastery for a solitary retreat in the desert. When he first comes upon Mary, he wonders whether she is real or imaginary, male or female. This creates suspense and excites curiosity about Mary's identity. Unlike the author of the *Menaea* Life, however, Almazov does not conceal Mary's name until her death, but instead has her reveal it

[5] This is also said to have happened when St. Anthony wished to bury the body of St. Paul the Hermit.

[6] Cf. George P. Fedotov, *The Russian Religious Mind*, 2 vols. (Belmont, Mass., 1975), 2: 316–17.

[7] No date is provided for the poem, but given that Almazov's other reworkings of saints' Lives, "Otshel'nik" and "Shchedryi bogach," both date from 1864, it seems likely that "Mariia Egipetskaia" was composed at about that time.

to Zosima almost immediately, with the addition of an instructive commentary: "Imia eto, / byt' mozhet, mne pokrovom tainym bylo,— / spaslo menia ot gibeli konechnoi" ("Perhaps this name was a secret cover for me,—it saved me from ultimate perdition") (414).[8] In this way, attention is drawn to the possible symbolic connotations of Mary's name, and narrative interest is sacrificed to didactic considerations. Indeed, Almazov's most distinctive changes and additions throughout the poem are didactic. When Mary asks Zosima whether her sins can be forgiven, he tells her that God long ago forgave her. Like an eighteenth-century raisonneur, the old monk provides a lengthy disquisition on her importance as a model, asserting that God wishes to use her experience to reveal the divine power of repentance. Mary's tacit acceptance of Zosima's interpretation of her life is evident when she later tells him that she has been praying for women like herself who fall into the grips of shameful passions at a tender age.

The markedly didactic tone of Almazov's poem may be motivated by the poet's desire to produce versions of saints' Lives suitable for popular consumption. His reworkings did in fact prove very accessible and appeared in large numbers in cheap editions.[9] A curious consequence of Almazov's emphasis on the didactic elements of Mary's story was the simultaneous sentimentalization of the saint's image, for the harsh ascetic of the ancient Life acquires a touch of ladylike sanctimoniousness. This does not change the essential meaning of the story, but merely serves to bring it more into line with less extreme religious tastes. The stringent asceticism practiced by many of the early Christian monks was never congenial to the less fanatical spirit of most Russians.[10] It seems unlikely that to dwell admiringly on Mary's outlandish ascetic accomplishments would ever have held much appeal for a Russian audience, but certainly by the nineteenth century it would not have evoked a responsive chord in most readers. In this connection, Dostoevsky's unflattering portrait of the ascetic monk Ferapont in *The Brothers Karamazov* is symptomatic. Almazov's emphasis on Mary as a symbol of penitence and redemption was doubtless more congenial to the mainstream of Russian religiosity.

Shakhova's version of the Life of Mary of Egypt, "The Power of

[8] The text of "Mary of Egypt" ("Mariia Egipetskaia") is found in Almazov, *Sochineniia* 1: 405–28.

[9] Almazov, *Sochineniia* 1: xvii.

[10] Fedotov, *Russian Religious Mind*, 1: 111.

Repentance (An Ascetic Poem)" ("Sila pokaiania [Asketicheskaia poema]"), is also based on the *Menaea* account.[11] Unlike Almazov, however, Shakhova departs from the *Menaea* in using a strictly chronological arrangement; she begins with Mary's conversion, only later shifting the focus of her narrative to Zosima's desert sojourn. Otherwise she follows the *Menaea* very closely, even emphasizing the miraculous elements of the story, which Almazov appears to have skirted, perhaps because of a greater sensitivity to possible scepticism on the part of his readers. Shakhova, on the other hand, describes in detail Zosima's amazement as Mary floats above the ground when she prays and as she walks across the water to meet him by the Jordan.

As the title of Shakhova's poem indicates, she also used Mary as an example of repentance rewarded. Yet unlike Almazov, her tone is less blandly didactic than shrilly vituperative. Mary's past is described in lurid detail and her rejection of this past is portrayed in an even more extreme fashion. Discussing Mary's self-tonsure before she crosses the Jordan, Shakhova compares her shorn hair to snakes lying curled in the dust, and continues:

Она,—ступив на них стопой,—
Вздрогнула, с чувством отвращенья,
Когда свершила над собой
Обряд святого постриженья . . .

(Treading on it with her foot, she flinched, with a feeling of revulsion, when she had completed the rite of holy tonsure) (218).[12]

The harshness of Shakhova's tone here and elsewhere is in marked contrast to Almazov's often saccharine sentimentality. Possibly Shakhova's own life and training as a nun made her particularly sensitive to the evils of feminine vanity, which may in turn have contributed to the passionate disgust sometimes evident in her poem.

The differences between Shakhova's and Almazov's versions of the Life of Mary of Egypt are ultimately less significant than their similarities. Both poems exemplify a preeminently conservative handling of the original hagiographical material: the language and style have been updated, but the focus and religious significance of the story are pre-

[11] In his edition of his aunt's works, Shakhov unfortunately provides no dates.

[12] The text of "The Power of Repentance (An Ascetic Poem)" ("Sila pokaiiania [Asketicheskaia poema]") is found in Shakhova, *Ss*, Pt. 3, 210–58.

served intact. Neither Shakhova nor Almazov appears to have wished to do much more than retell, rather than recast, the story of Mary.[13] In this regard, their poems differ greatly from a work like Anatole France's *Thais* (1891). In this novel, which was based on the legend of another penitent harlot, the author provides plausible and less than saintly motives for the monk Paphnutius' interest in the beautiful Thais, as well as a more coherent explanation for her desire for salvation than that provided by the original legend.

In discussing poetic reworkings of the Life of Mary, mention should also be made of the unfinished narrative poem "Mary of Egypt" ("Mariia Egipetskaia," 1845) by Ivan Aksakov, a prominent Slavophile. Aksakov apparently envisioned an ambitious work about the saint, but abandoned the idea, in part because he decided that only a better Christian than he could compose a Christian epic.[14]

The few pages of "Mary of Egypt" that Aksakov actually did write concern only the period before the saint's conversion; the fragment ends with a song the harlot sings to her fellow travellers on the ship to Jerusalem. The narrator admits that Mary "liubila greshnoe vesel'e" ("loved sinful gaiety") (145).[15] However, in contrast to Shakhova in particular, Aksakov depicts Mary's sinful youth with sympathy and admiration for her beauty. Had he completed his poem, its tone would undoubtedly have been much less preachy than either Shakhova's or Almazov's.

Almazov also produced a poetic version of the Life of Alexis, the Man of God, the other saint's Life mentioned by Zosima in *The Brothers Karamazov*. This Life achieved great popularity in both its literary and folk versions.[16] In the seventeenth and eighteenth centuries it was a frequent dramatic subject throughout Western Europe and Russia.[17] Almazov's poem draws on both the *Menaea* Life and the folk tradition.

Like the Life of Mary of Egypt, the Life of Alexis concerns an ascetic

[13] In the early part of this century, a prose version of the legend of Mary was produced by Aleksei Remizov. I have not discussed "Mary of Egypt" ("Mariia Egipetskaia," 1915) (not to be confused with Remizov's earlier work of the same name) here because it exhibits largely aesthetic concerns not shared to any significant extent by the nineteenth-century adaptations of legends and tales which are the primary subject of this chapter.

[14] Ivan Aksakov, *Stikhotvoreniia i poemy* (Leningrad, 1960), 278.

[15] The text of "Mary of Egypt" ("Mariia Egipetskaia") is found in Aksakov, *Stikhotvoreniia i poemy*, 143–50.

[16] Cf. V. P. Adrianova, *Zhitie Alekseia Cheloveka Bozhiia v drevnei russkoi literature i narodnoi slovesnosti* (Petrograd, 1917), 127, 144. The *Menaea* Life is found under March 17.

[17] Adrianova, *Zhitie Alekseia*, 149–52.

who accomplishes great spiritual triumphs outside the official church. A citizen of Rome in the early days of Christianity, Alexis so desires a life of celibacy and ascetic poverty that he steals away from his parents' home on his wedding night and makes his way secretly to Edessa. There he lives as a beggar for seventeen years until recognition of his ascetic accomplishments by those around him impels him to leave the city. As he sails across the Mediterranean, a storm carries his ship off course to Rome, and Alexis decides to return incognito to his parents' home. There he asks his unwitting father for a corner in which to live. Yet another seventeen years later, after Alexis' death, his saintliness is miraculously revealed to the city at large. Only then do Alexis' long-suffering parents and spouse learn that he has been living so close to them.

Like the Life of Mary of Egypt, this legend celebrates the virtues of humility and an exclusive commitment to Christ. It provides a classic expression of the idea voiced by Jesus in Matthew 16:24: "If anyone wants to be a follower of mine, let him renounce himself and take up his cross and follow me." Viewed in this light, Alexis' infliction of long years of grief on his family and his refusal to relent and identify himself even when he becomes a witness of that grief are not criticized. What is most important, the legend suggests, is Alexis' devotion to the spiritual path he has chosen, the way of extreme humility, of almost total abnegation of self.

Like "Mary of Egypt," Almazov's version of the Life of Alexis, "The Anchorite" ("Otshel'nik," 1864), is faithful to the plot and thematic intentions of the original legend. Even the lexicon is often reminiscent of a saint's Life. The formulae used in the description of Alexis' childhood might have been taken directly from a hagiographical text:

Стал отроком прекрасным, кротким, тихим;
Не по летам он разумом был мудр
И к книжному ученью прилеплялся.
И возлюбил он с самых ранних лет
Храм Божий и божественные книги . . .

(He became an excellent, meek, and quiet youth; he was wise in reason not according to his years and he clung to book learning. And from his earliest years he loved God's temple and the divine books) (355–56).[18]

[18] The text of "The Anchorite" ("Otshel'nik") is found in Almazov, *Sochineniia* 1: 355–70.

Similar formulations of the *puer senex* topos may be found in countless Lives.

As in "Mary of Egypt," Almazov stresses both didactic and sentimental elements in his story of Alexis. For example, he bases the laments of Alexis' parents and wife not on the *Menaea*, but on the folk version, which is distinguished by its greater emphasis on the poignancy of their sorrow.[19] The didactic element is most evident at the poem's conclusion, when the local patriarch delivers a sermon explaining why Alexis deserves to be called "Man of God" and to be included among the ranks of the saints. He cites especially Alexis' complete commitment to God and rejection of anything that smacks of worldly vanity. The passage is functionally very similar to Zosima's discourse on Mary's significance as a penitent. In both cases, the import of the original legend is made unmistakably explicit.

While severe asceticism did not often meet with enthusiasm, in their extreme humility and dedication to an independent conception of Christianity characterized by a literal acceptance of its tenets, Mary, Alexis, and other like-minded saints found favor with many Russians. As will be seen in the following chapter, the exaggerated denial of self, which may be called kenotic humility, proved especially attractive to the Russian spiritual imagination and found expression in numerous literary works other than adaptations of specific hagiographical legends and tales. Yet on one level the validity of the type of virtue practiced by Mary and Alexis was open to question; since their behavior was of no direct benefit to anyone but themselves, it could be construed as egotistical. Some nineteenth-century Russian writers were more attracted to the idea of a religion characterized by good works rather than one exclusively defined by faith and would probably have condemned these ascetics for their selfishness. In fact, in a story by Nikolai Leskov an anchorite comes under attack for his ostensibly self-centered existence. The protagonist of Almazov's third reworking of a saint's Life, "The Generous Rich Man" ("Shchedryi bogach," 1864), would probably have gained more approval from those who shared Leskov's conception of virtue. In this poem, Almazov treats the career of the Byzantine saint Philaretus the Merciful (d. 789).

According to some accounts, Philaretus was a rich husbandman at

[19] Cf. Adrianova, *Zhitie Alekseia*, 336.

Amnia in Paphlagonia who lost all he had to invading Saracens.[20] When Emperor Constantine VI married Philaretus' daughter, however, the fortunes of the impoverished farmer improved and he was made consul. According to the hagiographical tradition, Philaretus, like Mary and Alexis, espoused a primitively straightforward view of Christianity. Unlike these ascetics, he pursued the path of virtue in the bosom of his family and his convictions were most apparent in his charity. The *Menaea* Life describes him as a rich but extremely generous man who resembles Job in that he suffers a number of misfortunes and eventually loses most of his possessions. Yet this does not prevent Philaretus from expressing his charitable inclinations, even when this threatens the security of his family. On numerous occasions he gives away cattle, food, and other necessities of daily existence. When reproached, he tries to calm his family with promises of a secret treasure which will eventually be theirs. When imperial representatives from Constantinople appear seeking a wife for the emperor, it becomes clear what, or rather who, constitutes Philaretus' treasure. The Life suggests that because they are impressed by Philaretus' obvious good character, the envoys express an interest in his female offspring. His granddaughter Maria captures their attention, and in Constantinople her unspoiled goodness causes her to be chosen as the emperor's wife in preference to more sophisticated young women. While acknowledging that Philaretus and his family benefit greatly from their association with the royal family, the Life emphasizes that he continues to be as uninhibitedly generous as before.

Unlike the more somber legends of Mary and Alexis, the Life of Philaretus has the happy ending familiar from many folktales; the riddle of the secret treasure is explained, the prince wins the princess, and everyone lives profitably ever after. What this story shares with the other Lives reworked by Almazov is an unsophisticated protagonist whose practice of what he perceives as virtue is unhampered by practical considerations. In Philaretus' case this tendency becomes so marked as to verge on holy foolishness (*iurodstvo*): his apparently idiotic actions make religious sense. In his poem, Almazov draws attention to this aspect of Philaretus' activities. He lingers on the farmer's decision to

[20] The *Menaea* Life of Philaretus the Merciful is found under December 1. A popular version of his life was published a few years after Almazov's poem. See *Zhitie sviatogo Filareta Milostivogo* (Moscow, 1870). On Philaretus, see F. G. Holweck, *A Biographical Dictionary of the Saints* (St. Louis, Mo., 1924).

give away not only a cow, but also its calf, so that the two will not be separated. In a similar instance in one of Leskov's stories, a young woman decides to help a man she believes is about to steal fruit from her garden.

A concern for the caritative ideal had long been an important component of Russian spirituality. In this regard, the Russians' tremendous adoration for St. Nicholas the Wonderworker for his charitable rather than ascetic acts is significant.[21] In the case of Philaretus, the fact that he eventually reaps a material reward is irrelevant from a strictly religious point of view. His virtuous existence constitutes its own justification. In his reworking of the saint's Life, Almazov indicates that it is the type of virtue exemplified by Philaretus that is important, not the rewards his virtue brings him. Like "Mary of Egypt" and "The Anchorite," "The Generous Rich Man" is distinguished by a ponderously didactic tone. In this poem, however, the saint himself serves as his own interpreter through long, reference-laden discourses to his wife. The most overtly didactic incident occurs after Philaretus and his wife have acquired a luxurious residence in the capital. Philaretus instructs his wife to make all the necessary arrangements for entertaining the emperor and his nobles. When he arrives with a crowd of beggars, his wife innocently, and understandably, asks where the emperor is, to which Philaretus responds enigmatically: "On zdes', on zdes', sredi liubimtsev! / Da tol'ko zdes' temno, i my ne vidim" ("He is here, he is here, among his favorites! Only it's dark here, and we don't see") (398).[22] The motif of waiting on beggars, a classic metaphor for humility, was used by other Russian writers as well in their reworkings of hagiographical material.

If Philaretus' discourses prove too obscure, an unimaginative reader will find an explanation of his saintliness at the the end of "The Generous Rich Man" in the form of a short lecture by an angel to a hermit friend of Philaretus. His authoritative commentary resembles those by Zosima and the patriarch in Almazov's other hagiographical poems. Like them, the angel goes directly to the main point, saying that Philaretus' virtue consisted in his whole-hearted love for everyone. Faith, prayer, and works alone are not enough, continues the angel—for salvation, love is necessary.

[21] Fedotov, *Russian Religious Mind*, 1: 44.

[22] The text of "The Generous Rich Man" ("Shchedryi bogach") is found in Almazov, *Sochineniia* 1: 373–402.

Shakhova's and Almazov's poems represent one extreme of the possibilities for revising hagiographical material. In every case, their intention appears to have been to preserve the original meaning of the story while creating a more contemporary lexical and stylistic framework. As has been seen, Almazov also introduced a strongly didactic note into his poems, possibly because he feared that the broad audience he intended for his work might otherwise miss the larger significance of the saints he described. Yet neither Shakhova nor Almazov attempted to revitalize the religious thought of the original Lives or to give added psychological depth to the portraits of their saintly subjects. Their poems remain limited in their impact and their charm, such as it is, is antiquarian.

The Secularized Legends of Herzen and Aleksei K. Tolstoy

The majority of the nineteenth-century Russian writers who made use of hagiographical material did not pursue the conservative tack adopted by Shakhova and Almazov. In a much-quoted remark, Leskov wrote to the publicist and author Aleksei Suvorin that "the *Prolog* is rubbish, but in that rubbish there are pictures such as you couldn't make up."[23] Leskov's crudely direct formulation epitomizes the approach of many writers, who assumed a less reverential attitude than did Shakhova and Almazov and regarded hagiographical collections primarily as a fund of intriguing raw material. In the 1880s, the reworking of specific hagiographical legends and tales acquired a temporary popularity. This vogue can be at least partially attributed to the impact of Tolstoyanism, with its emphasis on simplicity of narration; hagiographical stories, many writers soon realized, could serve as perfect vehicles for the transmission of uncomplicated moral lessons. The primary tendency during this period was to exploit hagiography as a kind of literary Trojan horse, and religious views unacceptable to the mainstream of Russian Orthodoxy were clothed in the trappings of Christian legend in an attempt to disarm both the censor and, presumably, unsuspecting readers. The attempt was not always successful. Leskov, for example, had continual censorship problems because of his *Prolog* tales.[24]

[23] N. S. Leskov, *Ss*, 11 vols. (Moscow, 1956–1958), 11: 362.

[24] The most detailed discussion of Leskov's censorship problems is found in Stephen

By no means all of the writers who turned to hagiography during the nineteenth century wished to make a specifically religious point. Sometimes hagiography proved to be a viable form for the treatment of themes without a strong religious interest. This tendency manifested itself well before the 1880s, the heyday of hagiographical reworkings. Two of the earliest adaptations of saints' Lives, Alexander Herzen's story "The Legend of St. Theodora" ("Legenda o sv. Feodore," 1836) and Aleksei K. Tolstoy's narrative poem "John Damascene" ("Ioann Damaskin," 1858?), fall into this category. Both works exhibit a distinctly secular use of a religious subject.

In 1847 Herzen (1812–1870) left Russia for a life of self-imposed exile in the West, where he played a major role in attempts to influence the domestic Russian political situation from abroad. Herzen's departure was preceded by years of conflict with the tsarist establishment. It was in 1834, after having been arrested for seditious behavior and imprisoned in the barracks at Moscow's Krutitskii Monastery, that he spent time perusing the Gospels and the *Menaea*. About the latter, Herzen wrote to his cousin and future wife Natal'ia Zakhar'ina: "I am reading the *Reading Menaea* with enthusiasm; here were divine examples of self-sacrifice, here were men!"[25] As he became more closely acquainted with Orthodoxy, Herzen also began studying Italian in order to read *The Divine Comedy*. His captivation with Dante was such that the mid-1830s have sometimes been referred to as his "Dantean" period.[26] One of the fruits of these combined enthusiasms was a reworking of the *Menaea* legend of St. Theodora liberally sprinkled with references to the Bible and to Dante. It appears that Natal'ia may have been partially responsible for the composition of the story; "The Legend of St. Theodora" is dedicated to her and Herzen later claimed that he wrote it for her sake.[27] After he was sent into exile in provincial Viatka, he revised the story, but it remained unpublished until after his death.[28] The title of the story actually came from the editor of the post-

S. Lottridge, "Nikolaj Semenovič Leskov's *Prolog* Tales" (Ph.D. diss., Columbia University, 1970).

[25] Letter of 10 December 1834. See A. I. Gertsen, *Ss*, 30 vols. (Moscow, 1954–1964), 21: 28.

[26] A good discussion of this period is found in Frank Friedeberg Seeley, "Herzen's 'Dantean' Period," *Slavonic and East European Review* 33 (1954): 44–74.

[27] Letter of 16–21 July 1837. See Gertsen, *Ss* 21: 187.

[28] "The Legend" was first published by E. S. Nekrasova in *Russkaia mysl'*, 1881, no.

humous publication; Herzen generally refers to it simply as "The Legend."[29]

In his memoirs, Herzen speaks in a general way of his "mysticism" of this period.[30] Historians have disagreed as to how this should be interpreted and how appropriate it is to apply this term to Herzen's philosophical attitudes in the 1830s.[31] Reference is often made to the possible influence on him of Natal'ia and his new friend in exile, the architect Aleksandr Vitberg, both of whom had decidedly mystical leanings; Vitberg had strong ties to the Freemasons and had been given approval during the reign of Alexander I for a project commemorating the Russian victory over Napoleon that would have made use of Masonic motifs.[32] The degree to which Herzen was under the sway of the Saint-Simonians and their ideas of the New Christianity is also important in evaluating his "mysticism." Herzen himself characterizes these ideas as "mystical-social" and admits being captivated by them in the mid-1830s.[33]

In discussions of Herzen's possible mysticism, "The Legend of St. Theodora" often plays a role, particularly because Herzen produced comparatively few works in the mid-1830s. Treatments of this story by historians try to identify the sources of religious and philosophical commentary and make only cursory reference to the original *Menaea* legend. It has been argued very convincingly that, while there are superficial borrowings from Dante, many of the theories espoused by the intellectual abbot in "The Legend" reflect the influence of the "more exalted" Saint-Simonians, like Barthélemy Enfantin.[34] From a literary point of view, however, such observations do not furnish a complete picture. An understanding of Herzen's artistic intentions and thematic interests

12. An extensive discussion of the story from a literary point of view is found in Nicholas Rzhevsky, *Russian Literature and Ideology: Herzen, Dostoevsky, Leontiev, Tolstoy, Fadeyev* (Urbana, Ill. 1983), 34–37.

[29] A. I. Gertsen, *Polnoe sobranie sochinenii i pisem*, vol. 1 (Petrograd, 1919), 533. While the editor's title is ambiguous in Russian, prerevolutionary publications clarified that Theodora was the one meant through, for example, the use of an accent (Feodóre).

[30] Gertsen, *Ss* 8: 288.

[31] A good survey of the subject is found in Seeley, "Herzen's 'Dantean' Period," 56–64. Seeley discusses the views of E. H. Carr, Ia. El'sberg, P. Guber, and R. Labry.

[32] Martin Malia, *Alexander Herzen and the Birth of Russian Socialism* (New York, 1965), 168.

[33] Gertsen, *Ss* 8: 288.

[34] Malia, *Alexander Herzen*, 154.

demands comparison of his story with the original *Menaea* legend. This in turn may shed some light on the question of Herzen's mysticism.

The story of Theodore/Theodora, said to have lived at monastery "18" in the Thebaid in the fifth century, is one of the more doubtful of the *Menaea* legends. The saint's existence has been established, but her Life is regarded as fiction.[35] According to the story, as an extremely naive young woman Theodora adulterously betrays her beloved husband. Her remorse demands a severe act of repentance, and she decides to enter a monastery disguised as a man, understandably believing that this will frustrate her husband's attempts to find her. Once disguised, she convinces the abbot of an isolated monastery to accept her as a novice. Her first few years as a monk are filled with astonishing displays of virtuous and miraculous behavior, but trials are in store for Theodora. On a visit to another monastery, she is solicited by the abbot's daughter. Angered by the handsome young monk's refusal to sleep with her, the girl spitefully accuses Theodora of responsibility when she later becomes pregnant. Theodora's protestations of innocence are not believed, and when the child is born, the "father" and child are forced to live outside the monastery walls, where devils frequently torment the poor monk. Eventually the abbot relents, allowing the monk and child to return within the monastery walls, but only after her death is Theodora completely vindicated, when burial preparations reveal that she is a woman and thus incapable of impregnating anyone.

The legend of Theodora belongs to an entire cycle of early Christian legends concerned with male impersonators, young women who disguise themselves as monks, like Pelagia the Penitent of Antioch, Marina of Bithynia, and Margaret Reparata. Like Theodora, the latter two were accused of fathering a child. The modern sensibility may find the legend of Theodora particularly jarring, for her long-suffering virtue seems peculiarly pointless. Yet Theodora's repentance reflects precisely that idiosyncratic disregard for conventional, official routes to salvation that captured the imagination of many nineteenth-century Russians. In Theodora's case, while she is in the Church, she is most definitely not of it.

Its implausibility aside, the legend of Theodora has decidedly dramatic qualities, and it has been suggested that this may have been a

[35] The *Menaea* Life of Theodora is found under September 11. On the historical Theodora, see Holweck, *A Biographical Dictionary of the Saints*.

major reason that it attracted Herzen's attention.[36] In the original *Menaea* legend, it is clear that eventually the monk's feminine identity will be revealed, and narrative interest stems primarily from simple suspense as to when and how this will occur and from pleasurable anticipation of the shame that will be felt by Theodora's detractors. Herzen exploits the dramatic possibilities inherent in the story rather differently. He portrays Theodora from the beginning as a young man and does not reveal her true, female identity until after her death. This narrative device enables Herzen to keep alive the mystery of the child's paternity; at the crucial moment in the scene involving the abbot's daughter, there is a fade-out. The mystery is intensified by the fact that Theodore has in his possession a woman's belt. When confronted with it, he blushingly claims it as his own. Throughout the story, there are numerous hints as to the monk's real identity, so that the even slightly astute reader, or one familiar with the *Menaea* account, may guess the truth. The title of the story is naturally of help as well, but it should be remembered that this was not Herzen's chosen title.

One consequence of this narrative structure is that the point of view becomes less that of Theodore than of those around him; it would clearly be difficult to approach Theodore too closely without betraying his identity. During much of the story the focus shifts entirely to the abbot of Theodore's monastery. Even before the young monk arrives, the background and attitudes of the abbot are examined at length. The narrator sets the tone for this discussion with a brief description of the face of the fifty-year-old ascetic: "his face was pale and yellow; deep wrinkles on his forehead and his fiery eyes showed that strong passions burned in his soul and had not yet been extinguished" (88).[37] This hackneyed portrait might have been taken directly from a gothic potboiler, and it comes as no surprise that the ensuing biography of the abbot is highly romanticized.[38] His solitary youth in Antioch, his passion for philosophy, the inspiration he finds in Christian literature and the Christians—all are related in highly colored fashion, as is his conversion to Christianity: "there can be [only] one passion in a strong breast" (90).

[36] Raoul Labry, *Alexandre Ivanovič Herzen: Essai sur la formation et le développement de ses idées* (Paris, 1928), 169.

[37] The text of "The Legend" ("Legenda") is found in Gertsen, *Ss* 1: 81–106.

[38] On Herzen's romanticization of the legend of Theodora, see Opul'skii, *Zhitiia sviatykh*, 65–70.

From an intense and intellectual young man, the abbot becomes a severe yet just spiritual director. Sceptical of the fleeting enthusiasms of youth, he tests Theodore when he arrives by making him wait outside all night (another topos). Along with his scepticism, however, the abbot has a romanticized longing for a pure youth to serve as an intellectual companion, and for this reason he hopes that Theodore will pass his test. Thus, in Herzen's version of the story, the relationship between the abbot and Theodore and the strain that relationship undergoes when Theodore is accused of fornication become the central theme of the story. Herzen's abbot has implicit trust in Theodore's integrity and does not punish him until Theodore himself admits that he has deceived the abbot (he of course has in mind his assumed masculinity). Even after this the abbot seems to hear an inner voice asserting Theodore's innocence, and the eventual denouement comes as a bittersweet consolation.

The development of the relationship between the mature and sophisticated abbot and the idealistic young monk contributes to the narrative interest of "The Legend of St. Theodora," but it has little to do with religion in general or Christianity in particular. By shifting the focus from Theodore's search for sanctity to the role he plays in the abbot's life, Herzen diffuses the religious tension of the original legend. In fact, Theodore's silence begins to appear more than a little perverse. In Herzen's hands, the legend of Theodora becomes historical fiction rather than religious literature; the actual plot and the discussion of religion are not successfully integrated. The abbot devotes much thought to the intellectual implications of the monastic system, but his ideas have no connection with Theodora's self-sacrificing masquerade. As a consequence, treatment of religious questions in "The Legend" reminds one more of a philosophical tract than of inspired legend.

Herzen prefaces "The Legend of St. Theodora" with an explanation of how he became interested in a hagiographical theme. In the course of a prison stroll, the sight of the monasteries of Moscow carried his thoughts back to the heyday of Christian monasticism. He characterizes this early period in glowingly idealistic terms: "This life for an idea, life for the erection of a cross, for the redemption of man, seemed to me the highest expression of community spirit [*obshchestvennost'*]; it no longer exists and it is impossible now" (83). In the midst of further fulsome praises of medieval religiosity, Herzen imagines that he hears the hoots of derision typical of the nineteenth-century attitude to religion. In an earlier draft, he had mentioned Saint-Simon specifically as a source of mockery.[39] In this context, the assertion that "it no longer exists and it is impossible now," assumes a more precise relevance and suggests that Herzen's enthusiasm for the effusions of the Saint-Simonians was already checked by practical reservations. He continues: "Let us forget . . . our century, let's move on to those times of quiet contemplation, to those times of heaven on earth" (84). What is apparent here, and throughout the story, is that Herzen is describing a world that has no real validity for him as a guide to spiritual life in the present. Herzen does not appreciate Theodora's actions in the same way that Almazov and Shakhova appreciate the activities of Mary of Egypt, for example, and the thoughts of the abbot are lifeless. Thus, in spite of its superficially religious subject, "The Legend of St. Theodora" cannot serve as evidence of Herzen's purported mysticism. Instead, the story provides another demonstration that mysticism never gained full sway over his thoughts. Herzen himself later appraised "The Legend" as a failure as a religious document: "In prison . . . my need of the Gospel was strong; I read it with tears—but did not fully understand it; 'The Legend' is a proof of this; I comprehended the easiest part—the practical morality of Christianity, but not Christianity itself."[40] In other words, Herzen absorbed Christianity only as an ethical system. This helps to explain why Theodora's actions and indeed ascetic monasticism in general would have remained alien to him.

Count Aleksei K. Tolstoy (1817–1875), a distant relative of Leo Tolstoy, was a poet, playwright, and novelist whose humorous verse and historical dramas were very successful. Like Herzen's "The Legend of St. Theodora," Tolstoy's narrative poem "John Damascene" exemplifies the diversion of hagiographical material from its original religious purposes to more secular ones. The work is unusual among nineteenth-century reworkings of saints' Lives because it concerns an indisputably historical figure and one of the major Fathers of the Church.[41] John Damascene was known to Russians not only through his Life, but also as author of numerous hymns and the tale of Barlaam and Josaphat, a

[39] Gertsen, *Ss* 1: 465.

[40] Letter of 9–14 April 1837 to N. A. Zakhar'ina. See Gertsen, *Ss* 21: 158.

[41] The unfinished writings of Ivan Turgenev include a play very loosely based on the Life of St. Anthony of Egypt. See I. S. Turgenev, *Polnoe sobranie sochinenii i pisem*, vol. 3 (Moscow, 1962), 246–275. Because this work is not strictly speaking an adaptation of a hagiographical legend, it has not been discussed here.

variant of the legend of Buddha. Tolstoy's choice of saint was also unusual for, while John certainly espoused humility, he is not at all the typical meek, self-effacing, and unintellectual saint so dear to many Russians.

John Damascene lived during the late seventh and early eighth centuries, when Damascus was ruled by an Omayyad caliph and the Byzantine empire by fanatical iconoclasts. The caliph practiced religious toleration, and John held a high position in his court until Leo III (717–741), angered by John's opposition to iconoclasm, treacherously arranged for the caliph to believe John a traitor. According to some redactions of John's Life, the caliph in revenge ordered John's right hand cut off, but the saint's prayers caused his severed hand to grow back. John soon abandoned the secular world and entered the desolate Palestinian monastery of St. Sabas.[42] There his spiritual director enjoined a vow of silence upon him as a lesson in humility. When John broke his vow to compose a funeral hymn for a dead monk, he was punished by being assigned to clean the lavatories. Shortly afterwards the Mother of God is said to have appeared as his intercessor in a vision to John's spiritual director. John was released from his vow of silence and made a priest. He spent the rest of his life in the monastery writing hymns, stories, and theological treatises. Although anathematized by some of his contemporaries for his iconodulic views, he was later canonized.

In his reworking of the Life of John, Tolstoy generally ignores the purely religious aspects of the story. John's role in the battle against iconoclasm is barely mentioned in passing, and only as evidence of John's greatness, not for any religious purposes. Similarly, Tolstoy eschews the overtly miraculous features of the story: there is no mention of the hand-cutting episode. Tolstoy instead transforms John into a romantic hero, into the superior individual who stands far above the common herd, and uses the events of his life to glorify artistic creativity, not Christianity.

Tolstoy's John wishes to serve God, but this is less convincing as the driving force in his life than is his interest in the art with which he intends to serve God. His unhappiness at the caliph's court makes him beg the latter to release him: "Dozvol' dyshat' i pet' na vole" ("Permit

[42] The *Menaea* Life is found under December 4.

me to breathe and sing in freedom") (514).[43] The emphasis here is on his desire to pursue his artistic calling, not his religious avocation. When the caliph tries to persuade him to stay by offering him half his kingdom, John explains that a singer does not need such a gift. Typical of the romantic view of the artist is the notion here that he is above crass material concerns, that the opportunity to practice his art is all that matters.

Convinced by John's impassioned words, the caliph allows him to leave his service. In a manner reminiscent of many Byronic heroes, John vanishes without a trace. Soon afterwards, a wanderer appears at the gates of an isolated monastery, desiring refuge and informing the monks that their new brother has brought with him his "dar i gusli" ("gift and psaltery") (520). These assertions are distinguished neither by humility nor by religious fervor. Once again, the emphasis is on John's artistic talents, not his ostensibly religious purposes.

As in the original Life, the aspiring monk is enjoined to silence. Tolstoy's interpretation of this episode differs substantially from that found in the Life, however. John's spiritual director is narrow-minded and severe; while the other monks are reluctant even to presume to take such a famous man as John as a disciple, John's elder shows an embarrassing eagerness to humiliate the poet. In Tolstoy's poem, his injunction of silence has a spiteful ring:

Дух праздности и прелесть песнопенья
Постом, певец, ты должен победить!
Коль ты пришел отшельником в пустыню,
Умей мечты житейские попрать,
И на уста, смирив свою гордыню,
Ты наложи молчания печать!

(You must defeat the spirit of idleness and the charm of singing with fasting, singer! If you have come as a hermit to the desert, know how to trample worldly dreams, and humbling your pride, place a seal of silence on your lips!) (521).

John agrees to these conditions, although not with any noticeable enthusiasm. In fact, his enforced silence does not so much strengthen

[43] The text of "John Damascene" ("Ioann Damaskin") is found in A. K. Tolstoi, *Ss*, vol. 1 (Moscow, 1963), 513–34.

his soul as torment it. As Tolstoy presents it, the entire process is only an exercise in the frustration of John's talents.

When John compassionately agrees to break his vow in order to compose a funeral hymn for a fellow monk, the narrator takes the opportunity for a digression on the nobility of independent thought:

> Над вольной мыслью Богу неугодны
> Насилие и гнет.
> Она, в душе рожденная свободно,
> В оковах не умрет!

> (Coercion and oppression of free thought are not pleasing to God: born free in the soul, it will not die in fetters!) (525).

Implicitly, of course, this observation stands in direct opposition to one of the underpinnings of monasticism, unquestioning obedience to one's superior.

In Tolstoy's version of John's life, the hymn John composes for the monk's funeral is one now used by the Orthodox Church. The poem includes a paraphrase of this famous troparion.[44] Yet John's spiritual director is untouched by its beauty. He angrily drives John from the monastery, reviling him for his pride. Only the pleas of the other monks persuade the old man to allow John the opportunity to redeem himself. The elder is presented throughout in a wholly unfavorable light, as a rigid martinet who does not appreciate any kind of beauty. He does not even respond to the natural beauty around him, an unforgivable sin in the romantic canon. Instead, the elder delights in a self-mortifying asceticism and thoughts of death. The only positive action he performs is to beg John's forgiveness, which he does after the Mother of God orders him to lift his ban so that the world may profit from John's songs.

Although John uses his gift in the service of Christianity, the overall effect of Tolstoy's narrative poem subordinates religion to art. John's creative efforts are presented as implicitly superior to other types of religious activity; "the singer" is superior to the other monks by virtue of his talent, not through his religious commitment or ascetic feats. John's spiritual director, on the other hand, is not represented as the conventional venerable guide, but as a bigoted and misguided

[44] The Greek original of this troparion is found in Jacques Paul Migne, ed., *Patrologia Graeca*, 161 vols. (Paris, 1859–1889), 96: 1368.

thwarting influence. The monastic practice of self-effacing humility seems out of place; Tolstoy implies that when artistic talent is involved, modesty is inappropriate. Moreover, the continual insistence on the artists's need for freedom is a secular, not a religious theme. In short, "John Damascene" is not a religious poem, but a romanticized treatment of the artist in a religious setting. As in the case of "The Legend of St. Theodora," the original story has been given a secular orientation. Unlike Herzen's story, however, Tolstoy's poem develops its theme in a harmonious and integrated fashion.[45]

Leskov's Prolog Adaptations

The stories and narrative poems discussed so far are all based on Lives found in the *Reading Menaea*. As noted in Chapter One, these Lives tend to be more consistently biographical than the *Prolog* entries, which often seem to be episodes rather than Lives in the strict sense of the word. The same is true of many of the hagiographical legends and tales included in Aleksandr Afanas'ev's *Russian Folk Legends* (*Narodnye russkie legendy*, 1859) and similar collections. It is not surprising that writers of the 1880s with a religious axe to grind turned to these works rather than to the *Menaea*, for the greater sketchiness of the former provided more latitude for unorthodox thematic development. Some of these episodes were in themselves rather unorthodox.

Among the writers of the 1880s who reworked hagiographical material for their own religious purposes were Nikolai Leskov, Vsevolod Garshin, Leo Tolstoy, and Aleksei Suvorin. Of these, Leskov was the most enthusiastic about this type of literary composition; within about five years he wrote nine increasingly elaborate adaptations of *Prolog* stories.[46] In them, he runs the gamut of possibilities for reworking hagiographical material.

[45] Some of Tolstoy's contemporaries believed there was an autobiographical subtext to this poem. A career at court was as inimical to Tolstoy as to John, and in 1861 he was finally able to retire from government service. Cf. Tolstoi, *Ss* 1: 774; and F. D. Batiushkov, "Gr. Aleksei Konstantinovich Tolstoi," in D. N. Ovsianiko-Kulikovskii, ed., *Istoriia russkoi literatury XIX veka*, vol. 3 (Moscow, 1909), 410. Opul'skii discusses the possible autobiographical subtext in detail. See *Zhitiia sviatykh*, 80–81.

[46] They include: "The Tale of the God-pleasing Woodcutter" ("Povest' o bogougodnom drovokole," 1886), "The Tale of Fedor the Christian and His Friend Abram the Jew" ("Skazanie o Fedore-khristiane i o druge ego Abrame-zhidovine," 1886), "Pam-

Leskov (1831–1895) first gained popularity for his stories of ecclesiastical life, of which the most well-known is the novel *Cathedral Folk* (*Soboriane*, 1872). His relationship with Orthodoxy was always uneasy, and later in his life he became an adherent of Tolstoyanism, although his religious concerns often differed in emphasis from those of his mentor. Leskov liked the idea of serving as a literary guide to obscure or exotic spheres of Russian life. A desire to stake out the *Prolog* and the early Christian era as an area of personal expertise may have motivated his exhaustive examination of the *Prolog* at least in part.[47] This was accompanied by study of early Christian culture, particularly of the details of daily life. In researching the background for his stories, Leskov apparently made much use of the work of the Egyptologists Georg Ebers and Gaston Maspero.[48] Although few traces of the writings of Gustave Flaubert are evident in his stories, Leskov seems to have been familiar with "St. Julien l'hospitalier" (1876), "Hérodias" (1877), and *Salammbô* (1862) and in his concern with ethnographical verisimilitude he may have been influenced by the example of Flaubert.[49] In a review of Nikolai Barsukov's reference work *The Sources of Russian Hagiography* (*Istochniki russkoi agiografii*, 1882), entitled "Saints' Lives as a Literary Source" ("Zhitiia kak literaturnyi istochnik," 1882), he observed:

> But that in spite of the great difficulty in reconstructing the appearance of a saint according to the existing Lives, with a knowledge of history and a penetrating mind it is not impos-

falon the Mountebank" ("Skomorokh Pamfalon," 1887), "The Legend of Conscience-stricken Daniil" ("Legenda o sovestnom Daniile," 1888), "Beauteous Aza" ("Prekrasnaia Aza," 1888), "The Lion of the Elder Gerasim" ("Lev startsa Gerasima," 1888), "The Felon of Ashkelon" ("Askalonskii zlodei," 1888), "The Mountain" ("Gora," 1890), and "Innocent Prudentsii" ("Nevinnyi Prudentsii," 1891). Unlike the majority of the stories and poems discussed in this chapter, Leskov's *Prolog* tales have attracted a significant amount of attention by scholars. In addition to Stephen Lottridge's dissertation mentioned in n. 22, the most important treatments of the subject include sections of Valentina Gebel', *N. S. Leskov v tvorcheskoi laboratorii* (Moscow, 1945); Leonid Grossman, *N. S. Leskov: Zhizn', tvorchestvo, poetika* (Moscow, 1945); and Hugh McLean, *Nikolai Leskov: The Man and His Art* (Cambridge, Mass., 1977). Recent Soviet scholarship has not produced anything of comparable depth.

[47] Cf. Lottridge, "Leskov's *Prolog* Tales," 58. Opul'skii asserts that Leskov was "the Russian writer most well-read in hagiographical literature." See *Zhitiia sviatykh*, 137.

[48] For details, see Lottridge, "Leskov's *Prolog* Tales," 102.

[49] Grossman, *N. S. Leskov*, 226–27.

sible—this has been proven not only by Flaubert, but by N. I. Kostomarov as well.[50]

Presumably Leskov felt that he too possessed the necessary knowledge and penetration.

One of the fruits of Leskov's extensive study of the *Prolog* was a lengthy article entitled "Legendary Characters" ("Legendarnye kharaktery"), written in 1887 but unpublished until 1892. The article was long rejected by editors because it was considered immoral.[51] In it, Leskov claims that he has found precisely one hundred episodes from the *Prolog* suitable for narrative or plastic adaptation. He summarizes about thirty-five entries. Four of these later became the basis for the stories "Beauteous Aza" ("Prekrasnaia Aza," 1888), "The Felon of Ashkelon" ("Askalonskii zlodei," 1888), "The Mountain" ("Gora," 1890), and "Innocent Prudentsii" ("Nevinnyi Prudentsii," 1891).[52]

Leskov's ostensible purpose in compiling "Legendary Characters" was to disprove the notion that hagiographical stories are injurious to the reputation of women, which he called "a lie" (127).[53] His summaries are intended to show precisely the opposite, that very few *Prolog* women are portrayed as seductresses and those that are generally fail in attempts to woo men from the path of virtue. Instead, *Prolog* women are often victims of men's attentions rather than aggressors and, simultaneously, may exert a beneficial influence on their weaker male acquaintances. Yet, in spite of Leskov's protestations, he seems less concerned with the "woman question" than anxious to demonstrate his own expertise and the narrative potential of the *Prolog* stories. His subsequent use in "The Mountain" of one of the rare stories involving a would-be temptress is indicative; with characteristic inconsistency, his desire to correct the impression that hagiography displayed a negative attitude towards women did not extend to avoiding misogynist material.

In addition to the stories mentioned above, Leskov also based "The Tale of the God-pleasing Woodcutter" ("Povest' o bogougodnom dro-

[50] *Novoe vremia*, 17 August 1882.

[51] See McLean, *Nikolai Leskov*, 571–72, for discussion of the controversy.

[52] The article also includes summaries of the Life of Mary of Egypt and the story of Iakov the Faster and the harlot. The latter is echoed in Leo Tolstoy's story "Father Sergii" ("Otets Sergii," 1890–1898).

[53] The text of "Legendary Characters" ("Legendarnye kharaktery") is found in N. S. Leskov, *Pss*, 36 vols., 3d ed. (St. Petersburg, 1902–1903), 33: 126–95.

vokole," 1886), "The Tale of Fedor the Christian and His Friend Abram the Jew" ("Skazanie o Fedore-khristiane i o druge ego Abrame-zhidovine," 1886), "Pamfalon the Mountebank" ("Skomorokh Pamfalon," 1887) "The Legend of Conscience-stricken Daniil" (Legenda o sovestnom Daniile," 1888), and "The Lion of the Elder Gerasim" ("Lev startsa Gerasima," 1888) on *Prolog* narratives. With the exception of the last two, all have lay heroes and heroines. In "The Legend of Conscience-stricken Daniil" and "The Lion of the Elder Gerasim" the protagonists possess an ecclesiastical identity, but they are simple monks, not part of the upper reaches of the ecclesiastical hierarchy. Indeed, Daniil eventually opposes the ecclesiastical establishment. Such opposition is one of the hallmarks of Leskov's *Prolog* stories. In keeping with the tradition espoused by many Russian intellectuals, Leskov's protagonists are often "simple" people whose unsophisticated morality is superior to the more conventional religiosity displayed by those around them.

In their essentials, Leskov's attitudes about Christian morality at the end of the 1880s coincided with those of Tolstoy. Yet, although Leskov was very much under Tolstoy's sway for a few years, it seems likely that the great writer served less as a true initiator than as a catalyst in the development of Leskov's ideas.[54] Leskov himself described the relationship in these terms:

> When Tolstoy was writing *Anna Karenina*, I was already close to what I am saying now. I was already digging that heap which Lev Nikolaevich began to dig as well. But it's only that his light is brighter, and I followed him with my lampion. He has an enormous torch, while my little lampion is flickering. I am hurrying after him. I am hurrying![55]

Tolstoy would have agreed with this appraisal. In a conversation with Anatolii Faresov in 1898, he said: "Leskov was my follower, but not out of imitation. He had long been going in the same direction in

[54] William B. Edgerton, "Leskov and Tolstoy: Two Literary Heretics," *American Slavonic and East European Review* 12 (1953): 524–25. See also Lottridge, "Leskov's *Prolog* Tales," 82.

[55] Quoted in A. I. Faresov, *Protiv techenii: N. S. Leskov; ego zhizn', sochineniia, polemika i vospominaniia o nem* (St. Petersburg, 1904), 307–8. On the role played by Tolstoy in the development of Leskov's ideas, see Edgerton, "Leskov and Tolstoy," 524–25.

which I am now going."[56] The Tolstoyan inclinations of Leskov's *Prolog* tales are displayed in the glorification of a literal-minded morality that needs no commitment to offical Christianity and in an overt emphasis on active rather than contemplative spirituality.

In reworking *Prolog* narratives, Leskov may have been stimulated by Tolstoy's own reworkings of hagiographical material.[57] His first *Prolog* tale was published as part of an article which attempted to defend Tolstoy against accusations that his popular stories (*narodnye rasskazy*) contained subversive religious elements. In the introduction to his article, Leskov triumphantly proclaims that Tolstoy does know theology, that he is familiar with the *Prolog* (after all, gossips Leskov, the novelist Grigorii Danilevskii saw a copy of the *Prolog* in Tolstoy's study), and that there are many stories in the *Prolog* very similar in spirit to Tolstoy's stories.[58] In further support of these assertions, Leskov offers his own story "The Tale of the God-pleasing Woodcutter."

One of Tolstoy's stories mentioned by Leskov in his article is "Three Old Men" ("Tri startsa," 1886). Tolstoy's specific source is uncertain, but the story itself is a variant of a widespread hagiographical tale.[59] In Tolstoy's version, an archpriest happens to visit an island where he finds three pious but ignorant old men. He decides to remedy their ignorance by teaching them the Lord's prayer. After he leaves the island, however, the archpriest is amazed to see the old men pursue his boat across the water because they have forgotten part of the prayer. Impressed by their obvious sanctity, he assures them that their own method of prayer is pleasing to God and asks them to pray for "us sinners" (105).[60] In this instance, the superiority of unlettered spirituality to formal religion is made completely clear.

The message of "The Tale of the God-pleasing Woodcutter" is very similar. Leskov prefaces his story with the comment:

> I hope to show that not only is there nothing reprehensible if someone wishes to represent a simple man as capable of managing

[56] Faresov, *Protiv techenii*, 70–71.

[57] Cf. Lottridge, "Leskov's *Prolog* Tales," 63.

[58] The article, entitled "Luchshii bogomolets (Kratkaia povest' po prologu s predisloviem o 'tendentsiiakh' gr. L. Tolstogo)," is found in Leskov, *Ss* 11: 100–12. See 101–3, especially.

[59] For detailed discussion of other versions of the tale, see V. I. Sreznevskii's commentary in L. N. Tolstoi, *Pss*, 90 vols. (Moscow, 1928–1958), 25: 707–9.

[60] The text of "Three Old Men" ("Tri startsa") is found in Tolstoi, *Pss* 25: 100–5.

> his own path well by himself, but that it is possible to represent a simple man even doing things that are beyond the powers of ecclesiastics (103).

Leskov accomplishes his intention while simultaneously remaining faithful to the original *Prolog* account.

The original *Prolog* story concerns a terrible drought in an unspecified town.[61] To bring about rain, the local bishop is instructed by a "voice from heaven" to ask the first person he sees entering a certain town gate to pray for rain. Eventually an unprepossessing old woodcutter appears. After he has been convinced to pray, rain does appear. When asked about his manner of existence by the suitably awed bishop, the woodcutter insists that he lives sinfully, a typical expression of humility. His recapitulation of his habits reveals that the opposite is true. In revealing virtue through dialogue, this exchange is reminiscent of the first meeting between Mary and Zosima in the Life of Mary of Egypt.

The story of the woodcutter contains all the ingredients calculated to appeal to Leskov's Tolstoyan tastes. The woodcutter is simple, humble, and virtuous. In addition, his prayers are invidiously more efficacious than those of the other Christians in the story, most notably the bishop. Only the actual miracle of the rain would have been unlikely to gain Leskov's approval. As scholars have noted, in his reworking he underplays the miraculous aspect, leaving open the possibility that the rainfall may have been a coincidence.[62] In other respects, Leskov adheres to the original, while stressing those aspects that conform to his religious views. He dwells on the skepticism of the people regarding the woodcutter's ability to serve as an agent of salvation in order to emphasize the notion that virtue may choose an unassuming guise. When the bishop and his flock first catch sight of the old man, they look at one another and shrug their shoulders in bewilderment. Only the absence of anyone else causes the bishop to halt the woodcutter. Similarly, the failure of the bishop's faith is purposely underscored when the narrator innocently asks earlier in the story: "Who else could pray better than the bishop, and whose prayer could be more pleasing to God?" (104). Yet Leskov does not actively denigrate this ecclesiastic as he later does the character of the bishop in "The Mountain." In fact, his adaptation

[61] The *Prolog* story is found under September 8.

[62] Cf. McLean, *Nikolai Leskov*, 565.

of the *Prolog* original is generally more restrained than subsequent reworkings.

In several respects, "The Tale of the God-pleasing Woodcutter" exhibits in embryonic form tendencies that became full-blown in Leskov's later *Prolog* adaptations. It is indicative that "The Tale of the God-pleasing Woodcutter" occupies only five pages, while later stories are often several times as long. One reason for this was Leskov's fondness for melodramatic elaboration, which is apparent even in the relatively terse "Tale." The drought is described as "terrible and prolonged" (103), and its consequences are spectacularly horrendous. In later stories, Leskov's tendency towards melodramatic overkill became more pronounced. This effusiveness generally went hand in hand with an increased accumulation of ethnographical detail, something also characteristic of "The Tale of the God-pleasing Woodcutter." For example, when the old man mentions his habit of sleeping under churches, the narrator interrupts with a brief discussion of the architecture of early churches. In later stories, such information is generally integrated more skillfully into the fabric of the story.

"The Tale of the God-pleasing Woodcutter" is a reasonably straightforward reworking of the original *Prolog* entry; nothing major in the plot has been altered and no significant additions or omissions have been made. Yet Leskov's story differs radically from Shakhova's and Almazov's reworkings, for example: he emphasizes those aspects of the story that undermine the authority of the Church. Shakhova and Almazov, on the other hand, exalt untutored spirituality without criticizing the ecclesiastical establishment. Thus in their poems Zosima is a venerable figure, although implicitly his virtue is *not* as great of that of Mary of Egypt.

In "The Tale of the God-pleasing Woodcutter," Leskov does not dare suggest that official Christianity is spiritually bankrupt. He does so in "The Legend of Conscience-stricken Daniil," although still on firm *Prolog* ground. The story concerns a monk who is repeatedly captured by barbarians.[63] On the final occasion, he kills one of his captors in order to escape. Later this murder torments his conscience, and he visits several ecclesiastical dignitaries in search of spiritual advice. All assure him that he has committed no sin in killing a pagan. When he turns himself over to the secular authorities, they tell him the same thing.

[63] The *Prolog* story is found under June 7.

Yet he remains unconvinced and eventually discovers his own manner of penitence through caring for a leper.

Once again, it is easy to see why this story would have captured Leskov's interest: religious authorities are depicted not simply as spiritually inferior, but as erring sophists, and a simple monk proves himself more virtuous. In addition, the method chosen by the monk to express his repentance, the performance of good works, was undoubtedly attractive to Leskov. If Daniil had followed the example of Mary of Egypt and retreated into the solitary pursuit of ascetic perfection, Leskov would probably have been less enthusiastic about the story.

In "The Legend of Conscience-stricken Daniil," the basic plot has been much more extensively developed than in "The Tale of the God-pleasing Woodcutter," although Leskov was still supposedly attempting to emulate the simple style of Tolstoy's popular stories.[64] Leskov's "Legend" includes lengthy descriptions of Daniil's torments of conscience, which here assumes an anthropomorphic form, resembling the Ethiopian barbarian he had killed. His conscience often speaks to him in this guise and, even before he makes the rounds of the patriarchs, instructs him in morality. It tells him to embrace the severest kind of punishment, warning: "you killed a man, you plundered his estate and made his wife a widow and his children orphans. Do not seek justification in any kind of guile because it is not permitted to kill anyone" (10).[65] These warnings serve as an implicit commentary on the patriachs' "guile" and it is clear beforehand that Daniil cannot possibly accept their false interpretations. To paint the shortcomings of official Christianity in even blacker colors, Leskov exaggerates the baseness of the various patriarchs. Whereas in the *Prolog* they err only in suggesting that the barbarian was no better than an animal, in Leskov's version they compound this error: when Daniil innocently asks to be shown the relevant passage in the Gospels, the patriarchs haughtily rebuff him. Against this background of dishonesty, Daniil's unaffected morality appears in an even better light.

Thwarted in his search for punishment by both the ecclesiastical and the secular authorities, Daniil is advised by his conscience to look lower

[64] In the preface to "The Legend of Conscience-stricken Daniil" Leskov indicated that he intended the story in "the spirit of the popular [*prostonarodnye*] tales of L. N. Tolstoy." See Leskov, *Ss* 11: 714.

[65] The text of "The Legend of Conscience-stricken Daniil" ("Legenda o sovestnom Daniile") is found in Leskov, *Pss* 30: 3–20.

rather than higher for the solution to his dilemma. This suggestion is intended figuratively, but Daniil responds to it literally as well and, gazing towards the horizon, sees a leper. Understanding that charitable activity should always have been his goal, he devotes himself to the leper. Leskov's portrayal of this unusual form of repentance was possibly influenced by a similar episode in "St. Julien l'hospitalier."[66] The appearance at the very end of "The Legend" of an aspiring disciple gives Daniil the opportunity to enunciate his philosophy that one should serve others and be guided only by the teaching of Christ.

The didactic element in "The Legend of Conscience-stricken Daniil" is as pronounced as in Almazov's poems. Daniil's personified conscience, for example, is as much the mouthpiece of divine truth as the monk Zosima in "Mary of Egypt." The difference is that Leskov's adaptation of the *Prolog* original, here as in the case of "The Tale of the God-pleasing Woodcutter," serves to undermine respect for the Church. Almazov's didacticism intends only to clarify, while Leskov's is decidedly revolutionary.

As Leskov continued to rework *Prolog* narratives, his attack on the Church became more direct. In "The Mountain," his longest and most elaborately developed *Prolog* tale, he uses a technique familiar from the two stories discussed above, exaggerating implications of the original to support his own views. The gloves have been removed, however, and the Church and conventional Christians are presented in a negative light.

The *Prolog* entry on which "The Mountain" is based tells of an Egyptian gold merchant who, when sexually tempted by a female pagan, cuts out his right eye in literal obedience to the words of Matthew 5:29: "If your right eye should cause you to sin, tear it out and throw it away; for it will do you less harm to lose one part of you than to have your whole body thrown into hell."[67] Somewhat later, the local Mohammedan ruler initiates a new wave of persecution against the Christians, cynically ordering them to demonstrate their faith by moving a nearby mountain. All is not lost, however, for the gold merchant's rejected lover conveniently mentions his act of piety to the local bishop. The bishop recruits the gold merchant to pray, the mountain moves, the Christians are saved from persecution, and many pagans convert.

[66] Cf. McLean, *Nikolai Leskov*, 573; and Grossman, *N. S. Leskov*, 226.

[67] The *Prolog* story is found under October 7.

From the beginning of "The Mountain," Leskov deliberately establishes an opposition between the gold merchant Zeno and the other Christians in Alexandria. Zeno, it seems, acquired his brand of Christianity from an itinerant Syrian and does not share many of the views of the Alexandrians. When threatened with destruction, the latter prove shallow in their faith. The wily patriarch (a creation of Leskov's) and the wealthier members of the congregation steal away from the city, while the bishop appears for the most part an ineffectual coward, and his lower-class parishioners an unruly mob. When they reach the mountain, these second-rate Christians exhibit an exaggerated regard for ritual and quarrel over the proper way to pray. Zeno assures them that "it is only necessary that the hands of those praying be pure of self-interest and the soul free from every evil and lifted to heaven by the thought of eternity" (378).[68] In true Tolstoyan, and Leskovian, fashion, he points to the superiority of content to form, of faith to ritual.

At the end of "The Mountain," Zeno and the patriarch discuss the nature of faith, and Zeno draws an analogy between faith and a bowstring:

> I have remembered the words of Amasis: the bowstring on a bow is weak, until an arrow is placed on it and it is stretched with the hand. When it is necessary that it be taut, it will be taut and will strike hard; but if it is continually stretched and held in tension, it will become thin and its strength will weaken (389).[69]

This is an intriguing conception, but not a view of faith calculated to appeal to adherents of Orthodox theology. Yet it epitomizes the moral flexibility that Leskov demands from his *Prolog* heroes and heroines.

In Leskov's eyes, superior spiritual qualities were not necessarily dependent on a commitment to Christianity or a product of it. The protagonists of his *Prolog* tales include not only maverick Christians,

[68] The text of "The Mountain" ("Gora") is found in Leskov, *Ss* 8: 303–89.

[69] The reference here is to the observation attributed to the Egyptian king Amasis in the *History* of Herodotus, Book 2: "Archers string their bows when they wish to shoot, and unstring them after use. A bow always kept strung would break, and so be useless when it was needed. It is the same with a man; anyone who was always serious, and never allowed himself a fair share of relaxation and amusement, would suddenly go off his head, or get a stroke. It is because I know this that I divide my time between duty and pleasure." See Herodotus, *The Histories*, trans. Aubrey de Selincourt, revised A. R. Burn (Great Britain, 1972), 198.

but also remarkable pagans and adherents of other religions. In three stories, "Beauteous Aza," "The Tale of Fedor and Abraham," and "The Felon of Ashkelon," non-Christians are shown to be just as virtuous if not more so than the majority of the Christians they encounter. As in some other stories, Leskov did not have to make substantial changes in the original plot of "Beauteous Aza" in order to bring it into harmony with his own religious philosophy. The *Prolog* tells how a wealthy young pagan woman comes upon an intended suicide in her garden.[70] After learning of his terrible financial plight, the young woman gives him her entire fortune. As for the now destitute young woman, ignorance of any useful skills drives her into a life of prostitution. When she later decides to convert to Christianity, this naturally makes it difficult for her to convince proper Christians to condone her baptism. By miraculous dispensation, however, angels in human form serve as her sponsors and she is baptized immediately before her death. Her saintly act of generosity is subsequently revealed to the other Christians.

It is understandable here as well why Leskov might have selected this story for adaptation: the virtue of the young woman does not depend on membership in the Church and takes the form of self-denying service to others, regardless of the consequences to herself. These are precisely the features of the story on which Leskov dwells. For example, when Aza initially stumbles upon the desperate debtor, she thinks that he is stealing fruit from her garden and, in a manner reminiscent of Philaretus the Merciful, she resolves to help him.[71] Like Philaretus, Aza is also described as having always been generous to the poor. Leskov thus implies that the disposal of her fortune is not an isolated quixotic gesture, but the logical outcome of her beliefs.

In Leskov's hands, Aza becomes a mouthpiece for non-partisan religious sentiments. As a pagan, she is ideally suited to this role. When the Hellene she intends to help reminds her that he is of another faith, Aza responds that this is a matter for the priests, but that she believes that "dirt soils the foot of a Greek woman just as it does anyone else's foot, and a red-hot coal burns everyone in the same way" (295).[72] Sim-

[70] The *Prolog* story is found under April 8.

[71] Her behavior is also reminiscent of that of Macarius the Elder, who helped thieves rob his cell, even running after them with an overlooked pair of sandals. See Jacques Lacarrière, *Men Possessed by God: The Story of the Desert Monks of Ancient Christendom*, trans. Roy Monkcom (Garden City, N.Y., 1964), 119.

[72] The text of "Beauteous Aza" is found in Leskov, *Ss* 8: 291–302.

ilarly, when her deceased parents' friends later criticize her for having acted senselessly and, even worse, on behalf of people of another faith, Aza retorts: "not a race or a faith, but people were suffering" (296). None of this enviable broadmindedness is evident in the *Prolog*.

Leskov stresses the fact that Aza's act of charity amply compensates for her sins even more than the author of the *Prolog* account. The epigraph to the story is taken from I Peter 4:8: "Love covers a multitude of sins." The old man who indoctrinates Aza in the tenets of Christianity is supposedly a friend of Isaac the Syrian, a Byzantine mystic much admired by Leskov.[73] He quotes this verse and assures Aza that Christ has written her sin in the sand and left it for the wind to blow away. The import of his remarks is evocative of Zosima's to Mary of Egypt—the virtuous harlot need not fear. As occurs so often in Leskov's stories, however, "good" Christians are in a minority, and the contemptible majority persist in their rigid narrowmindedness. After Aza's death, the old man corrects them when they refer to her as a fornicatrix, telling them that the fornicatrix has been buried in the ground, while "the daughter of consolation" (302) has entered heaven; he refers here to her "righteous soul."[74]

Leskov was much enamored of the theme of the superiority of an individual morality independent of the religious establishment and, concomitantly, of the idea that Christianity is not inherently superior to other faiths. The original *Prolog* entry on which "Beauteous Aza" is based lends itself to the development of this thought, and Leskov makes the point even more forcefully through a slight change in the ending of the story. Thus Aza is not baptized before her death, but is instead carried off by the angels in her baptismal robes immediately afterwards. In this way Leskov manages to suggest that virtue will be recognized, whatever its formal status. A slight plot change thus broadens the meaning of the story considerably. As will be seen, in other of Leskov's

[73] For discussion of Leskov's admiration of Isaac the Syrian, see James Y. Muckle, *Nikolai Leskov and the "Spirit of Protestantism"* (Birmingham, England, 1978), 132. Fedor Dostoevsky was also an admirer of Isaac the Syrian, of whose ascetic discourses he owned a Russian translation published in 1854. On the possible impact of the thought of Isaac the Syrian on Dostoevsky's writings, most notably *The Brothers Karamazov*, see especially Sergei Hackel, "The Religious Dimension: Vision or Evasion? Zosima's Discourse in *The Brothers Karamazov*," in Malcolm V. Jones and Garth M. Terry, eds., *New Essays on Dostoyevsky*, (Cambridge, 1983), 145–47, 159–60.

[74] Lottridge, "Leskov's *Prolog* Tales," 138.

Prolog tales a change in the ending of the original gives a vastly different significance to the new version. The same technique was employed, with similar effect, by both Garshin and Tolstoy.

In "Beauteous Aza" Leskov develops the idea of a virtue independent of Christianity without making many changes in the *Prolog* original. In both "The Tale of Fedor and Abram" and "The Felon of Ashkelon," however, he takes extensive liberties with the original in order to develop themes similar to that of "Beauteous Aza."

The *Prolog* account of the merchant Fedor and his Jewish friend is essentially a tale of conversion.[75] Fedor, who continually loses shipments because of nautical disasters, is forced to borrow money from an obliging Jew. As a pledge he cites his faith in Christ. Eventually the Jew is miraculously repaid and, after witnessing other examples of the power of Fedor's religion, he converts.

In an afterword to his reworking of this story, Leskov insisted on its veracity and on the fact that he was now presenting it "in a new exposition . . . for the possible pleasure of the friends of peace and philanthropy who have been outraged by the impatient breath of brother-hatred [*bratonenavidenie*] and rancor" (111).[76] In its implication that Leskov was faithful to the original, this statement is decidedly misleading, for his "new exposition" is a story with an entirely different moral emphasis from that of the original. In the *Prolog*, it is very clear that Christianity is inherently superior to Judaism. Leskov had not always been tolerant of the Jews, but by the 1880s such a chauvinistic sentiment did not correspond to his more open-minded views.[77] In his reworking, all traces of an exalted appraisal of Christianity have disappeared.

The narrative possibilities latent in the friendly relationship between a Christian and a Jew may initially have drawn Leskov's attention to the *Prolog* entry. In Leskov's story, this friendship assumes center stage. In their youth, Fedor and Abram are the closest of friends. This idyll is undermined by the growing movement within the Byzantine empire for separate educational institutions for children of different faiths. The major

[75] The *Prolog* story is found under October 31.

[76] The text of "The Tale of Fedor the Christian and His Friend Abram the Jew" ("Skazanie o Fedore-khristiane i o druge ego Abrame-zhidovine") is found in Leskov, *Pss* 30: 88–111.

[77] For an account of Leskov's shifting attitudes toward the Jews, see McLean, *Nikolai Leskov*, 418–35.

commentator on this pernicious development is the pagan philosopher Panfil (Leskov's creation), who declares that evil stems not from a multiplicity of faiths, but from the belief that one faith is superior.

The remainder of "The Tale of Fedor and Abram" serves to illustrate the theme enunciated by Panfil. The boys begin to fight with each other and their friendship comes to an end. Yet they are not entirely corrupted by their environment; many years later Fedor defends Abram when he sees him tormented by Christian bullies. This incident marks the beginning of a renewed but secret friendship between the two youths. In their discussions of religion, they eventually come to conclusions similar to those of Panfil.

Within this framework of the need for religious tolerance, Leskov retells the events of the *Prolog* story. According to his version, when Fedor begins to incur heavy financial losses, his Christian acquaintances interpret this as a sign of God's anger at his friendship with a Jew. Only Abram comes to Fedor's aid, not because of a desire for financial gain, as in the *Prolog*, but out of true friendship. Similarly, when Fedor swears by Christ, Abram is touched because he knows how fervently his friend believes in God, but he also assures Fedor he will not doubt his faith even if he fails in his venture.

While according to Leskov's version Fedor conveniently has little to lose whatever happens, ultimately he does repay Abram. In Leskov's story, the transaction is deprived of miraculous overtones. As in the *Prolog*, Abram pretends he has not received the money owed him, but both Abram's motives and Fedor's reaction differ from those described in the original. Instead of confronting Abram, Fedor indulges him, and Abram explains that he had wanted to see whether Fedor would accuse him of "Yiddishness" (*zhidovstvo*); the reason for his suspiciousness is not provided. Yet he is naturally delighted by Fedor's self-sacrificing reaction and declares that he sees that the latter is as meek as his teacher Jesus. Both protagonists thus prove much more virtuous and selfless than their *Prolog* originals. Finally, in a complete reversal of the ending of the *Prolog* story, Abram does not convert, and instead Fedor and Abram found a non-denominational home for children. Rather than glorify Christianity, "The Tale of Fedor and Abram" thus extols the independent-minded virtue of two individuals. Moreover, just as might be expected from Leskov's protagonists, their virtue takes the form of disinterested good works.

The belief that Christianity is not inherently superior to other faiths and that the morality of an uncommitted individual may surpass that of official believers is central to "The Felon of Ashkelon" as well. As in "The Tale of Fedor and Abraham," Leskov takes substantial liberties with the original in order to make this point.

The *Prolog* legend of the so-called felon of Ashkelon is simple and to the point.[78] A merchant in the town of Ashkelon is imprisoned because of his debts. While visiting him in prison, his wife attracts the attention of a wealthy almsgiver, who offers to buy her husband's freedom in exchange for sexual favors. She says that she must ask her husband, who refuses even to consider allowing his wife to be dishonored. The wealthy visitor leaves the scene, and a robber who has overheard everything that has happened is so impressed by the couple's virtue that he tells them where his loot is hidden, thus enabling the husband to go free.

In Leskov's version of the legend, the story does not end with the couple's refusal.[79] Instead, the Byzantine official who lusts after the beautiful Teniia lingers in Ashkelon, and she is subjected to a series of pressures from the local scoundrel. The competition of some stunning Nubian striptease artists causes her to lose her job singing and playing at the local tavern, she is denied permission to see her husband, the wrath of the other prisoners is turned against the couple, her mother-in-law tries to persuade her to meet the official's demands, offering her an oblivion-inducing concoction of blue mushrooms to ease her surrender, and, worst of all, her husband begins to waver. In the nick of time the robber, who is not just an ordinary robber, but the murderer of forty men, tells Teniia where his money is hidden. With this she is able to buy not only her husband's freedom, but also that of all the other imprisoned debtors.

The religious moral of Leskov's story draws its force from the fact that Teniia manifests such staunch virtue as a pagan, while her husband and other supposed Christians emerge as Christians in name only. In spite of numerous additions, the plot of "The Felon of Ashkelon" remains essentially unchanged in Leskov's version. Yet by altering such an important detail about the personality of his heroine, the writer completely undermines the original meaning of the *Prolog* legend. He transforms the story of a Christian couple rewarded for their virtue into

[78] The *Prolog* story is found under June 14.

[79] The text of "The Felon of Ashkelon" ("Askalonskii zlodei") is found in Leskov, *Pss* 30: 29–87.

the tale of a pagan whose natural religion is superior to the formal Christianity of those around her. This interpretation of the legend undermines the exclusive validity of Christianity.

"The Felon of Ashkelon" appeared in November 1889. On Christmas day of the same year, Aleksei Suvorin (1833–1911), who is remembered primarily as an editor, published his own version of the legend, "Ashkelon Fidelity" ("Askalonskaia vernost' "), in his own newspaper *New Times* (*Novoe vremia*).[80] In a footnote Suvorin states that he had not read Leskov's story until his own was completed. He modestly claims that his task was the easier of the two because he paid little attention to the everyday side of life, on which Leskov dwelt with "particular love," an understatement to put it mildly.[81] Suvorin goes on to say that the two stories have nothing in common but their themes. Even this statement may be an exaggeration.

While Leskov gives new meaning to the story of the felon of Ashkelon by changing the religious affiliation of the heroine, Suvorin does so by creating another major character and by drastically altering the plot. As in the original legend, Suvorin's heroine Neana refuses to sleep with the wealthy pagan Diomed, and the felon tells Neana and her husband Fedor where his loot is hidden. Here the resemblance between the two works ends. Fedor, who subscribes to the theory that what he doesn't know won't hurt and may even help him, is annoyed that his wife does not simply accede to Diomed's demands without informing him. The felon tells the couple about his money not because he is impressed by their virtue, but because he overhears Fedor berating Neana and takes pity on her. Most significantly, Neana refuses Diomed's offer only *after* she has learned about the felon's gold. This shift in the original chronology points to the shallowness of Neana's Christian convictions.

These differences between "Ashkelon Fidelity" and the *Prolog* legend represent only the beginning of Suvorin's quarrel with the view of Christianity implicitly propounded by the ancient legend. The mouthpiece for his most serious reservations is found in the new character Agrippa, a young, handsome Christian acquaintance of Neana and Fedor. At the very beginning of the story, he suggests to Neana that it

[80] The text of "Ashkelon Fidelity" ("Askalonskaia vernost") is found in *Novoe vremia*, 25 December 1889.

[81] Suvorin's footnote is reprinted in Leskov, *Ss* 11: 746.

is wrong to ask her husband whether she should sleep with Diomed. According to Agrippa, the Pauline claim that a woman belongs to her husband means that she should preserve her virtue regardless of her husband's wishes. Such an interpretation is in marked contrast to the more overtly male chauvinistic *Prolog* legend. Later Agrippa warns Neana that she should refuse the felon's ill-gotten gold because it represents as much of a temptation as Diomed's offer. Neana does not follow her friend's advice on either occasion, but events seem to justify his fears.

In the course of the story it becomes clear that neither Agrippa's nor Neana's faith is perfect. Much is made of Neana's childishness and naiveté throughout; she is innocent, but she is also unthinking. Agrippa, on the other hand, suffers from unacknowledged feelings of lust for Neana but deludes himself into believing that for him Neana is just another phenomenon of natural beauty. Yet when Neana and Agrippa go together to retrieve the felon's gold, suitable circumstances and their lack of moral vigilance combine to drive them into each other's arms.

As Suvorin describes it, only after this disastrous development are the two aspiring Christians able to discover true faith. In a fit of repentance, Agrippa anonymously donates the stolen gold to free Fedor and turns himself in to the prison authorities, falsely claiming that he had been in league with the now executed felon. In a further twist, the suspicion arises that perhaps Fedor is also a criminal (hence the anonymous donation). In order to squelch this rumor, Neana convinces Diomed, who now turns out to be a "good" pagan, to claim that he paid for Fedor's release. This will naturally make everyone assume that she did sleep with Diomed, but such is the form that Neana's atonement for her adultery must take.

The point of this extraordinarily convoluted version of the legend is apparently to demonstrate that sin and repentance through self-sacrifice are necessary prerequisites for true Christianity. In their pre-fall state, Agrippa has too abstract an understanding of Christianity, while Neana is as innocent (and as immature) as a child. Significantly, at the end of "Ashkelon Fidelity" Fedor recognizes Neana's newly acquired spiritual maturity and stops bullying her.

While Leskov's version of the legend is a radical attack on the unique superiority of Christianity, Suvorin's story is rather an attempt at an emended interpretation. While "Ashkelon Fidelity" does not call into question the ultimate validity of Christianity, it does suggest that the ancient legend was marred by theological errors. In Suvorin's somber Christian worldview, there is no place for the simple mechanism of virtue and reward: Christianity demands sacrifice.

The case of this legend and its reworkings exemplifies why the *Prolog* may have been a less popular source of hagiographical material than the *Menaea* among more conservative and more Orthodox writers. In a critical review of Leskov's version of the legend, Viktor Burenin, the conservative publicist, poet, and dramatist, condemned Leskov for ruining the "conciseness, veracity, and simplicity, . . . and the sincere and chaste tone" of the original.[82] Similar accusations were leveled at the writer by other contemporaries.[83] More importantly, Burenin criticizes even Leskov's choice of legend, saying that "not all the legends in this 'apocryphal' source are equally instructive; on the contrary, in the content of some of them distortions of pure Christian morality are perceptible." Burenin considers this true of the legend of the felon, noting with especial disapproval the couple's acceptance of the felon's ill-gotten gains. It will be remembered that this is precisely one of the aspects of the original that Suvorin chose to modify in his story. One wonders whether Burenin, who was a member of the editorial board of *New Times* and whose article appeared in that newspaper three days before Suvorin's story, approved of the latter. In the case of Leskov, he declared that the writer would do better to limit himself to producing modern Russian translations of the *Prolog* legends.

Yet Leskov clearly wished not to update old spiritual messages but to adapt them to his own intentions. His claim that the *Prolog* was apocryphal was spurious; a new edition of the collection was published by the Orthodox Church in 1895–1896 (St. Petersburg). Leskov probably made such claims in an effort to minimize the significance of his changes to the original legends.[84] These changes multiplied rapidly as he continued to rework. As has been seen, one recurrent theme is the superiority of good works to a life of contemplation. This theme finds most explicit expression in "Pamfalon the Mountebank." In this story Leskov makes particularly effective use of a device exploited by Tolstoy

[82] V. Burenin, "Kriticheskie ocherki," *Novoe vremia*, 22 December 1889.

[83] See, for example, the vicious attack by A. I. Bogdanovich in "Leskov—pisatel'—anekdotist," in his *Gody pereloma, 1895–1906: Sbornik kriticheskikh statei* (St. Petersburg, 1908), 78. The article first appeared in *Mir bozhii*, January 1897.

[84] Cf. McLean, *Nikolai Leskov*, 563.

and Garshin as well, the transformation of a story's meaning through the alteration of its ending. Such changes produce a retroactive revision of the moral philosophy of the original legend or tale.

In the *Prolog* legend on which "Pamfalon the Mountebank" is based, the old stylite Theodulus is instructed to make the acquaintance of one Cornelius of Damascus as an example of a virtuous man.[85] In familiar fashion Cornelius insists on his own sinfulness, but tells a story which indicates the opposite. In this display of humility, he resembles the woodcutter in "The Tale of the God-pleasing Woodcutter." Cornelius' virtuousness stems from his accomplishment of many good deeds, most notably the donation of a large sum of money to a woman whose husband had been imprisoned. Impressed and reassured by his story, Theodulus returns to his column.

Leskov's changes to the story involve the character of the stylite, now called Ermii. At the beginning of the story, the narrator describes Ermii's anchoretic existence and comments that "according to contemporary conceptions this was considered pleasant and pleasing to God" (178).[86] This tendentious appraisal leaves no doubt as to Leskov's own opinion of hermit life. The negative impression engendered here is later unwittingly reinforced by Pamfalon. It transpires that Ermii was once an official; ignorant of the identity of his elderly visitor, Pamfalon asserts that if Ermii had still been in office, a certain hapless woman might not have ended up in such desperate straits. "Cruel old man! May heaven forgive him his hermitic pride" (220), concludes Pamfalon. Ultimately Ermii does recognize that the path he chose was wrong. At the end of the story he returns to the site of his hermit life, not to continue as a stylite, but in order to help the local people, having realized that "man should serve man" (230). A similar conclusion is reached by some of Tolstoy's heroes, like Father Sergii in the story of the same name.

Not content with the drastic transformation produced by the changed ending, Leskov fills "Pamfalon the Mountebank" with characters and incidents designed to lend further support to his thesis that good works count for more than other expressions of virtue. The story includes a generous prostitute whose kindness is juxtaposed to the lack

[85] The *Prolog* story is found under December 3.

[86] The text of "Pamfalon the Mountebank" ("Skomorokh Pamfalon") is found in Leskov, *Ss* 8: 174–231.

of charity and even downright viciousness of several upper-class Christian ladies. Moreover, Pamfalon's example proves instructive not only to Ermii, but also to the unfortunate woman mentioned above, who realizes that his unfeigned charitable spirit is superior to her rigid and unproductive morality.

In his story "Two Brothers and Gold" ("Dva brata i zoloto," 1885), Tolstoy also suppressed the ending of the *Prolog* original in order to develop a theme similar to that of "Pamfalon the Mountebank"—the importance of good works as an expression of true religiosity. The *Prolog* legend describes the different reactions of two brothers, both hermits, who stumble across some gold.[87] One brother runs away from their find, while the other takes it, uses it for positive purposes, and then returns to the desert, filled with pride at his achievement. On the way he meets an angel who explains that his brother's action was actually superior to his own because his brother tried to please God, while he was concerned with pleasing men.[88] He is told that before he can see his brother, he must repent, and an unseen voice instructs him to become a stylite in Edessa. After fifty years of this existence he is given the gift of distinguishing between the righteous and the sinful.

Tolstoy purges this story of all sectarian elements. The brothers are no longer portrayed as monks, but as lowly workers. Nor is there any mention of either brother becoming a stylite. Such an occupation would have seemed as futile to Tolstoy as it did to Leskov. Instead, Afanasii, who had taken great pride in the praise he won for his material generosity, reaches the conclusion that "not by gold, but only by labor can one serve God and people" (30).[89] In his spiritual evolution, Afanasii calls to mind Leskov's Ermii.

In their condemnation of the contemplative anchoretic life, Leskov and Tolstoy did not simply express idiosyncratic religious ideas, but also echoed a widespread prejudice among nineteenth-century European intellectuals. One of the most hostile formulations of this attitude was

[87] The *Prolog* story is found under January 7.

[88] In "Father Sergii" ("Otets Sergii"), Sergii concludes about his childhood friend Pashenka: "Pashenka is exactly what I should have been, and what I was not. I lived for people, on the pretext of living for God; and she lives for God, imagining that she lives for people." See Tolstoi, *Pss* 31: 44.

[89] The text of "Two Brothers and Gold" ("Dva brata i zoloto") is found in Tolstoi, *Pss* 25: 28–30.

provided by the British historian William Lecky in 1869 in his appraisal of early Christian monasticism:

> There is, perhaps, no phase in the moral history of mankind of a deeper or more painful interest than this ascetic epidemic. A hideous, sordid, and emaciated maniac, without knowledge, without patriotism, without natural affection, passing his life in a long routine of useless and atrocious self-torture, and quailing before the ghastly phantoms of his delirious brain, had become the ideal of the nations which had known the writings of Plato and Cicero and the lives of Socrates and Cato.[90]

One suspects that Leskov and Tolstoy would have approved of this assessment.

Reworkings of Legends and Tales by Garshin and Leo Tolstoy

It was noted in Chapter One that in addition to collections such as the *Prolog* and the *Reading Menaea*, a fruitful source of hagiographical material available to nineteenth-century Russian writers was collections like Aleksandr Afanas'ev's *Russian Folk Legends*, which enjoyed great success with the reading public. The Bollandist Hippolyte Delehaye's useful distinction between hagiographical legends and tales should be mentioned in this regard. According to his definition, a legend is always linked to a specific place, while a tale lacks any association with specific people or places.[91] By the addition or deletion of such details, a legend may become a tale and vice versa. Afanas'ev's collection is a good example of this process because it often includes both legendary and folk variants of a hagiographical narrative. For example, the legend of Aggei, king of Filuian, becomes the tale of a nameless rich man of unknown domicile. In reworking this account for his story "The Tale

[90] William Edward Hartpole Lecky, *History of European Morals from Augustus to Charlemagne* (London, 1869), 2: 107. I have been unable to discover whether Leskov was familiar with Lecky's work. Tolstoy was acquainted with another book by Lecky, *History of the Rise and Influence of Rationalism in Europe* (1865), which appeared in Russian translation in 1871. See Tolstoy's note of 20 May 1889 in Tolstoi, *Pss* 50: 83.

[91] Hippolyte Delehaye, *The Legends of the Saints*, trans. Donald Attwater (New York, 1962), 7. See also René Aigrain, *L'hagiographie: ses sources, ses méthodes, son histoire* (Poitiers, 1953), 130.

of Proud Aggei" ("Skazanie o gordom Aggee," 1886), Garshin relied more on the legend. In his dramatic reworking of the same subject, Tolstoy relied much more on the folk variant.

In Afanas'ev's version of the story of Aggei, God decides to punish the proud ruler because he denies the validity of the Gospel claim, "The rich shall become poor and the poor shall become rich."[92] While hunting, Aggei leaves his clothes on a river bank to swim after a deer sent by God to distract him (in medieval literature the deer is often a symbol of Christ).[93] Meanwhile, his place is taken by an angel in disguise, and Aggei is later unable to prove that he is in fact himself. He is forced to leave the city and eventually must hire himself out as a servant to a band of beggars. Several years later at a feast at his one-time palace, Aggei and the angel have a tête-à-tête. After the angel realizes that Aggei is truly repentant, he restores the former ruler to his throne.

One of the Russian writers who reworked the legend of Aggei was Vsevolod Garshin (1855–1888), best known for his stories of morbid or deranged states of mind like "The Red Flower" ("Krasnyi tsvetok," 1883), a tale of a lunatic asylum. Like Leskov, Garshin succumbed for a time to the lure of Tolstoyan morality. This interest is evident in "The Tale of Proud Aggei." Although he emphasizes the pathetic element in the story—the beggars are blind as well as poor, for example—he takes few liberties with the plot until the end of the story, even retaining much of the lexicon of the original. Yet the ending of Garshin's story completely reverses that of the legend found in Afanas'ev's collection: when the angel offers to return the throne, Garshin's Aggei refuses, to the great approval of his heavenly interlocutor. Aggei spends the rest of his life looking after "the poor, the weak, and the oppressed" (298).[94]

[92] I have been unable to locate this precise citation in the Gospels. The sentiment expressed, however, corresponds to statements made in Luke 1:52–53, 6:20–26. See also I Samuel 2:7, James 1:9–11. Afanas'ev's version of the legend of Aggei, "Povest' o tsare Aggee i kako postrada gordostiiu," is found in A. N. Afanas'ev, *Narodnye russkie legendy* (Moscow, 1859), 84–87; the folk variant appears on 172–76. According to Leonard A. Magnus, a translator of the story of Aggei, "Filuyan is a fabulous city found in the cantations and mystical rites of the Russian peasants. It is, however, probably derived from the Greek θύλη." See *Russian Folk-Tales* (London, 1915), 335.

[93] Iuliia Sazonova, *Istoriia russkoi literatury: Drevnii period* (New York, 1955), 2: 155.

[94] The text of "The Tale of Proud Aggei" ("Skazanie o gordom Aggee") is found in V. M. Garshin, *Sochineniia* (Moscow, 1960), 289–98.

Like Ermii ("Pamfalon the Mountebank") and Afanasii ("Two Brothers and Gold"), he has learned the importance of doing good for others.

When Garshin read this story at a meeting of the Neophilological Society at St. Petersburg University, the young members of his audience, displeased with the modified ending, objected that Aggei's attitude betrayed Buddhistic, egotistical tendencies and that as a wise ruler he would have been able to achieve more good than as a beggar.[95] To view Aggei's decision to renounce his throne in this light may be extreme, but the alteration in the ending does give the story a very different religious slant. Of paramount importance in Garshin's version of the legend is the unceasing practice of humility, the actual humbling of oneself. In the earlier version, the sense of humility alone appears sufficient to establish virtue. As in "Two Brothers and Gold," in "The Tale of Proud Aggei" to do good is not enough; one must act from a position of humility. While in the original version Aggei's virtue is rewarded by the restoration of his original status, in Garshin's story his virtue is indeed its own reward. Garshin does not match Leskov in implying that paganism can be superior to Christianity, but he does argue in favor of a radical humility in the secular sphere that would be unacceptable to some adherents of Orthodoxy.

Tolstoy apparently worked on a dramatic version of the legend until he learned about Garshin's piece.[96] His unfinished play was first published in 1926.[97] Tolstoy relied more extensively on the folk variant of the story. In this version, the proud and impious *pan* (landowner) is attacked by robbers, who strip him and leave him tied to a tree.[98] When rescued by shepherds, the *pan* responds with shocking ingratitude and incurs their wrath as well. Some passing beggars take pity on him, provide him with clothing, and allow him to accompany them to his hometown. There the *pan*'s wife, convinced that such a scruffy derelict cannot possibly be her husband, orders him whipped and buried alive. There is no suggestion here of moral rebirth, and the crudely violent ending implies that the *pan* received his just deserts.

Tolstoy's play follows the outline of this plot, while adding other revealing encounters. In scene after scene, the *pan* displays his unsavory

[95] This incident is recounted by I. Shliapkin in *Russkii bibliofil*, 1913, no. 4: 83–84.

[96] Cf. N. K. Gudzii's commentary on Tolstoy's play in Tolstoi, *Pss* 26: 855–57.

[97] It appeared in L. N. Tolstoi, *Neizdannye rasskazy* (Paris, 1926).

[98] *Pan* may mean specifically a Polish landowner or, as here, any well-to-do landowner.

character, an unfortunate combination of the bully and the braggart. Should the reader be slow to grasp the point, Tolstoy provides comments like the following: "You're a robber just like us, but of another kind" (492).[99] Yet, while the *pan* appears lacking in any redeeming qualities, Tolstoy does not allow his life to come to a violent end. Instead, he borrows the motif of an angelic surrogate from the literary version and retains the encounter between the two, as well as the repentance of the *pan* and his consequent restoration to his former position. In the final scene, the *pan* and his wife are seen waiting on beggars, a common metaphor for humility also used in Almazov's "The Generous Rich Man." Yet ironically, because the *pan* regains his former wealth, the ending of Tolstoy's play actually seems less Tolstoyan than that of Garshin's story.

Tolstoy clearly intended to show that the *pan* had learned from his mistakes and thus merited another opportunity to adopt a life of virtue. Yet, as in some of Tolstoy's other later works, most notably "Father Sergii" ("Otets Sergii," 1890–1898), the protagonist's corruption is so convincing that one is sceptical about his regeneration. In this case, the *pan* never once reveals any self-doubt until the moment of his transformation. The ending of the play thus appears forced in a way that Garshin's story, with its implicit maturing process, does not.[100]

The importance of good works is the theme of another story by Tolstoy based on a hagiographical tale, one recounted to him by the storyteller Vasilii Shchegolenok.[101] In this tale, an old man who makes a pilgrimage to Jerusalem imagines that he sees there another old man who had been unable to accompany him. Yet when he returns home, his friend swears that he has actually been looking after a poor family, not making journeys abroad. The message is clear; his charity has enabled him symbolically, if not actually, to reach Jerusalem.

As with many of the *Prolog* legends adapted by Leskov, it is obvious

[99] The text of Tolstoy's play [Dramaticheskaia obrabotka legendy ob Aggee] is found in Tolstoi, *Pss* 26: 488–502.

[100] A reworking of the legend of Aggei was also produced by Aleksei Remizov in "Tsar' Aggei" (1917). As in the case of Remizov's reworking of the Life of Mary of Egypt, I have not discussed this story because it reflects almost exclusively aesthetic concerns and hence does not lend itself to discussion in the present context.

[101] See V. I. Sreznevskii's commentary on "Dva starika" in Tolstoi, *Pss* 25: 703. Sreznevskii notes that Tolstoy may also have been familiar with a story on this theme by A. F. Kovalevskii, "Podvig palomnichestva i podvig chelovekolubiia" (1871).

why Tolstoy would have found this tale an attractive subject for reworking. In his version, "Two Old Men" ("Dva starika," 1885), an endorsement of good works, implicit in the original, is more fully and explicitly developed. Efim and Elisei both set out for Jerusalem, but only Efim, who has a rigid, loveless view of Christianity, actually reaches his destination. Elisei spends all his travel money helping famine victims. When he returns home after his abortive trip, he conceals the true reason for the loss of his money. When Efim learns of his good deed and tries to discuss it, Elisei is evasive, and Efim realizes that he should mention neither Elisei's act of charity nor his own vision in Jerusalem; in true Tolstoyan spirit, virtue is best left unacknowledged. Efim now understands the meaning of existence, recognizing that God has ordered everyone "to pay his quitrent with love and good deeds" (99).[102] Such thoughts would undoubtedly have met with the approval of Aza, Aggei, Daniil, Ermii, Pamfalon, and several of the other characters discussed in the preceding pages.

WITH THE EXCEPTION of Aleksei K. Tolstoy, all of the writers discussed in this chapter chose for adaptation the Lives or episodes from the Lives of unsophisticated, humble saints frequently lacking in elaborate formal ties to the Orthodox Church. This broad coincidence in subject matter seems to reflect both the longstanding Russian penchant for nonconformist displays of sanctity as well as the enthusiasm for supposed "simplicity" of character to which many nineteenth-century Russian intellectuals succumbed. In some cases, a dissatisfaction with the Church is readily apparent. There are important divisions among the writers who made use of the *Menaea*, the *Prolog*, and other hagiographical literature, however, both in the particular virtues they chose to emphasize and in the aesthetic methodology they employed in adapting their sources for contemporary consumption. These two aspects of the process of revising hagiographical material prove to be closely related, for a conservative or radical approach in one area is generally matched by a similar approach in the other.

The writers treated in this chapter seem to have a tacit disagreement as to the necessity for good works. Shakhova and Almazov admire both the largely contemplative, ascetic existence of Mary of Egypt or Alexis, the Man of God, and the continual and active generosity practiced by

[102] The text of "Two Old Men" ("Dva starika") is found in Tolstoi, *Pss* 25: 82–99.

Philaretus the Merciful. Tolstoy and his like-minded contemporaries, on the other hand, often implicitly rebuke those who seek virtue through contemplation. Largely through their choice of subject, writers like Tolstoy and Leskov argue for a virtue marked by disinterested good works. Good works may outweigh the seemingly minor detail of a formal commitment to Christianity—hence the virtuous pagans who haunt the pages of Leskov. While Shakhova and Almazov affirm their protagonists' idiosyncratic devotion to an exclusively Christian conception of goodness, Tolstoy, Leskov, and Garshin are more critical. All these writers, conservatives and radicals alike, share a fondness for humility as a source of virtue, but they differ as to its proper mode of expression.

The degree of commitment to Orthodoxy of each writer appears to have influenced not only the choice of saints, but also the techniques employed in revising hagiographical material. Almazov and Shakhova apparently considered the original *Menaea* Lives to be sacrosanct; the two writers act primarily as simple transmitters, rather than as interpreters. The writers drawn to hagiography in the 1880s, on the other hand, were willing if not downright eager to tamper significantly with the original sources in order to communicate the desired message. This betrays not simply a search for the most effective development of one's theme, but a radically different attitude to hagiography. In this regard, a comment made by Leskov in "Saints' Lives as a Literary Source" is illuminating: "In the Lives of Russian saints, in spite of their great interest, there is one large shortcoming that has long been noticed—in them the individualism of the person being glorified is scarcely visible."[103] Here is the same lack of religious awe that evoked his irreverent remark about the *Prolog* cited earlier. Leskov was aware that this pragmatic attitude to hagiography might expose him to imputations of sacrilege. For this reason, presumably, he upheld the "apocryphal" status of the *Prolog* or implied, as in the case of "The Tale of Fedor and Abram," that he had transmitted a legend intact even when that was patently untrue. Leskov's unsubmissive attitude towards hagiography was shared by Tolstoy, Garshin, and even Suvorin.

The question of Orthodoxy or of particular conceptions of virtue becomes a moot point when one considers the cases of Herzen and Aleksei K. Tolstoy. Where these writers differ most from the religious con-

[103] *Novoe vremia*, 17 August 1882.

servatives like Almazov and Shakhova and the moral radicals of Leskov's ilk is in their subordination of religious issues to other questions. This is most apparent in the case of Tolstoy's "John Damascene," where religion serves merely as backdrop to a treatment of the needs and rights of the artist. Herzen's "The Legend" is also psychological rather than religious in focus.

Broadly speaking, the stories and poems discussed in this chapter fall into three main categories. The poems of Shakhova and Almazov exemplify an aesthetic and a religious conservativism. There is nothing in Shakhova's "The Power of Repentance" to which even the ecclesiastical reader could object. The many hagiographical reworkings of the 1880s, on the other hand, typify the use of traditional religious material to convey diverse and controversial religious messages. As has been seen, this approach may result in the complete reversal of the original meaning of a given legend or tale, as in several of Leskov's stories, Garshin's "The Tale of Proud Aggei," and Tolstoy's "Two Brothers and Gold." Finally, a third category appears almost to ignore the religious issues raised by the original, neither assenting nor dissenting, but instead exploiting the plot of the original legend or tale for purposes not primarily religious. Thus, both "John Damascene" and "The Legend of St. Theodora" are relatively indifferent to religious questions.

Except for a brief flurry of general interest during the 1880s, shared by Tolstoy, Leskov, Garshin, and Suvorin, the direct reworking of hagiographical texts, like the poetic adaptations of the Lives of saintly princes, never achieved popularity. Nor are the adaptations of saints' Lives the most artistically successful productions of writers like Tolstoy and Leskov. Yet hagiographical reworkings are by no means a peripheral area of nineteenth-century Russian literature, as is indicated by the interest they provoked from several prominent writers of diverse views, as well as from more obscure figures like Elisaveta Shakhova. Moreover, the interest in hagiographical reworkings throughout the nineteenth century testifies to the fact that Russian writers both continued to read hagiographical collections like the *Menaea* and the *Prolog* and also perceived such works as viable vehicles for contemporary concerns. That these writers regarded the Lives of saints with fresh enthusiasm indicates the vitality of the hagiographical tradition in modern Russian culture.

In considering the mainstream of Russian literature and culture, perhaps the most significant feature of the reworkings discussed in this chapter involves the kinds of saintly personalities they glorified. Their nearly consistent adulation of humble, unassuming, and sometimes even illiterate holy men and women is extremely revealing. The modern Russian literary works which draw upon hagiography in creating their own, "modern" protagonists, grant these traits great importance and often relegate the question of good works to the background. It was stated at the beginning of this chapter that in *The Brothers Karamazov*, Father Zosima mentions with especial approval the Lives of Mary of Egypt and Alexis, the Man of God. The following chapter will show that the exaggerated humility displayed by these two saints was shared by many of the saintly characters found in nineteenth-century literary works.

CHAPTER FOUR

Neo-Hagiography: The Saintly Monk and the Holy Fool in Modern Dress

Be humble and heaven and earth will be subjected to you.
Zosima Verkhovskii of Tobol'sk

His simplicity had an admixture of cunning: that traditional Russian psychological mechanism known as *iurodstvo.*
Ilya Ehrenburg

In july 1903 Serafim of Sarov, a renowned mystic of the late eighteenth and early nineteenth centuries, was canonized at his isolated northern monastery. Hundreds of thousands of visitors attended the elaborate ceremony. Among the dignitaries who carried the coffin of the saint was Nicholas II, who had been instrumental in hastening the canonization process. Nicholas took a personal interest: according to tradition, the imperial family had directly experienced the beneficent power of Serafim's prayers.[1]

These events, on the eve of the empire's collapse, epitomize the role played throughout Russian history by monastic saints and holy men. Far from peripheral to Russian society and culture of the Middle Ages, these unusual figures often served as significant critics or supporters of princely activities. A good example is the blessing Sergii of Radonezh gave Prince Dmitrii Donskoi of Moscow (late fourteenth century) to aid his efforts to oust the Mongols from the Russian lands. The psychological importance of such support should not be underestimated. In later centuries, when the Church had lost much of its former political power,

[1] Valentine Zander, *St. Seraphim of Sarov*, trans. Sister Gabriel Anne, S.S.C. (London, 1975), 139. Serafim was a popular saint among Russian intellectuals as well. See Nicholas Zernov, *The Russian Religious Renaissance of the Twentieth Century* (London, 1963), 208.

revered monks continued to engage the attention of prominent Russians. In the nineteenth century great public interest was aroused by the unusual elders at the monastery of Optina Pustyn' in central Russia, Leonid Nagolkin (1768–1841), Makarii Ivanov (1788–1861), and Amvrosii Grenkov (1812–1891). Makarii's visitors included Nikolai Gogol and the Slavophile philosopher Ivan Kireevskii; Amvrosii met with the writers Fedor Dostoevsky and Leo Tolstoy and the religious philosophers/writers Vladimir Solov'ev, Konstantin Leont'ev, and Vasilii Rozanov. Leont'ev even ended his life as a monk.[2] Monks like these elders were tremendously popular with the humble elements of the laity. The numerous pilgrims and other visitors—peasants, merchants, members of the upper classes—have been described not only in accounts of the lives of holy men by their admiring disciples, but also in literary form, ranging from the sympathetic portrayal in *The Brothers Karamazov* to the cynical exposé in Joseph Kallinikov's *Women and Monks*.

Outside the monasteries, nineteenth-century Russians were often exposed to another type of sanctity in the holy fools (*iurodivye*)—itinerant ascetics who frequently behaved in bizarre but ostensibly meaningful ways. Holy fools had occupied an important position among Russian saints since the Muscovite period, but by the nineteenth century they had fallen into disfavor with ecclesiastical and civil authorities and were often persecuted by the police. They were venerated by the peasants and evoked feelings ranging from reverence to scepticism and contempt in the educated.

The saintly monk and the holy fool entered the mainstream of nineteenth-century Russian literature in direct and transmuted forms. Within the sphere of what I have termed neo-hagiography, their features exemplified the most popular conception of goodness. Works throughout the century contain many characters who are either themselves monks and holy fools or whose features were heavily influenced by the traditional portrayals of these figures. As with direct adaptations of hagiographical material, the writers who used these models ranged from the conservative to the radical, the devout to the sceptical. The analysis of this literary development constitutes an important part of the discussion of hagiography and modern Russian literature and is the

[2] Cf. Sergius Bolshakoff, *Russian Mystics* (Kalamazoo, Mich., 1977), 188. On visits to Russian monasteries and convents by nineteenth-century writers and thinkers, see also Zernov, *The Russian Religious Renaissance*, 54–55.

subject of this chapter. The saintly monk and the holy fool will be discussed together, as the distinguishing characteristics of these two types often overlap. Many writers noticed this, most notably Dostoevsky.

The portrayal in literature of modern saintly figures was greatly influenced by the hagiographical tradition. As mentioned above, this tradition is remarkable for its stereotyping effect. From the eleventh to the twentieth century, accounts of Russian monastic saints and holy men by believers, whether contemporary disciples or later writers, exhibit tremendous consistencies. For example, certain shared features connect Feodosii of the Kievan Cave Monastery (d. 1074), the most popular monastic saint of the Kievan period, with Tikhon of Zadonsk, an eighteenth-century mystic. Like Feodosii, Tikhon supposedly shunned childhood amusements for the sake of study, an early indication of his saintly inclinations.[3] Similarly, like Feodosii and many others, Amvrosii of Optina Pustyn' was credited with an ability to foretell the future.[4] Numerous other examples of such topoi can be adduced.

An appreciation of the significance of topoi for typical saints' Lives is essential to an analysis of neo-hagiography of the nineteenth century, for otherwise the conventional may be perceived as novel. Among Russian writers, Dostoevsky in particular exploited this aspect of the hagiographical tradition. Similarly, an awareness of the dominant spiritual features of the holy fool and the major types of saintly monks may help to reveal the extent to which nineteenth-century writers upheld ideals of positive behavior that reflected traditional perceptions. A thorough overview of the development of Russian monasticism and its interrelationship with hagiography and the rise of "holy foolishness" can provide the necessary background for a discussion of the modern "saints." These range from characters in Ivan Turgenev's story "Living Relics" ("Zhivye moshchi," 1874) to those of Maxim Gorky's novel *Mother* (*Mat'*, 1906).

The Russian Hagiographical Tradition

From the earliest period of Russian hagiography on, many of the topoi associated with monastic saints were inherited from Byzantine saints'

[3] Cf. Bolshakoff, *Russian Mystics*, 62.

[4] Cf. John B. Dunlop, *Staretz Amvrosy: Model for Dostoevsky's Staretz Zossima* (Belmont, Mass., 1972), 61–62.

Lives. Among the Lives that circulated in Kievan Rus' were those of Nicholas the Wonderworker, bishop of Myra in the fourth century; John Chrysostom, the famed preacher and patriarch of Constantinople (d. 407); the courageous hermit Basil the Younger (d. 952); the holy fool Andreas Salos (d. circa 940); Alexis, the Man of God (fifth century); and the renowned early monks Anthony of Egypt (d. 356) and Sabas of Palestine (d. 532).[5] The Lives of Anthony and Sabas in particular provided not only a rich fund of topoi, but also models for different types of monastic existence.

The Lives of Anthony and Sabas, composed respectively by Bishop Athanasius of Alexandria (d. 373) and the sixth-century monk Cyril of Scythopolis, exploit many of the same motifs.[6] Both saints are depicted as the offspring of respectable Christian parents and show an early disdain for worldly things. As hermits, they achieve great ascetic feats and resist the blandishments of demons. Both exert a positive, almost supernatural, influence on wild animals. When they gain renown, Sabas and Anthony become known for their remarkable humility, ability to effect cures and miracles, and peaceful and joyful deaths. All of these features became commonplaces in medieval Russian hagiography.

In spite of their similarities, however, Sabas and Anthony exemplify vastly different approaches to the monastic way. While both saints were ascetics who began by confronting the devil alone in the desert and later often attracted emulators, Anthony is remembered as the archetypal solitary hermit, Sabas as the founder of a half-coenobitic, or loosely communal, type of monastic establishment, the laura. The driving interest of Sabas, who, according to his Life, abandoned the eremitic existence by divine instruction, was in founding communities of monks, which he did with remarkable success. The impact of these communities on the subsequent development of monasticism in many countries was tremendous.[7] The essence of the Palestinian ideal as

[5] Dmitrij Čiževskij, *History of Russian Literature from the Eleventh Century to the End of the Baroque* ('s-Gravenhage, 1962), 21; and N. K. Gudzy, *History of Early Russian Literature*, trans. Susan Wilbur Jones (1949; reprint, New York, 1970), 28.

[6] The Life of Anthony is found in Jacques Paul Migne, ed., *Patrologia Graeca* 161 vols. (Paris, 1857–1889), 26: 835–976. The Life of Sabas is found in Eduard Schwartz, ed., *Kyrillos von Skythopolis*, Texte und Untersuchungen zur Geschichte der altchristlichen Literatur, vol. 49, no. 2 (Leipzig, 1939), 85–200.

[7] Cf. Derwas J. Chitty, *The Desert a City: An Introduction to the Study of Egyptian and Palestinian Monasticism under the Christian Empire* (Oxford, 1966), 180.

exemplified by Sabas and his confreres was an accessible moderation in monastic existence. Anthony, on the other hand, is linked inextricably to the awesome ascetic feats so characteristic of early Egyptian and Syrian monasticism.[8]

The majority of early Russian monks found the Palestinian approach, with its "humanizing of the ascetic ideal," more congenial.[9] Russia did have its own Antonii, a solitary ascetic involved in the founding of the Kievan Cave Monastery. But it is symptomatic of the comparative lack of appeal for Russians of the physically rigorous type of monasticism that his Life was lost long ago. The bleakness of the existence led by Antonii and his few like-minded successors has been grippingly depicted by Rainer Maria Rilke in *The Book of Hours* (*Das Stunden-Buch*, 1905):

> Those saints, Lord—something of them you must know?
> They felt the thickest of monastic walling
> was still too close to laughter and to bawling
> and dug themselves into the earth below.
> Each with his breathing and his light consumed
> the little air his trench had got to give,
> forgot the age and features he'd assumed
> and like an all-unwindowed house would live
> and died no more, as thought he'd long been dead.[10]

A very different approach was adopted by Antonii's student, Abbot Feodosii of the Kievan Cave Monastery (1008?–1074), whose popular Life was one of the seminal works of Russian hagiography. In composing the Life of Feodosii, the monk Nestor made use of numerous translated Lives, including those of Anthony; John Chrysostom; the monastic reformer Abbot Theodore of Studion (d. 826); Bishop Theodore of Edessa (d. 848), who had been a monk in one of Sabas' establishments; and, most especially, the Lives of John the Hesychast (d. 558), who spent much of his later life as a recluse in Sabas' laura; Theodosius the Cenobiarch (d. 529), the founder of the first coenobitic monastery; Euthymius the Great (d. 473), a Palestinian abbot whom Sabas

[8] For more detailed comparison of Palestinian, Egyptian, and Syrian monasticism, see George P. Fedotov, *The Russian Religious Mind*, 2 vols. (Belmont, Mass., 1975), 1: 113.

[9] Fedotov, *Russian Religious Mind*, 1: 113.

[10] Rainer Maria Rilke, *Selected Works*, trans. J. B. Leishman (Norfolk, Conn., 1960), 2: 75.

admired; and Sabas himself. The Lives of Euthymius and Sabas were especially important for Nestor.[11] The predominantly Palestinian orientation of the Lives that influenced the Russian writer should not be considered fortuitous.[12] In its moderation, the ideal advanced by Feodosii had much in common with that of the Palestinian saints. With Feodosii, Russian monks embraced a monasticism of harmonious balance between manual labor and ascetic and spiritual achievements.

From the point of view of the subsequent development of the Russian monastic ideal, perhaps the most important feature of Feodosii's spirituality is what George Fedotov has called "the dominant motif in Russian spirituality," kenoticism.[13] Kenoticism may be defined as the imitation of Christ's extraordinary humility. The term kenosis goes back to the statement made in Philippians 2:6–8, which describes Christ's renunciation of his divine attributes:

> "His state was divine, yet he did not cling to his equality with God but emptied himself (ἑαυτὸν ἐκένωσεν) to assume the condition of a slave, and became as men are; and being as all men are, he was humbler yet, even to accepting death, death on a cross.

How profound this renunciation was has been the subject of much dispute among theologians.[14] Paul introduces this appraisal of Christ in his letter to the Philippians in order to inspire others to emulate this humility:

> There must be no competition among you, no conceit; but everybody is to be self-effacing. Always consider the other person to be better than yourself, so that nobody thinks of his own interests first but everybody thinks of other people's interests instead. In your minds you must be the same as Christ Jesus (Philippians 2:3–5).

In Nestor's Life of Feodosii, the kenotic attitude is succinctly captured:

[11] Fedotov, *Russian Religious Mind*, 1: 112.

[12] Cf. Fedotov, *Russian Religious Mind*, 1: 113.

[13] George P. Fedotov, *A Treasury of Russian Spirituality* (Belmont, Mass., 1975), 14. I am much indebted to Fedotov's brilliant and idiosyncratic work, *The Russian Religious Mind*, for first acquainting me with the importance of kenoticism for the Russian spiritual tradition.

[14] For more detail, see the discussion of kenosis in William L. Reese, *Dictionary of Philosophy and Religion* (Atlantic Highlands, N.J., 1980).

> he possessed true humility and great meekness, for in this he imitated Christ, the true God, who said: "Learn from me, for I am gentle and humble in heart" [Matthew 11:29]. Contemplating such humility, he therefore humbled himself and considered himself the last of all.[15]

This is expressed in Feodosii's demeanor, appearance, and actions. The abbot dresses so poorly that he is mistaken for a beggar. He also works assiduously at all sorts of menial tasks and happily endures the ridicule that sometimes ensues.

Neither the attitude expressed here nor its manifestations originated with Feodosii. Humility had long been considered an essential monastic virtue and, as regards Feodosii's humility, much of his humble behavior is couched in topoi.[16] In the Life of Sabas, for example, the saint is initially forbidden to enter the palace of Emperor Anastasius because his poor clothing serves to disguise his exalted identity. Yet what distinguishes Feodosii from his predecessors, Fedotov convincingly argues, is the importance of the kenotic ideal in his spiritual Weltanschauung. With Feodosii, kenoticism becomes not simply an aspect of the monastic existence, but its focal point. After his Life was written, an emphasis on humility persisted as a central element in many monastic Lives, while ascetic accomplishments, though never denied importance, often receded into the background.

The Mongol invasion and occupation of the early thirteenth century dealt a devastating blow to Russian monasticism, particularly its urban variety. In the fourteenth century a revival began to take place under the leadership of one of Russia's most famous monastic saints, Sergii of Radonezh (1314–1392). As in the heyday of Egyptian and Palestinian monasticism, the focus of monastic life during the era of "the northern Thebaid" shifted away from urban areas to the wilderness—in this case to Russia's northern forests. A common pattern for the evolution of a monastic community during this period was the emigration of a hermit or two to an isolated area, the eventual development of a skete-type

[15] Dmitrij Tschižewskij, ed., *Das Paterikon des Kiever Höhlenklosters* (Munich, 1964) (reprint of *Kievo-Pechers'kii paterik*, ed. D. I. Abramovich [Kiev, 1930]), 46. On the significance of kenosis for Feodosii, see Fedotov, *Russian Religious Mind*, 1: 128, especially.

[16] Examples of early Christian saints of whom excessive humility was characteristic include St. Sisoes and St. Isadora. See Jacques Lacarrière, *Men Possessed by God: The Story of the Desert Monks of Ancient Christendom*, trans. Roy Monkcom (Garden City, N.Y., 1964), 101.

existence, and finally the organization of a larger coenobitic community. There were also urban monasteries, but their spiritual importance was much less than their eventual political significance.

Like Feodosii, Sergii was motivated by a strong sense of humility. Many of the same topoi are ascribed to Sergii. Thus his deliberately simple garb also keeps others from recognizing him as an important personage. Another famous example of Sergii's humility is his initial refusal to become abbot of his monastery on the grounds that he is unworthy. Humility, one notes, is not always synonymous with obedience.[17] The refusal to accept ecclesiastical honors is a frequent topos. In an earlier century, the monk Ammonius had cut out his tongue in an attempt to avoid being consecrated as bishop in an Egyptian city, and in the same century as Sergii, Andrew Corsini (1301–1373) tried to avoid being made bishop of Fiesole by running away. As with Feodosii, what is involved in the case of Sergii is a question of degree and focus.

Unlike Feodosii, however, Sergii appears to have been privy to a variety of mystical experiences, a comparatively new development in Russian monasticism. A mystical orientation became a frequent characteristic of Sergii's spiritual successors. From Sergii on, one of the two important strains in Russian monasticism often combined kenoticism and mysticism, emphasizing internal spiritual achievements more than external observances and ascetic feats. This strain became associated with the Russian variant of Hesychasm, a mystical movement centered on the Jesus prayer that acquired much popularity throughout the Orthodox world in the thirteenth and fourteenth centuries. The adherents of Hesychasm in Russia were generally found among the monks who sought peace in the northern forests on the other side of the Volga and have therefore frequently been called the Transvolgan hermits.

In their attempted fidelity to the kenotic ideal, the Transvolgans often resisted the accumulation of monastic property; hence they are frequently called the non-possessors. A reverence for humility also meant that the Transvolgans, while intolerant of heretical views, were loathe to assume the role of judging and condemning others as heretics.[18] These were some of the issues that divided the Transvolgans, led

[17] Cf. Fedotov, *Russian Religious Mind*, 2: 208.

[18] In an article on the controversy between the Transvolgans and the Josephites, J. Fennell emphasizes that the Transvolgan defense of the Judaizers was based on humanitarian rather than doctrinal grounds. See "The Attitude of the Josephians and

by the mystic Nil Sorskii (1433–1508), from many of their monastic peers.[19] The latter are often called the Josephites, after the abbot Joseph of Volokolamsk (c. 1439–1515), their most well-known leader and author of a strict monastic rule. Joseph himself had been greatly influenced by the example of the severe and revered abbot Pafnutii of Borovsk (d. 1477).[20]

Unlike the Transvolgans, the Josephites were convinced that they could better observe the caritative ideal if their monasteries had large holdings. They also favored a relentless persecution of suspected heretics. The differences between the two groups were symptomatic of a more profound disagreement, of radically differing conceptions of the monastic existence. The Josephites were much more concerned with external manifestations of piety, with monastic ritual, than with the mystical approach linked to kenoticism. Joseph's monastic rule emphasized the total submission of the individual to the community and the primacy of external discipline over internal spirituality.[21] The monastic institutions of the Josephites exhibited a much greater rigidity and ritualization of behavior, and their severely regulated existence left no room for the potentially anarchic individualism of the Transvolgans.

From the fifteenth century on, these two very different and essentially incompatible trends dominated Russian monastic life. The Josephites soon allied themselves with the increasingly powerful Muscovite princes. The theory of Moscow as the third Rome originated among the Josephite monks,[22] and it was believed that Ivan the Terrible's birth was caused by a prayer offered to Pafnutii of Borovsk.[23] In the middle

the Trans-Volga Elders to the Heresy of the Judaisers," *Slavonic and East European Review* 29 (1951): 495.

[19] On Nil Sorskii's kenoticism, see especially George A. Maloney, *Russian Hesychasm: The Spirituality of Nil Sorskii* (The Hague, 1973), 45, 204. Nil was much admired by some nineteenth-century liberals. See James Y. Muckle, *Nikolai Leskov and the "Spirit of Protestantism"* (Birmingham, England, 1978), 140; and Ia. S. Lur'e, "K voprosu ob ideologii Nila Sorskogo," *TOdl* 13 (1957): 182.

[20] The life of Pafnutii is found in the *Reading Menaea* under May 1.

[21] J. Meyendorff, "Partisans et ennemis des biens ecclésiastiques au sein du monachisme russe aux XVe et XVIe siècles," *Irénikon* 29 (1956): 29. An excellent formulation of the differences between the Josephites and the Transvolgans as expressed in hagiographical literature is found in A. Kadlubovskii, "Ocherki po istorii drevne-russkoi literatury zhitii sviatykh," *Russkii filologicheskii vestnik* 47 (1902): 44–90.

[22] Meyendorff, "Partisans et ennemis," 34.

[23] Čiževskij, *History*, 238.

of the sixteenth century the Josephites succeeded in crushing the Trans-volgans, and many of the latter were condemned as heretics.[24] It is fitting that the Josephite victory seems to have been essentially a formal one; though able to dominate the ecclesiastical establishment, they produced comparatively few holy men.[25]

In the seventeenth century the Church and monasticism suffered the devastating effects of the schism, which split the Orthodox community into the Old Believers and adherents of the official church. Throughout the seventeenth and eighteenth centuries monasticism was also periodically attacked by the government, which wished to curb the influence and numbers of the monks. Because of this persecution, some monks emigrated, including Paisii Velichkovskii (1722–1794), who spent most of his life in monasteries on Mount Athos and in Rumania. Perhaps the greatest service Paisii, who was much influenced by Nil Sorskii, performed for Russian monasticism was to translate the *Philokalia*, an anthology of Eastern Orthodox ascetic and mystical literature (published in Venice in 1782), into Church Slavonic.[26] Paisii's translation, known in Slavonic under the title of *Dobrotoliubie* (*Love of Good*) appeared in Russia at the end of the eighteenth century. In the late nineteenth century Bishop Feofan Govorov (1815–1894) produced an extensive Russian version of this work.[27] The *Dobrotoliubie* was also a source of inspiration for the unknown author of the widely read *Otkrovennye rasskazy strannika dukhovnomu svoemu ottsu* (*The Frank Tales of a Wanderer to His Spiritual Father*), which appeared in several editions during the nineteenth century. Through the *Dobrotoliubie* and by his own example Paisii did much to repopularize the institution of *startsy*, elders or spiritual directors, and to revive an interest in a monastic approach more oriented toward the internal than the external.[28] Through his disciples as well, Paisii had a great deal of impact on nineteenth-century Russian monasticism, and a mysticism linked to kenoticism again became

[24] Fedotov, *Russian Religious Mind*, 2: 380.

[25] Cf. Fedotov, *Russian Religious Mind*, 2: 381. Two of the more well-known Josephite holy men were Daniil of Pereiaslavl' (d. 1540) and Gerasim of Boldino (d. 1554). On the ultimately greater spiritual reverence enjoyed by Nil Sorskii as opposed to Joseph of Volokolamsk in particular, see Maloney, *Russian Hesychasm*, 235.

[26] On the *Philokalia*, see *Encyclopedic Dictionary of Religion* (Washington, D.C., 1979).

[27] *Dobrotoliubie v russkom perevode dopolnennoe* (Moscow, 1895).

[28] On the influence of Nil Sorskii on Paisii, see Maloney, *Russian Hesychasm*, 33, 236.

important in Russian spiritual life. The elders of Optina Pustyn' can be considered the spiritual descendants of Feodosii and Sergii.

From its beginning in the eleventh to the twentieth century, Russian monasticism was thus dominated by two conflicting trends, one more ascetic and severe, concerned with external demonstrations of piety, the other less concerned with strict observance of ecclesiastical conventions, often more inward-directed, and grounded in a keen sense of humility. While the precise forms taken by these two tendencies varied from century to century, many basic features remained constant. These features reappeared with remarkable regularity in hagiographical literature, often in the form of topoi.

Of the two trends, it was the gentler, less severe one that proved more popular among the Russians. The great appeal of kenoticism to Russian religious thinking over the centuries is borne out by the popularity of kenotic features among certain lay saints, namely the holy fools. Holy fools had been venerated in Byzantium for many centuries, and, as mentioned above, one of the earliest translated Lives concerned a holy fool, Andreas Salos. In sheer numbers, however, the holy fools achieved an unprecedented popularity in Russia. The height of this popularity came between the fifteenth and sixteenth centuries, when twenty-five holy fools were canonized, but they continued to enjoy veneration in some circles until the end of the Russian empire and even later.[29]

The biblical inspiration for holy foolishness comes from I Corinthians 3:18: "Make no mistake about it: if any one of you thinks of himself as wise, in the ordinary sense of the word, then he must learn to be a fool before he can be really wise."[30] The essence of Russian holy foolishness is a feigned madness which both fosters humility in the holy fool and also provides him or her with a persona which may speak the truth more directly than allowed by normal social conventions.[31] The Kievan Cave

[29] Cf. Fedotov, *Russian Religious Mind*, 2: 316.

[30] On the Pauline origins of holy folly, see Fedotov, *Russian Religious Mind*, 2: 321; and Natalia Challis and Horace W. Dewey, "Divine Folly in Old Kievan Literature: The Tale of Isaac the Cave Dweller," *SEEJ* 22 (1978): 262.

[31] A good definition of the "passive" and "active" sides of holy folly is provided by A. M. Panchenko in "Smekh kak zrelishche," in D. S. Likhachev and A. M. Panchenko, eds., *"Smekhovoi mir" drevnei Rusi* (Leningrad, 1976), 101. Cf. also E. Golubinskii, *Istoriia russkoi tserkvi*, 2d ed. (Moscow, 1904; The Hague, 1969), vol. 1, pt. 2, 656–57.

Monastery Paterikon story of Monk Isaakii illustrates the self-oriented aspect of holy folly very clearly. According to the paterikon, Isaakii was lured into bowing to disguised demons and paid for this lapse with a long illness. After his recovery, Isaakii, "not desiring human glory, began to practice holy foolishness and to do mischief, now to the abbot, now the monks, now laymen."[32] This humility-inspired route led him to great spiritual achievements. Isaakii's story provides effective criticism of "excessive asceticism linked with the absence of humility."[33] During the Muscovite period, the other-directed aspect of holy foolishness assumed a great importance. Famous sixteenth-century holy fools like Vasilii the Blessed of Moscow and Ioann "Big Cap" are said to have dared to reproach the tsars themselves. At this time, the holy fools were often credited with both great spiritual insight and the gift of prophecy.[34]

Unlike Isaakii, a monk who remained in one monastery, the typical holy fool of later years was a layman and a wanderer. One of the distinguishing characteristics of such holy fools was their bizarre dress, which often included some of the paraphernalia of the harsher forms of asceticism, like chains. They tended to dress in ragged and scanty clothes; this, in the harsh Russian climate, was an ascetic achievement in itself, as was their frequent habit of sleeping outdoors or on church porches. The significant feature of the behavior of holy fools towards others often lay in their apparently ridiculous, but supposedly purposive actions. For example, Vasilii the Blessed threw stones at the homes of the good, but kissed the houses of the evil because devils lurked about the one, while angels lamented inside the latter.[35]

Fedotov calls the existence led by the holy fool "the most radical form of Christian kenoticism."[36] A central concern of both holy folly and kenotic monasticism is self-humiliation as the path to spiritual salvation. The kinship between the two movements is underscored by the fact that the kenotic monastic saint may share external features with the holy fool, such as a fondness for poor garb; sometimes he may, like Isaakii, adopt holy foolishness as a means of ensuring his own humility. For example, Kirill of Beloozero (d. 1427), one of the protégés of Sergii

[32] *Paterikon*, 188.

[33] Čiževskij, *History*, 46.

[34] Cf. Čiževskij, *History*, 247.

[35] Fedotov, *Russian Religious Mind*, 2: 338.

[36] Fedotov, *Russian Religious Mind*, 2: 321.

of Radonezh, in his early days at a Moscow monastery, purposely behaved in a foolish and unseemly fashion to avoid praise. This was not uncommon among monks even as late as the nineteenth century; both Paisii Iarotskii (1821–1893) and Feofilii Gorenovskii (1788–1853) of the Kievan Cave Monastery practiced holy foolishness.[37]

The boundary between the kenotic monk and the holy fool is a fairly fluid one. In their shared and persistent popularity, they may be viewed as complementary manifestations of a similar religious spirit. This helps to explain why, in the neo-hagiography of the nineteenth century, the two types may coexist in the same work or even in the same character.

How sensitive nineteenth-century Russian writers were to the importance of certain spiritual types for Russian cultural history is suggested by Alexander Pushkin's *Boris Godunov* (1825), which is set in the Time of Troubles at the turn of the seventeenth century. Both a holy fool (Nikolka) and a virtuous monk (Pimen) figure in this play. In his famous Pushkin speech of June 1880 Dostoevsky spoke of Pimen thus:

> About the type of the Russian monk-chronicler, for example, it would be possible to write an entire book in order to show all the importance and all the significance for us of this majestic Russian image found by Pushkin in the Russian land, depicted by him, sculpted by him, and placed before us now forever in its indisputable, humble, and majestic spiritual beauty.[38]

While Dostoevsky's speech may, as Isaiah Berlin suggests, provide an excellent example of the attempt to impute one's own attitudes to another, the assertion that Pimen represents an important spiritual type is certainly valid.[39] The monk is not thoroughly developed as a saintly figure and indeed functions primarily as an observer and commentator rather than as an active participant in events. Yet to a large extent he conforms to the ideal described in the preceding pages.

As the archetypal monk-chronicler, Pushkin's Pimen is both courageous and humble. The monk himself indulges in the traditional topos of humility regarding his annalistic activities and, in conversation with young Grigorii, the future pretender to the throne, takes no personal

[37] Bolshakoff, *Russian Mystics*, 114.

[38] F. M. Dostoevskii, *Ss*, vol. 10 (Moscow, 1958), 452–53.

[39] For Berlin's observations, see "The Hedgehog and the Fox," in his *Russian Thinkers* (New York, 1978), 23.

spiritual credit for his entrance into the monastery. Pimen's aura of humility is such that even the secular-minded and ambitious Grigorii notices it and speaks of the older monk's "vid smirennyi, velichavyi" ("humble, majestic appearance") (18).[40] This humility also expresses itself in the calm and reasoned manner in which Pimen speaks and in his consistent lack of fanaticism in evaluating all that he has witnessed. This does not mean that Pimen is tolerant of vice. As with many kenotic monks, the counterpart to his humility is a lack of awe for authority. Just as Feodosii fearlessly criticized rapacious and violent princes, so Pimen faithfully chronicles political truth as he perceives it. Grigorii draws attention to the courage implicit in this activity when he says: "Boris, Boris! vse pred toboi trepeshchet, / . . . A mezhdu tem otshel'nik v temnoi kel'i / Zdes' na tebia donos uzhasnyi pishet" ("Boris, Boris! Everything trembles before you . . . but meanwhile a hermit in a dark cell writes a terrible denunciation of you here") (23). It is also significant that in his appraisal of events, Pimen reveals the perspicacity generally attributed to saintly monks.

The character of the holy fool Nikolka also conforms to traditional stereotypes. In creating Nikolka, Pushkin appears to have been influenced by various accounts of holy fools in Karamzin's *History of the Russian State*.[41] In the tenth volume of the *History*, Karamzin describes how a revered holy fool castigated the tsar Boris Godunov (1598–1605) and foretold great misfortunes for him, and how Boris endured this criticism silently and did not dare to do him the least evil (10: 169). By analogy, Karamzin repeats the story that Vasilii the Blessed did not hesitate to reproach Ivan the Terrible (1533–1584), bravely shouting in the city squares about his cruel deeds (10: 169). In a footnote to this discussion Karamzin mentions another Muscovite holy fool, Ioann "Big Cap," so called because he wore not only iron chains, but also a heavy cap (10: n. 469). In discussing Vasilii the Blessed's assault on Ivan, Karamzin also refers to his treatment in the ninth volume of the *History* of a confrontation between the tsar and the holy fool Nikola of Pskov. Pushkin may have made use of this material as well.[42] According to this

[40] The text of *Boris Godunov* is found in A. S. Pushkin, *Pss*, 16 vols. (Leningrad, 1937–1949), 7: 1–98.

[41] Cf. N. Granovskaia, "Iurodivyi v tragedii Pushkina," *Russkaia literatura*, 1964, no. 2: 92. The text of Karamzin's *History* referred to here is the edition published in St. Petersburg in 1892 (reprint, The Hague, 1969).

[42] Granovskaia, "Iurodivyi v tragedii Pushkina," 93–94.

story, Nikola, who "under the protection of his holy foolishness was not afraid to expose the tyrant's bloodthirstiness and sacrilege" (9: 98), offered Ivan some raw meat when the tsar visited him. When Ivan objected that as a Christian he did not eat raw meat during Lent, Nikola retorted: "You do worse: you feed on human flesh and blood, forgetting not only the fast, but God as well" (9: 98). Frightened by Nikola's threats, Ivan did not unleash his full wrath on the city of Pskov.

Pushkin's Nikolka appears to be derived from several historical fools. He shares his name with Nikola and, like Ioann "Big Cap," wears an iron cap. Like Nikola, Vasilii the Blessed, and the anonymous fool who confronts Boris, he does not hesitate to criticize the tsar for his crimes. His approach especially resembles that of Nikola of Pskov. Yet Nikolka is above all a representative of a type. In this context, an apposite comment was made by Karamzin in response to Pushkin's request for the Life of Ioann "Big Cap" or of any other holy fool: "All holy fools are alike."[43] In a sense, of course, so they are. Pushkin's Nikolka exhibits all the traditional characteristics of the type. In his iron cap and chains, he reveals the harshly ascetic inclinations of the fool, while the apparent ridiculousness of his behavior provokes the taunts of children. Yet when Boris appears, Nikolka reveals that combination of insight and lack of fear so typical of the fool, saying: "The little children hurt Nikolka's feelings . . . Order them slaughtered, as you slaughtered the little tsarevich" (78). Out of respect or fear or both, Boris refuses to allow the boyars to seize Nikolka, and instead asks the holy fool to pray for him. Yet Nikolka persists in his condemnation of Boris for his supposed slaughter of the child Prince Dmitrii of Uglich (1582–1591), the youngest son of Ivan the Terrible, saying: "No! No! It is forbidden to pray for a Herod-tsar (*tsar' Irod*)—the Mother of God doesn't allow it" (78).

The figures of Pimen and Nikolka attest to the nineteenth-century awareness of the historical stereotypes of the saintly monk and the holy fool. The major difference between Pimen and Nikolka and the other characters discussed in this chapter is that Pushkin's characters operate within the context of historical fiction. This difference is especially pertinent where the figure of the holy fool is involved. Until the demise of the Russian empire, saintly monks continued to enjoy a certain prestige among all religious segments of the population; the fortunes of holy

[43] Pushkin, *Pss* 13: 224.

fools, however, suffered a decided decline. During the period in which *Boris Godunov* is set, fools were accorded much respect. By the nineteenth century, this was often no longer true.[44] Two semi-autobiographical works by the very dissimilar writers Leo Tolstoy and the radical Gleb Uspenskii, *Childhood* (*Detstvo*, 1852) and "Paramon the Holy Fool" ("Paramon iurodivyi," 1877), well illustrate the contemporary position of the holy fool. A brief consideration of the fools in these writings will help evaluate how the type reverberated in nineteenth-century works of a neo-hagiographical slant.

The holy fools Grisha and Paramon found in these two works exhibit the traditional external characteristics of the type. Both are laymen of peasant origin who spend their lives wandering from place to place. Their asceticism manifests itself in chains and tattered clothing; Paramon even wears an iron hat. The narrator of *Childhood* observes that Grisha's enigmatic pronouncements "are considered by some people to be prophecies" (17).[45] The narrator of "Paramon the Holy Fool" is more outspoken in his appraisal of the fool's speech:

> He had concocted or contrived a few phrases . . . which in all probability were supposed to express some thought, but because of the illiteracy of the peasant-ascetic, didn't signify anything except nonsense (242).[46]

In neither case does the narrator suggest that the holy fool should be credited with the remarkable insight often attributed to the type in the Middle Ages.

In both works, the holy fool is presented from a child's point of view. In *Childhood*, Nikolai Irtenev initially approaches Grisha in a spirit of curiosity rather than religious awe. This is partially because of the differences of opinion in his family regarding holy fools. Nikolai's father is skeptical to the point of contempt about the sanctity of such wanderers, while his mother believes in their spiritual insight and wishes

[44] On the decline of the status of the holy fool, see Panchenko, "Smekh kak zrelishche," 180, 183.

[45] The text of *Childhood* (*Detstvo*) is found in L. N. Tolstoi, *Pss*, 90 vols. (Moscow, 1928–1958), 1: 1–95.

[46] The text of "Paramon the Holy Fool" ("Paramon iurodivyi: Iz detskikh let odnogo propadshego") is found in G. I. Uspenskii, *Ss*, 9 vols. (Moscow, 1955–1957), 1: 237–61. The story is based on Uspenskii's memories of his childhood years in Tula. See 1: 529.

Grisha to be treated with kindness. Such differences reflect the range of opinions among educated nineteenth-century Russians. When Nikolai actually witnesses Grisha at his prayers, rather than being amused as he had anticipated, he is convinced of Grisha's true religiosity:

> O, great Christian Grisha! Your faith was so strong that you felt the nearness of God, your love so great that the words poured from your lips by themselves—you did not verify them with your reason. (35).

Paramon is also portrayed as deeply and sincerely religious. The narrator goes so far as to call him a "holy man" (237) and asserts that Paramon's sanctity is immediately perceived by everyone in the household. In spite of this, the narrator expresses ambivalence about Paramon, characterizing him as "clumsy, uneducated, ignorant . . . , with his strange theory of salvation by means of physical sufferings" (238). At the same time he claims that one of his dearest memories is of this "saintly simpleton" (*prostiak sviatoi*) (238).

The major point of "Paramon the Holy Fool" is political rather than religious; Paramon is used as a foil to expose an atmosphere of fear during the reign of Nicholas I.[47] As a runaway peasant, Paramon lacks proper documents, and the family of the narrator is cowed by the local police officer into denying him shelter. In keeping with the traditional lack of awe for authority exhibited by the holy fool, Paramon is the only one who does not reveal any fear before the policeman.

Both Grisha and Paramon are unquestionably sincere in the adoption of their painful and demanding existence and are truly kenotic in voluntarily undertaking a radical form of self-humiliation. And yet, unlike many holy fools of an earlier era, they are not generally credited with spiritual insight and certainly do not exhibit any. Thus their ability to influence others has been undermined. While their religious commitment remains admirable, they have been, as it were, demythologized. No longer the charismatic denouncers of hidden vice, they appear nothing more than virtuous but ignorant peasants.[48]

This disparity between medieval and contemporary perceptions of the figure of the holy fool proves important in analyzing the type in

[47] Because of this aspect of the story, its separate publication was forbidden by the censorship in 1898. See Uspenskii, *Ss* 1: 529.

[48] A similiarly unvarnished portrayal of a holy fool is found in Ivan Turgenev's "A Strange Story" ("Strannaia istoriia," 1870).

nineteenth-century Russian literature. The tension between views creates a wide variety not only in the kinds of "foolish" personalities but also in the writers' attitudes to the type. This is particularly noticeable in the case of Dostoevsky. Moreover, since the saintly monk may exhibit traces of holy foolishness, the complex cluster of perceptions surrounding the holy fool may have an impact on portrayals of this type as well.

Saintly Personalities in the Novels of Dostoevsky

The nineteenth-century Russian author most remarkable for his efforts in neo-hagiography was Fedor Dostoevsky (1821–1881). In his major novels, this deeply religious writer made increasing use of hagiographical features and stereotypes in creating his characters. It has often been noticed that the types that most interested him were precisely the saintly monk and the holy fool.[49] Once again, it is important to recognize the fluidity of the boundary between these two modes of sanctity, for all of Dostoevsky's saints partake to some extent of kenotic values.

In considering Dostoevsky's characters, the impact of the holy fool provides a logical point of departure, both chronologically and thematically. Roughly speaking, characters modelled on holy fools tend to appear more frequently in the earlier novels, while those evocative of saintly monks are found in the later novels, most notably *The Brothers Karamazov*. More importantly perhaps, the characters who derive predominantly from the tradition of the saintly monk are in general more extensively developed as hagiographical personalities. The analysis of the later characters will benefit from a discussion of the less fully exploited saintly characters who preceded them.

There are many characters in the novels of Dostoevsky who exhibit some of the traits of holy fools. In fact, the claim has been made that "all of his meek types are holy fools in disguise, and the predatory,

[49] See, for example, Sven Linnér, *Staretz Zosima in The Brothers Karamazov: A Study in the Mimesis of Virtue* (Stockholm, 1975), 87. There are, of course, other saintly figures who appear in Dostoevsky's writings, for example, the virtuous harlot, a type that finds most striking embodiment in the character of Sonia Marmeladova (*Crime and Punishment*). However, I have limited myself here to the saintly monk and the holy fool. On the impact of kenotic values on Dostoevsky's spiritual development, see, for example, Nicholas Rzhevsky, *Russian Literature and Ideology: Herzen, Dostoevsky, Leontiev, Tolstoy, Fadeyev* (Urbana, Ill., 1983), 68–73.

those who refused or did not dare to take the big step, are the potential ones," i.e., potential holy fools.[50] While this claim may possess some validity, it is too broad to be entirely helpful. Some of Dostoevsky's characters, including Prince Myshkin in *The Idiot* (*Idiot*, 1868), Semen Iakovlevich and Mariia Lebiadkina in *The Possessed* (*Besy*, 1872), and Lizaveta in *The Brothers Karamazov*, are more clearly patterned on the figure of the holy fool, and it is these that will be treated here.

With the possible exception of Semen Iakovlevich, none of the characters mentioned above can be termed a holy fool in the strict medieval, hagiographical sense of the word because their foolishness is devoid of premeditation. From a religious point of view holy foolishness presumes a conscious desire to adopt unconventional, ascetic behavior as a form of humility. Some argue about whether many of the historical holy fools, even canonized ones, were actually severely disturbed, with no control over their actions, but it is not essential to answer that question here.[51] Rather, what is important is the way in which the fool was traditionally perceived and how that compares to the way Dostoevsky's characters are portrayed.

Stinking Lizaveta, the mother of Fedor Karamazov's presumed illegitimate son Smerdiakov, provides an extreme example of the holy fool deprived of inner spiritual content. In her appearance and behavior, she is extraordinarily evocative of the traditional holy fool. She goes about barefoot and scantily clad even in winter and sleeps on the ground or the church porch. That this results from unconscious choice rather than necessity is borne out by the failure of some of those who regard her as a holy fool to dress her more warmly. No one teases Lizaveta, even the local boys. Instead, like the holy fools of tradition, she is allowed to wander freely in and out of people's houses. Though frequently presented with money and food, she reveals the lack of interest in material goods characteristic of the fool and often gives these things away, subsisting on black bread and water alone.

[50] Ewa M. Thompson, "The Archetype of the Fool in Russian Literature," *Canadian Slavonic Papers* 15 (1973): 263.

[51] On the similarity between the behavior ascribed to holy fools and the symptoms of autism, see Natalia Challis and Horace W. Dewey, "The Blessed Fools of Old Russia," *Jahrbücher für Geschichte Osteuropas* 22 (1974): 2–5, especially. Panchenko distinguishes between "innate" [*prirodnoe*] and "voluntary [*dobrovol'noe*] *iurodstvo* ('for the sake of Christ')." See Panchenko, "Smekh kak zrelishche," 95. It was the latter which gained currency in hagiography.

Yet Lizaveta lacks the spiritual insight which is generally considered the internal counterpart to the external strangeness of the fool. Instead, she simply exists, without purpose or motive. The description of her face indicates this: "Her twenty-year-old face, healthy, broad, and rosy, was completely imbecilic; her gaze was fixed and unpleasant, although mild" (90).[52] Even more than Grisha and Paramon, Lizaveta represents the debasement of the image of the holy fool. More than anything else, Lizaveta attests to the persistent belief among some segments of Russian society that idiots have been touched by God.

How lacking Lizaveta's existence is in true spiritual foundations is in a sense borne out by the character of her son. With his affected clothing and manners and purposely obfuscatory speech, Smerdiakov seems almost a parody of a holy fool. Yet Smerdiakov possesses no ethical sense. His personality provides eloquent testimony to the fact that eccentric behavior may not always stem from moral fervor.

Like Lizaveta, the holy fool Semen Iakovlevich who appears briefly in *The Possessed* bears witness to the respect of some laymen for this distinctively Russian form of sanctity. Yet, as in the case of Lizaveta, Semen Iakovlevich seems spiritually flawed, although for somewhat different reasons. At first glance he appears to conform to the stereotype much more than Dostoevsky's other fools, both in his behavior and in the way he is regarded by those around him. Though differing from many saintly fools in having a semi-permanent residence, the home of a merchant who cares for all his physical needs, he shows little interest in material goods, distributing or handing over to the local monastery the many gifts he receives and living very simply, consuming only fish soup, potatoes, and tea. In his seemingly capricious and senseless, but supposedly meaningful behavior, Semen Iakovlevich very much resembles the holy fool of convention. For example, he orders tea for only some of his many visitors. While his choice seems to lack rhyme or reason, his visitors and attendants generally believe it to be profoundly significant.[53] How credulous his observers are regarding such apparently random actions is well illustrated by the following episode: a poor

[52] The text of *The Brothers Karamazov* (*Brat'ia Karamazovy*) is found in Dostoevskii, *Pss*, 30 vols. (Leningrad, 1972–), vols. 14 (Books 1–10) and 15 (Books 11–12 and Epilogue). Unless otherwise noted, all citations are to *Pss* 14.

[53] This detail would appear to be borrowed from the description of a monastic holy man given in *Skazanie o stranstvii i puteshestvii po Rossii, Moldavii, Turtsii i Sviatoi Zemle postrizhennika Sviatye Gory Afonskie Inoka Parfeniia* 4 vols. (Moscow, 1855), 1: 288.

gentlewoman complains that her children are taking her to court; Semen responds with a gift of several loaves of sugar. Both the woman and the crowd who witness this believe there is some meaning to this, but no one is certain what it might be. Nor is any explanation forthcoming concerning Semen Iakovlevich's unprintable response to another woman's request for a prophecy. While lewd or indecent behavior or speech was often associated with holy fools, such antics were also supposed to be accessible to moral interpretation. No such interpretation is offered in Semen's case.[54]

The narrator of *The Possessed* is not a devout believer himself and is in fact a member of a group that visits Semen seeking amusement, not guidance. Still, nothing described in the episode involving the fool lends credence to his holiness. His behavior appears not only decidedly bizarre, but also devoid of religious purpose. Semen certainly behaves like a holy fool, but his actions lack moral depth. He serves less as an example of a contemporary holy fool the equal of Vasilii the Blessed or Nikola of Pskov than as a sign of the decay of the institution of holy fools by the late nineteenth century. Thus the fool's strange yet meaningful behavior accompanied by deep spiritual insight yields to simple eccentricity, and the audience's devout belief is replaced by an easy credulousness. There is no reason to think that Semen Iakovlevich is a complete charlatan, but neither is he a saint.

Moving beyond Lizaveta and Semen Iakovlevich, whose similarity with the traditional holy fool is largely external, one finds more profound echoes of the holy fool in less conventional guises, specifically in the characters of Mariia Lebiadkina and Prince Myshkin. Both appear to suffer from more or less severe psychological disturbances, and it seems unlikely that their behavior is assumed or intentional. At the same time, both reveal the startling flashes of spiritual intuition that characterize the holy fool of hagiography. Nor do they completely lack external similarities with the type.

The appearance and manner of Mariia Lebiadkina, the crippled sister of the debauched Captain Lebiadkin and the secret wife of Nikolai Stavrogin, are very reminiscent of the holy fool. This is made especially clear when she visits the local cathedral:

[54] On lewd and scandalous behavior in fools, see Fedotov, *Russian Religious Mind*, 2: 317–18.

> Sneers and even surprise accompanied [Mariia] . . . She was unhealthily thin and limped, was overly powdered and rouged, with a completely bare neck, without a shawl or a coat, wearing only an old dark dress, in spite of the cold and windy September day, with a completely bare head . . . she walked with her eyes modestly lowered, but at the same time smiling gaily and archly (122).[55]

In her inadequate clothing, Mariia exhibits a disregard for the elements, one of the forms of asceticism usually ascribed to holy fools. Her appearance is also marked by touches of the bizarre, such as excessive make-up and an inappropriate smile, that are likely to provoke ridicule from many onlookers. Such conspicuous oddness is also reminiscent of the holy fools.

Mariia's verbal behavior too is in keeping with that of a traditional holy fool. Her discourse is completely uninhibited, and she shocks those around her by her embarrassing directness. When she first meets the sister of a friend in Varvara Stavrogin's drawing room, she exclaims: "Well, Shatushka, your sister's not like you. How can my [brother] call such a charming creature the serf girl Dashka?" (132–33). Dasha Shatov has long since risen above her humble beginnings and Mariia's repetition of her dissolute brother's sneering words is inappropriate and unwelcome. More importantly, Mariia's comments to Dasha and her observations to Stavrogin concerning the people gathered at his mother's house that afternoon betray not only a devastating frankness, but also that uncanny insight into character often imputed to holy fools. She captures the essence of Varvara Stavrogin's arrogant pride when she remarks: "His [Stavrogin's] mother should be an abbess; I'm afraid of her, even though she gave me the black shawl" (216). As for the shawl, when Stavrogin visits Mariia, he sees that the shawl is neatly folded, but not in use. Like Lizaveta and Semen Iakovlevich, Mariia shows little interest in material possessions.

Mariia's ability to discern people's true natures extends to the mysterious Stavrogin as well. Captivated by fantasies about the character of the "real" Stavrogin, her "Prince," she accuses Stavrogin of being the

[55] The text of *The Possessed* (*Besy*), excluding Chapter 9, is found in Dostoevskii, *Pss* 10. Mariia's status as a holy fool, in particular, her characteristic insight, is mentioned in F. I. Evnin, "Roman *Besy*," in N. L. Stepanov, ed., *Tvorchestvo F. M. Dostoevskogo* (Moscow, 1959), 247.

Pretender Grishka Otrepev when she perceives that he does not match her expectations. This reference to the first False Dmitrii (1605) evokes precisely that period when holy fools commanded a great deal of respect. Mariia's accusation is especially interesting because it demonstrates that, unlike many of the other characters in *The Possessed*, she is not misled by Stavrogin's mask, but recognizes the shoddy personality within. She is wrong in believing in the existence of a noble prince, but astonishingly correct in realizing that Stavrogin is a kind of impostor. Her perception is even more specific: she also recognizes that Stavrogin has murderous intentions towards her; this is the purport of her insistence that he has a knife in his pocket. Mariia even reveals a kind of prescience here, for it is indeed a knife that is shortly thereafter used as her murder weapon.

In her external strangeness and internal perceptiveness, Mariia much more fully resembles the holy fool of hagiography than does either Semen Iakovlevich or Lizaveta. Yet those around her generally treat her with little respect. Even those who feel compassion for her, like the former serf and religious nationalist Shatov, consider her mentally unbalanced and discern no religious implications in her behavior, despite her own overt religiosity. Still, no matter how peculiar her general demeanor, Mariia consistently reveals a certain piety; when she visits the church she retains her own sort of dignity, and in her room she keeps a lamp burning before an icon. Mariia is indeed psychologically disturbed, but she is also an unacknowledged holy fool. The depth of her spirituality is measured not only by her insight, but also by her gift of tears. Describing how she followed the advice of a certain old woman and wept and prayed as she kissed the earth, she tells Shatov: "there was nothing bad in those tears—and even if you have no sorrow, all the same the tears will run from your eyes out of happiness alone. The tears will run by themselves" (116). Her inspired tears tie Mariia very firmly to the Russian hagiographical tradition.

At first glance, Prince Myshkin of *The Idiot* appears to have little in common with the traditional holy fool. It has been observed that he does evoke the type because he arrives in Russia "without possession or station."[56] Soon, however, as a wealthy member of high society, Myshkin leads an existence that does not at all reflect the poverty or

[56] Howard H. Keller, "Prince Myshkin: Success or Failure?" *Journal of Russian Studies* 24 (1972): 19.

lack of social status typical of the lives of many fools. Like Mariia Lebiadkina, however, Myshkin proves to have both external and internal connections with the type. His character grows very much out of the Russian hagiographical tradition, a link aptly symbolized by his command of medieval calligraphy.

Externally, Myshkin's affinity with the holy fools is most evident in his clothing. His first appearance in the novel draws attention to the strangeness of his apparel:

> [Myshkin] was forced to endure on his shiveringly cold back all the sweetness of a damp Russian night, for which he was obviously not prepared. He was wearing a fairly wide, thick cape with a huge hood, exactly like those that travellers often use in the wintertime somewhere far abroad, in Switzerland or, for example, in northern Italy . . . But what was suitable and completely satisfactory in Italy turned out to be not completely suitable in Russia (6).[57]

Somewhat later the wealthy merchant's son Rogozhin, who claims to have taken a liking to the prince, offers to outfit him properly. Much later in the novel, he reminds the prince of their first meeting and again mentions his odd clothing. Moreover, it eventually becomes apparent that it is not simply the nature of his clothing, but how he wears it that distinguishes the prince, for even when he acquires more conventional clothing, his appearance remains slightly bizarre:

> his entire dress was different, sewn in Moscow and by a good tailor; but even this dress had a shortcoming: it was made in too fashionable a style . . . and for someone who was not at all interested in it, so that if anyone overly fond of laughing had looked carefully at the prince, he would have found something to smile at (159).

Clothing that invites attention and ridicule is a hallmark of the holy fool, as is disregard for the elements. Moreover, the mockery that the prince provokes only begins with his clothing; his behavior in general often serves as a source of amusement.

The opening episode on the train adds other touches of the holy fool to the portrait of Myshkin. Though not a foreigner, Myshkin has a

[57] The text of *The Idiot* (*Idiot*) is found in Dostoevskii, *Pss* 8.

distinctly non-Russian air about him and has spent the past few years abroad. According to hagiographical accounts, many holy fools were of foreign origin. His seeming foreign thus links Myshkin to the type as well.[58] On the train the prince confesses that he has had no carnal knowledge of women. This also ties him to the holy fools, who, like other Russian saints, were implicitly chaste. Rogozhin, with his intensely devout merchant background, is inspired by Myshkin's admission to observe: "Well, if that's the case, . . . you're completely a holy fool, Prince, and God loves such as you" (14).

As in the case of Mariia Lebiadkina, Myshkin's external strangeness is paralleled by an uncanny and unexpected insight into the behavior of those around him.[59] He confounds Nastas'ia Filippovna by telling her she is not the woman she pretends to be. Similarly, he sees through the machinations surrounding Burdovskii, who claims to be the illegitimate son of Myshkin's wealthy benefactor Pavlishchev, and thus demonstrates the deceptiveness of his apparent naiveté. The other characters in the novel notice his talent for penetrating the motives and personalities of others. Burdovskii's friend Keller makes perhaps the most illuminating comment: "such artlessness, such innocence as were unheard of even in the golden age, and suddenly at the same time you pierce a person like an arrow, with such a very profound psychology of observation" (258). This surprising, even shocking, perceptiveness, links Myshkin to both holy fools and saintly monks.

Much more than Mariia Lebiadkina, Myshkin exhibits the kenotic humility characteristic of the holy fools and many saintly monks. He willingly refers to himself as an idiot and shows himself ready to assume guilt needlessly. For example, he blames himself for having suggested that he and Burdovskii have suffered from the same illness and for having publicly offered him money. His humility also expresses itself in his attitude toward class distinctions. Like kenotic types, he does not accept the concept of social inferiors. This is brought out in an early episode involving the well-to-do General Epanchin's servant, with whom Myshkin wishes to converse and whom he succeeds in upsetting

[58] Robin Feuer Miller, *Dostoevsky and The Idiot: Author, Narrator, and Reader* (Cambridge, Mass., 1981), 66. On this aspect of holy foolishness, see Fedotov, *Russian Religious Mind*, 2: 327.

[59] Cf. Joseph Frank, "A Reading of *The Idiot*," *The Southern Review* 5 (1969): 309; and Zinaida Malenko and James J. Gebhard, "The Artistic Use of Portraits in Dostoevskij's *Idiot*," *SEEJ* 5 (1961): 244.

precisely because he does not observe the normal social boundaries. Finally, the prince's humility is also evidenced by his unwillingness to judge others, an unwillingness he tries to communicate to proud Aglaia Epanchina, one of the young daughters of the general, when he tells her, in true biblical spirit, not to cast stones at Nastas'ia Filippovna.[60]

How much of an impression Myshkin's humility makes on the other characters in *The Idiot* is ironically indicated by their sarcasm. The young consumptive Ippolit claims that he was amused by the boy Kolia's apparent decision to imitate the prince in his "Christian humility" (328). Similarly, in encouraging Myshkin to go off with Nastas'ia Filippovna, Aglaia tells him: "Then sacrifice yourself, it becomes you so" (363). In both instances, a certain cynicism betrays a recognition of Myshkin's kenotic mode of existence.

The remarks made by Aglaia and Ippolit point as well to one of the major weaknesses in the personality of the prince, a weakness common indeed to some extent to all of Dostoevsky's "foolish" characters. Myshkin is good, but his holy foolishness has little positive effect on those around him. As portrayed by Dostoevsky, holy foolishness proves much less efficacious a form of spiritual commitment than is suggested by medieval hagiography or, it may be added, by historical fiction of the type of *Boris Godunov*. For characters in Dostoevsky's world who exemplify a more active, productive kind of virtue, one must look to those inspired by a different hagiographical model, namely the kenotic monk.

Dostoevsky's first attempt at portraying a saintly monk was made in the notorious ninth chapter of *The Possessed*, in which Stavrogin confesses to the local holy man Tikhon his sexual and other crimes against the twelve-year-old Matresha. Although Dostoevsky had intended this chapter to serve as a pivotal point in the novel, he was forced by the conservative publicist Mikhail Katkov to exclude it from the first, serial publication of *The Possessed* in *The Russian Messenger* (*Russkii vestnik*). Nor did the writer try to include the chapter in subsequent editions of the novel. It has remained extant in the form of proofs prepared in 1871 and a manuscript copy done by Dostoevsky's wife Anna from an unknown manuscript.[61]

[60] On Myshkin's reluctance to judge others because of his humility, see Romano Guardini, "Dostoevsky's Idiot, A Symbol of Christ," *Cross Currents* 6 (1956): 362, and Nadejda Gorodetzky, *The Humiliated Christ in Modern Russian Thought* (London, 1938; New York, 1973), 65.

[61] On the complex history of this chapter, see Dostoevskii, *Pss* 12: 237–46.

The genesis of the character of Tikhon is connected with the figure of the eighteenth-century monk Tikhon of Zadonsk (1724–1783), who was much admired by nineteenth-century Russian intellectuals, including Nikolai Gogol, Ivan Kireevskii, Leo Tolstoy, Gleb Uspenskii, and Maxim Gorky.[62] Dostoevsky's interest in the saint can be traced to 1861, when Tikhon's relics were found in the provincial city of Voronezh.[63] He intended to have Tikhon play a major role in an ambitious work he planned, but never wrote, *The Life of a Great Sinner* (*Zhitie velikogo greshnika*). In a letter written to the poet Apollon Maikov in 1870, he said that in the second part of the work he wished to present as "the main figure Tikhon of Zadonsk, under a different name of course, but also as a bishop who will be living in retirement in a monastery."[64] A few months later, when he had already begun *The Possessed*, Dostoevsky wrote to Katkov: "In general I am afraid that much is beyond my powers. For the first time, for example, I want to touch upon one category of characters, still little touched by literature. As the ideal of such a character I am taking Tikhon of Zadonsk."[65]

Tikhon of Zadonsk, whom Fedotov has described as a "westernizing kenotic," came from a poor but pious family.[66] After completing the seminary in Novgorod, he taught for several years before becoming a monk and eventually a bishop. He was familiar not only with more traditional Orthodox ecclesiastical literature, but also with the writings of western writers, most notably the German theologian Johann Arndt (1555–1621).[67] After serving for several years in an episcopal capacity, he sought permission to retire. He spent the last thirteen years of his life at the Monastery of Zadonsk, where he led a scrupulously humble existence and became increasingly inclined to mysticism.[68]

[62] Nadejda Gorodetzky, *Saint Tikhon of Zadonsk: Inspirer of Dostoevsky* (Crestwood, N.Y., 1976), 217, 219. See also her introduction to Tikhon Zadonskii, *Tvoreniia izhe vo sviatykh ottsa nashego Tikhona Zadonskogo* (St. Petersburg, 1912; Holland, 1970).

[63] R. Pletnev, "Serdtsem mudrye (O 'startsakh' u Dostoevskogo)," in A. L. Bem, ed., *O Dostoevskom. Sbornik statei*, vol. 2 (Prague, 1933), 75.

[64] Letter of 25 March 1870. See F. M. Dostoevskii, *Pis'ma*, ed. A. S. Dolinin, vol. 2 (Moscow, 1930; The Hague, 1968), 264.

[65] Letter of 8 October 1870. See Dostoevskii, *Pis'ma* 2: 289.

[66] Fedotov, *Treasury of Russian Spirituality*, 182.

[67] Georgii Florovskii, *Puti russkogo bogosloviia* (Paris, 1937), 123.

[68] On the life and thought of Tikhon of Zadonsk, see, for example, Gorodetzky, *Saint Tikhon*; Bolshakoff, *Russian Mystics*, 61–78; Florovskii, *Puti russkogo bogosloviia*, 123–25; Igor Smolitsch, *Russisches Mönchtum: Entstehung, Entwicklung und Wesen* (Würzburg, 1953), 516–20.

Tikhon's existence during the Zadonsk period of his life was described in detail by his two cell-attendants, Vasilii Chebotarev and Ivan Efimov.[69] Like other such accounts, they are marked by credulousness and the pronounced influence of hagiographical conventions. Only occasionally do they allude to less saintly aspects of Tikhon's character, like his melancholy and irritability. The monk who emerges from these descriptions, the saint revered throughout Russia, is a decidedly kenotic type thoroughly in keeping with the tradition of Feodosii of the Kievan Cave Monastery and Sergii of Radonezh.

As described by his disciples, Tikhon exhibits many typical kenotic characteristics. Chebotarev speaks at length of his humility and voluntary poverty, focusing on his simple clothing and his habit of giving away any money and clothing presented to him. He also refers to Tikhon's fondness for the peasants, which extends to waiting upon them himself. Efimov comments that often peasant visitors did not realize "with whom they were talking, for his simple attire disguised his bishop's rank."[70] Here in modified form is a familiar topos. Tikhon's humility also expresses itself in an eagerness to assume blame for supposed sins. The most famous example of this occurs when Tikhon gently attempts to convince a bad landowner not to mistreat his serfs. When the landowner slaps him, Tikhon begs his forgiveness "for having led him into such a temptation."[71] Dostoevsky made use of this archetypally kenotic display in an episode involving Prince Myshkin in *The Idiot*.[72]

Dostoevsky's Tikhon shares a number of features with his historical model. Both are bishops living in retirement without the wholehearted patronage of their abbots and some of their fellow monks. Chebotarev refers to the many offenses patiently endured by Tikhon; the narrator of

[69] These reminiscences, "Zapiski o sviatitele Tikhone ego keleinikov Vasiliia Ivanovicha Chebotareva i Ivana Efimova," are found in *Tvoreniia izhe vo sviatykh otsa nashego Tikhona Zadonskogo*, 1: 3–55.

[70] Efimov, "Zapiski," 33.

[71] This episode is recounted in the translation of Efimov's reminiscences found in Fedotov, *Treasury of Russian Spirituality*, 211. Fedotov's translation is based on the text found in the edition of Tikhon's works published in Moscow, 1898–1899. This episode is omitted from the 1912 edition. It is also described, however, in Arkhimandrit Ignatii, *Kratkie zhizneopisaniia russkikh sviatykh* (St. Petersburg, 1875). See Dostoevskii, *Pss* 9: 512.

[72] Cf. W. Komarowitsch, *F. M. Dostojewski. Die Urgestalt der Brüder Karamasoff. Dostojewskis Quellen, Entwürfe und Fragmente* (Munich, 1928), 74.

The Possessed writes of his Tikhon's abbot: "It was said that the father archimandrite, a man severe and strict regarding his duties as Father Superior and, in addition, well-known for his erudition, even entertained towards him some supposedly hostile feeling and censured him . . . for his casual life and almost for heresy" (6).[73] In his rigidity and severity, the archimandrite appears distinctly Josephite. Neither the historical nor the fictional Tikhon arouses suspicions of true heresy, but both do exhibit a broad range of interests alien to their narrow-minded associates. Even the reverent Chebotarev admits that his mentor occasionally enjoyed discussing military operations with noblemen. This interest is more fully developed in Dostoevsky's Tikhon; the bishop has in his cell a book on the last war and a map on which he follows the campaigns described. Moreover, the narrator observes that Tikhon has in his possession not only religious books, but "theatrical compositions, 'and perhaps even worse' " (7). Thus, while the two Tikhons are undoubtedly similar in their comparative broadmindedness, the portrayal of Dostoevsky's Tikhon emphasizes those features which distinguish him from a convention-ridden Josephite.

As regards the guiding philosophy behind Tikhon's behavior, the chapter in *The Possessed* in which the retired bishop appears does not include such striking demonstrations of his humility as do Chebotarev's and Efimov's accounts of Tikhon of Zadonsk, but it does succeed in communicating Tikhon's underlying kenotic spirit. When Stavrogin questions the prelate about whether his faith is capable of moving a mountain, the latter responds: "God will command, and I will move it" (10). His entire demeanor is characterized by a humility which reveals itself in behavior slightly evocative of holy foolishness. It is precisely in these traces of holy foolishness that Dostoevsky's Tikhon most departs from his historical model, although not in a fundamental way. Dostoevsky's Tikhon has been described as an "interaction" of the models of the elder and the holy fool.[74] This is an understandable development; as the sources of their spirituality overlap, the border between the kenotic monk and the holy fool is easily crossed.

The question of the nature and extent of Tikhon's holy foolishness is a complex one. Even before Dostoevsky's monk appears one learns that there is something odd about him that even his admirers wish to con-

[73] The text of Chapter 9 of *The Possessed* (*Besy*) is found in Dostoevskii, *Pss* 11: 5–30.

[74] Linnér, *Staretz Zosima*, 87.

ceal, "some sort of weakness of his, perhaps holy foolishness" (6). The narrator gives a physiological explanation for this suspicion, claiming that Tikhon suffers from rheumatism and nervous fits. When the bishop appears in his simple cassock, he does give a strange impression, as if he were "somewhat ill, with a vague smile and a strange as it were bashful look" (6). This slight peculiarity in his glance reappears from time to time in his conversation with Stavrogin; together with his occasional halting manner of speech, it is a major source of his external resemblance to the holy fool. While this highly circumscribed oddness is far from rendering Tikhon a classic example of holy foolishness, it does establish a link with the type.

Tikhon's eccentricity, reminiscent of holy foolishness, focuses attention on his gift of insight. While both saintly monks and holy fools were often known for almost clairvoyant penetration, the insight of the fools was particularly commanding because it stemmed from such an unexpected source. Dostoevsky exploits this aspect of holy foolishness with great skill in his portrait of Tikhon. "You damned psychologist" (30), Stavrogin finally says to the unassuming monk, and it is apparent throughout the chapter that Stavrogin finds Tikhon's perceptiveness especially jarring given his slightly peculiar demeanor. This is made most clear at the beginning of their conversation:

> it suddenly seemed to him that Tikhon was dropping his eyes as it were shamefully and even with some sort of unnecessary ridiculous smile. This momentarily aroused aversion in him; he wanted to get up and leave, the more so because Tikhon, in his opinion, was definitely drunk. But he [Tikhon] suddenly raised his eyes and looked at him with a glance so steadfast and filled with thought, and at the same time with such an unexpected and enigmatic expression that he almost flinched (7).

Tikhon's affinity with monks of the more moderate tradition is also reflected in the advice he gives Stavrogin. Far from endorsing the latter's intention of publicizing his crimes, Tikhon suggests milder measures—and not simply because he mistrusts Stavrogin's motives. The tenor of his Christianity is balanced and compassionate. He speaks to Stavrogin of forgiveness and discourages him from throwing his existence into an upheaval: "Why spoil things? Why such inflexibility?" (28). Stavrogin's intended step might be worthwhile if it were inspired by humility, says Tikhon, but with uncanny insight he observes: "A desire for martyrdom and self-sacrifice is attempting to vanquish you; subdue this desire of yours . . . put to shame all your pride and your demon!" (29). Tikhon proposes that Stavrogin instead submit to the tutelage of a certain elder he knows and respects, but this solution lacks the peculiar sort of notoriety Stavrogin seeks.

The notion that the better part of virtue may be the superficially less demanding feat is characteristic of the kenotic tradition. Monks of this persuasion would shun the extreme, and dangerously ostentatious, accomplishments of, for example, a saint like Simeon the Stylite; this Byzantine saint subjected himself to severe physical deprivations and spent decades living at the top of a pillar. The idea at work here stems once again from the belief that humility, the avoidance of attention, is the true source of virtue. In his advice to Stavrogin, Tikhon clearly indicates his adherence to the school of Feodosii and Sergii. This moderation distinguishes such monks from their more fanatical opponents.

Tikhon functions in *The Possessed* as a model of virtue and exposes Stavrogin's desire to confess his crime for what it really is, a gesture of pride. But Tikhon's impact on the action of the novel is limited, partially because he is unable to influence Stavrogin, who is only angered by the monk's insight.[75] In his spiritual beauty, Tikhon is a worthy companion to Dostoevsky's later Zosima, but in terms of his organic role in the novel Tikhon is much less important.

Between completing *The Possessed* and writing *The Brothers Karamazov*, Dostoevsky produced *The Adolescent* (*Podrostok*, 1875), a novel that is often given scant attention. The novel is, however, crucial to a discussion of Dostoevsky's hagiographically inspired characters. The wanderer Makar Ivanovich represents a significant stage in Dostoevsky's development of the saintly personality. In Makar Ivanovich, several hagiographical elements find expression. Moreover, in the tenor of his religiosity Makar Ivanovich has much in common with both Tikhon and Zosima.

The type of the wanderer (*strannik*) has been described as the "moral cousin" of the holy fool.[76] This appraisal of the wanderer has a certain external validity. Like a holy fool, a wanderer gives up the security of a fixed residence for a life possessing low social status. In addition, the wanderer exhibits a similar indifference to material goods. Makar Iva-

[75] Cf. Pletnev, "Serdtsem mudrye," 77.

[76] Thompson, "Archetype of the Fool," 246.

novich fits this model. The details surrounding the three thousand rubles offered to him by the landowner Versilov underscore his lack of personal acquisitiveness. Versilov seduces Makar Ivanovich's wife, then offers him money. Versilov is surprised when Makar Ivanovich accepts and even duns him for the money, but it later transpires that the old man intends the entire sum, with accumulated interest, for his wife, not himself. In essence, however, the character of the wanderer in general and that of Makar Ivanovich in particular differ greatly from that of the holy fool. Makar Ivanovich does not exhibit the extreme ascetic tendencies typical of the holy fool, for example, or cultivate bizarre and apparently ridiculous behavior. In fact, as a hagiographical personality, he proves to have much in common both with the stereotype of the saintly monk and, among Dostoevsky's characters, with Zosima in particular.

The character of Makar Ivanovich is marked by a great humility complemented by a sense of the importance of forgiveness.[77] The narrator of *The Adolescent*, Versilov's illegitimate son Arkadii, says that what is attractive about Makar Ivanovich is his "extraordinary candor and lack of the least vanity" (308).[78] As with Tikhon and Zosima, the external sign of this is his smile, which Arkadii describes as "calm and sedate" (301). In Makar Ivanovich's personal life, this attitude manifests itself in his forgiveness of his wife, which even extends to his assumption of the greater part of the responsibility for what has happened among his wife, Versilov, and himself. Such eagerness to accept blame is distinctively kenotic. On a more mundane level, Makar Ivanovich's pervasive humility reveals itself in the tolerance he shows for Arkadii's adolescent musings and in the diffidence he manifests when his physical weakness is callously disregarded by Arkadii's sister Liza. At her request, he tries to stand even though he really cannot.

One of the most clearcut similarities between Makar Ivanovich and Zosima is their common inclination towards didactic monologues. The inclusion of such discourse in the novels links them to hagiography.[79]

[77] In his discussion of *The Adolescent*, Nicholas Rzhevsky observes that Makar Ivanovich "speaks for and acts out a natural, emotional Christianity based on humility and love of others." See Nicholas Rzhevsky, "*The Adolescent*: Structure and Ideology," *SEEJ* 26 (1982): 38.

[78] The text of *The Adolescent* (*Podrostok*) is found in Dostoevskii, *Pss* 13.

[79] Rostislav Pletnev, "Der Stil als Ausdruck der religiösen Weltanschauung Dostoevskijs," *Jahrbücher für Kultur und Geschichte der Slaven* 9 (1933): 521.

Similarly, both Makar Ivanovich and Zosima reveal a fondness for the legends of the saints as pedagogical aids, and it is noteworthy that the only Life specifically mentioned by Arkadii is the Life of Mary of Egypt, one of the two singled out by Zosima as especially moving. In addition, an important key to the spiritual philosophy of both men is found in their perception of the biblical patriarch Job. Neither views Job in a tragic or pessimistic light. Each focuses instead on the positive implications of the denouement of his story, on the victory over egotism that the patriarch's submission represents. Discussing his acceptance of approaching death, Makar Ivanovich says:

> may God's name be blessed; only I would like to look my fill on all of you. Even long-suffering Job, looking at his new children, was comforted, but did he forget the former ones, could he forget them—this is impossible. Only with the years is sadness as it were mixed with happiness, will it be transformed into a bright yearning. Thus it is in the world: every soul is both tried and comforted (330).

This serene acquiescence is an outgrowth of profound humility. At the same time, however, Makar Ivanovich is by no means as "simple" as his cheerful submissiveness might suggest. Arkadii describes his "artlessness" and "subtlety" (309) and observes that there is something of the propagandist about him. As with many of Dostoevsky's other saintly characters, Makar Ivanovich's humility accompanies a spiritual perceptiveness, which in his case is most evident in didactic discourses of the type cited above.

The most fully developed and successful of Dostoevsky's hagiographical creations is Father Zosima of *The Brothers Karamazov*. Zosima shares a number of spiritual traits with both Tikhon and Makar Ivanovich, but he lacks the slight air of ineffectuality that typifies Tikhon in particular. Rather, Zosima is an effective proponent of the active love he preaches, and his influence within the world of *The Brothers Karamazov* is substantial.

The question of the historical models for Zosima has occupied a number of scholars and has resulted in a long list of possibilities.[80] Heading the list is Amvrosii Grenkov, the third of the great elders at

[80] A concise overview of some of these possible prototypes is provided in Victor Terras, *A Karamazov Companion* (Madison, Wisc., 1981), 29.

Optina Pustyn' who were guided by the spiritual system revived by Paisii Velichkovskii. Born in 1812, Amvrosii was the son of a village sacristan. He attended the Tambov seminary, but appparently never considered becoming a monk until after a serious illness.[81] He eventually entered Optina and became a disciple of the elder Leonid Nagolkin. After Nagolkin's death he was guided by Makarii Ivanov, whose publication efforts in the sphere of patristic literature he aided and subsequently continued himself.[82] Amvrosii was the resident elder at Optina from 1862 until his death in 1891.

During his later years at Optina Amvrosii was continually besieged by visitors of all sorts seeking spiritual guidance. These he received with unfailing kindness, in spite of his chronic ill-health. With the notable exception of Leo Tolstoy, Amvrosii's intellectual visitors were generally impressed by his demeanor and conversation.[83] Dostoevsky, who went to see the elder in 1878 after the death of his son Alesha, found him immensely consoling. According to his wife Anna, the words that Zosima uses to comfort the peasant woman who has lost her child were ones Amvrosii told Dostoevsky to communicate to her.[84]

The descriptions of the monastery where Zosima is domiciled and of his routine are undoubtedly evocative of Amvrosii and Optina Pustyn'. On the other hand, the manner of existence pursued by Zosima resembles the life of virtually any popular elder. A more compelling similarity between the historical and fictional elder is that both are cheerful and outgoing as young men and retain this disposition into old age; not for them the melancholy of Tikhon of Zadonsk, for example.[85] In addition, both are educated men with strong intellectual interests.[86] The fact that both are said to possess the gift of tears has also been cited.[87] This of course also represents a common topos. Finally, Amvrosii's

[81] On Amvrosii, see Bolshakoff, *Russian Mystics*, 188–89; Smolitsch, *Russisches Mönchtum*, 509–10; Metropolit Seraphim, *Die Ostkirche* (Stuttgart, 1950), 308–19.

[82] On publications directed by Makarii and Amvrosii, see Sergii Chetverikov, *Optina pustyn': Istoricheskii ocherk i lichnye vospominaniia* (Paris, 1926), 49, 65; and Dmitry F. Grigorieff, "Dostoevsky's Elder Zosima and the Real Life Father Amvrosy," *St. Vladimir's Seminary Quarterly* 11 (1967): 29.

[83] On Tolstoy's reaction to Amvrosii, see Chapter Six.

[84] A. G. Dostoevskaia, *Vospominaniia* (Moscow, 1981), 329.

[85] On similarities between the personalities of Amvrosii and Zosima, see Linnér, *Staretz Zosima*, 91.

[86] Linnér, *Staretz Zosima*, 92.

[87] Linnér, *Staretz Zosima*, 91.

humility should be noted, for it too finds an echo in Zosima's personality and teachings in *The Brothers Karamazov*.[88] A remarkable and repeated assertion made by Amvrosii concerning the power of humility is quoted by the émigré scholar Rostislav Pletnev: "As soon as a man humbles himself, his humility immediately sets him on the threshold of the Heavenly Kingdom."[89] Zosima has no less an appreciation of the importance of humility.

Certainly the image of Amvrosii must have been vivid in Dostoevsky's mind during the composition of *The Brothers Karamazov*. Yet the similarities between Amvrosii and Zosima are sufficiently limited and general as to permit many other hypotheses about possible prototypes for Dostoevsky's elder. It has been suggested that among the elders of Optina Pustyn', not only Amvrosii, but also Leonid Nagolkin may have affected the portrayal of Zosima. Leonid, who was directly influenced by a disciple of Paisii Velichkovskii, was the resident elder at Optina from 1829 until 1841. He was employed by a merchant before becoming a monk at the age of nearly thirty and became an abbot within a few years. Under the guidance of Paisii's disciple Fedor, Leonid came to realize that his mystical quest was incompatible with an abbacy and resigned. After spending almost twenty years at other monasteries, he finally settled at Optina.[90] Although he encountered a great deal of resistance from more conservative monks, Leonid was finally able to pursue the practice of *starchestvo* (eldership) unhindered.

The best piece of evidence in favor of the influence of Leonid on the character of Zosima is that Dostoevsky's personal library included the Life of Leonid published in 1878.[91] The religious scholar F. I. Udelov argues that it was here that Dostoevsky found discussion of unproductive monks like Ferapont as well as descriptions of the kind of service to people exemplified by Zosima's activities.[92] He also cites Leonid's more relaxed attitude towards food and medicines as a model for Zosi-

[88] Dmitry F. Grigorieff, "Dostoevsky's Elder Zosima," 26.

[89] Cited in Pletnev, "Serdtsem mudrye," 87.

[90] On Leonid Nagolkin, see Bolshakoff, 177–78; Smolitsch, *Russisches Mönchtum*, 505–7; Metropolit Seraphim, *Die Ostkirche*, 298–302.

[91] *Zhizneopisanie Optinskogo startsa ieromonakha Leonida* (Moscow, 1876). See L. Grossman, *Seminarii po Dostoevskomu* (Leningrad, 1923), 43. A contemporary description of Leonid is also provided by Parfenii, *Skazanie o stranstvii*, 1: 280–83.

[92] F. I. Udelov, "Dostoevskii i Optina Pustyn'," *Vestnik russkogo studencheskogo khristianskogo dvizheniia* 99 (1971): 8–9.

ma's own tolerance.[93] More importantly, Udelov implies that Zosima's flexible perception of the boundary between the monastery and the world, as witnessed by his advice to Alesha, reflects Leonid's own attitude, although he does admit that there are numerous other possible sources for this idea.[94]

As in the case of Amvrosii, many of the attitudes and experiences associated with Leonid are typical of monks of the kenotic tradition, who are often known for their greater tolerance and frequently encounter opposition from conservative monks of the Josephite tradition. It is interesting to note that Ferapont has in fact been labelled a "degenerate type of Josephite," an apt designation given his narrow-minded obsession with excessive fasts and other ascetic externals.[95] This does not imply that Dostoevsky was not influenced by his reading of the Life of Leonid or, for that matter, by his visit to Optina Pustyn' to see Amvrosii. The point is merely that in considering the impact on Dostoevsky of these holy men, whose images were conventionalized by their followers even during their lifetimes, care must be taken not to attribute too much individuality, and hence too much influence, to any one of them.

In view of Dostoevsky's avowed interest in Tikhon of Zadonsk, it is not surprising to find him also cited as a model for Zosima. Nadejda Gorodetzky in particular has devoted much attention to similarities between the two, which she finds less in the specific details of their lives than in their beliefs and attitudes. Among these, she mentions their shared emphasis on active love, their criticism of the greed of the clergy, their attitude toward children, their comments on judging others, and their perceptions of hell.[96] In short, according to Gorodetzky, the entire tenor of Zosima's Christianity was heavily influenced by Tikhon.[97] Dostoevsky himself would doubtless have agreed to a certain extent with this appraisal. In a letter written in August 1879 to

[93] Udelov, "Dostoevskii i Optina Pustyn'," 9–10.

[94] Udelov, "Dostoevskii i Optina Pustyn'," 10–11. On similarities between Zosima and Leonid, see also Sergei Hackel, "The Religious Dimension: Vision or Evasion? Zosima's Discourse in *The Brothers Karamazov*," in Malcolm Jones and Garth M. Terry, eds., *New Essays on Dostoyevsky* (Cambridge, 1983), 156.

[95] Grigorieff, "Dostoevsky's Elder Zosima," 27.

[96] Gorodetzky, *Saint Tikhon*, 227.

[97] Komarowitsch also comments on how fully the spiritual essence of Tikhon is realized in *The Brothers Karamazov*. See *Urgestalt der Brüder Karamasoff*, 102.

the editor Nikolai Liubimov, Dostoevsky commented on the chapter, "About the Holy Scripture in the Life of Father Zosima" ("O sviashchennom pisanii v zhizni ottsa Zosimy") and declared: "This chapter is enraptured and poetic, its prototype is taken from certain sermons of Tikhon of Zadonsk, and the naiveté of its account from the book about the wanderings of Monk Parfenii."[98] The second work mentioned here by Dostoevsky, *A Tale about Wandering and Journeying through Russia, Moldavia, Turkey, and the Holy Land* (*Skazanie o stranstvii i puteshestvii po Rossii, Moldavii, Turtsii i Sviatoi Zemle*, 1855) by Monk Parfenii, was also part of the writer's library.[99] Dostoevsky had apparently discovered Parfenii's book, which contains much material about the author's contact with various holy men, including Leonid Nagolkin, in the 1860s.[100] Traces of Parfenii's adventures are perceptible not only in *The Brothers Karamazov*, but in earlier works as well. Pletnev has done a detailed comparison of the precise episodes in the various novels apparently influenced by Parfenii.[101] For example, the discussion early in *The Brothers Karamazov* of a monk whom not even the patriarch of Constantinople can release from his obligations to his elder seems to have been largely borrowed from a story in Parfenii's book. As regards the tone of the itinerant monk's account, it reflects the unselfconscious and somewhat credulous style characteristic of much hagiographical literature.[102]

It seems reasonable to assume that in creating Zosima Dostoevsky was influenced by his personal knowledge of Amvrosii, as well as by his reading of and about Leonid Nagolkin, Tikhon of Zadonsk, and possibly others, including Zosima (Verkhovskii) of Tobol'sk (1767–1835), the founder of a monastery near Moscow whose biography has many points of resemblance with Zosima's.[103] This does not mean, however,

[98] Letter of 7 August 1879. See Dostoevskii, *Pis'ma*, vol. 4 (Moscow, 1959), 92.

[99] See Grossman, *Seminarii po Dostoevskomu*, 44.

[100] Komarowitsch, *Urgestalt der Brüder Karamasoff*, 64.

[101] R. Pletnev, "Dostoevskij und der Hieromonach Parfenij," *Zeitschrift für slavische Philologie* 14 (1937): 30–46. See also his "La légende chrétienne dans l'oeuvre de Dostoievsky," *Etudes slaves et est-européennes* 6 (1961): 141–50.

[102] On Zosima's hagiographical style of discourse, see Orest Miller, *Russkie pisateli posle Gogolia*, 4th ed., vol. 1 (St. Petersburg, 1886), 284; and M. Bakhtin, *Problemy poetiki Dostoevskogo*, 2d ed. (Moscow, 1963), 334.

[103] M. S. Al'tman, Erik Krag, and R. Pletnev all mention Zosima (Verkhovskii) of Tobol'sk (1767–1835). See Al'tman, "Iz arsenala imen i prototipov literaturnykh geroev Dostoevskogo," in V. G. Bazanov and G. M. Fridlender, eds., *Dostoevskii i ego vremia* (Leningrad, 1971), 215; Krag, *Dostoevsky: The Literary Artist*, 2d ed. (Oslo, 1976), 266–

that Zosima is simply a composite figure based on a handful of eighteenth- and nineteenth-century monks. Just as Dostoevsky was interested in Tikhon of Zadonsk as the representative of a type, so he seems to have viewed the creation of Zosima in this light as well. In the same letter cited above, he says of Zosima:

> He could not express himself in other language or in another spirit than that which I gave him. . . . I took his person and figure from the Old Russian monks and prelates: together with deep humility [they had] limitless naive hopes for the future of Russia, about its moral and even political predestination. Didn't St. Sergii and the metropolitans Petr and Aleksii really always, in this sense, have Russia in mind?[104]

As the Swedish scholar Sven Linnér observes in his study of Zosima, Dostoevsky wanted "to base himself on a tradition."[105] It is possible to define that tradition as the kenotic one initiated by Feodosii of the Kievan Cave Monastery and brought to completion by the elders of Optina Pustyn'. Given this, a productive approach to the figure of Zosima and, one might add, to that of Alesha as well, is to analyze not only their relationship to particular historical monks of the eighteenth and nineteenth centuries, but also their conformity to hagiographical conventions in general and the kenotic world view in particular. In this light, both Zosima and Alesha, while far from typical, have strong ties to the saintly monk of tradition.

Unlike the usual saint's life, Zosima's story is not presented in strict chronological order. Instead, the reader initially meets him near the end of his life, in the famous and scandalous family meeting at the monastery. Despite such an unorthodox introduction to the holy man and the fact that much of his life is later narrated by himself, various stages of Zosima's life reflect hagiographical topoi.

A significant part of a saint's Life is often his childhood, and thus it is in the case of Zosima.[106] His autobiographical reminiscences begin

67; Pletnev, "Serdtsem mudrye," 84–85. Al'tman notes that in 1860 there appeared *Izrecheniia startsa skhimonakha Zosimy i izvlecheniia iz sochinenii ego* (Moscow, 1860), whose title is reminiscent of that of the second chapter of Book Six of *The Brothers Karamazov*.

[104] Dostoevskii, *Pis'ma* 4: 91–92.

[105] Linnér, *Staretz Zosima*, 93.

[106] Cf. V. V. Kuskov, "Motivy drevnerusskoi literatury v romane F. M. Dostoevskogo

with an episode that illustrates the piety of his family background, reference to which is a traditional component of saints' Lives. Zosima's mother exhibits a conventional religiosity throughout, and his brother Markel ultimately emerges as another devout believer. This comes about in an unusual fashion: Markel first wrestles with atheism, then, immediately before his death, becomes an iconic embodiment of joyful Christianity. Markel's change and his new beliefs prefigure the later transformation of Zosima. Like Zosima, Markel reveals a profound sense of humility and responsibility for others that is accompanied by a tremendous joy in life, which expresses itself, among other ways, in the saintly gift of tears. His demeanor before his death is characterized by the radiant peacefulness generally ascribed to dying saints. This is later true of Zosima as well.

Within the life of Zosima, Markel serves as a hagiographical figure. The function he performs for his brother is that of an idealized image of virtue. The depth of Markel's influence on his brother's spiritual development is indicated by Zosima's summary comment: "I was young, a child, but in my heart everything remained indelibly, the feeling was harbored. In due course everything was bound to rise up and respond. Thus indeed it happened" (263).

The impact of his brother's epiphany and death is only one of Zosima's spiritual experiences as a child. He is also profoundly affected by his exposure to the Bible. An enthusiasm for religious literature and enjoyment of reading are often associated with the saints, and in this Zosima is no exception. "To my memories of home I also add my memories of sacred history, which . . . although still a child, I was very curious to know" (264), recalls Zosima, adding that he learned to read from a children's version of the Old and New Testaments. Yet even before he learns how to read, Zosima reacts intensely to the liturgical reading of a particular biblical passage. Such a reaction also constitutes a topos and traditionally serves as a prelude to the saint's decision to pursue a religious life. One thinks of saints like Anthony of Egypt, whose imagination was gripped by Matthew 19:21: "If you wish to be perfect, go and sell what you own and give the money to the poor, and you will have treasure in heaven; then come, follow me."

The biblical passage that impresses Zosima so deeply is the story of

'Brat'ia Karamazovy'," *Vestnik Moskovskogo universiteta*, Series 10 (*Filologiia*), 1971, no. 5: 26.

Job.[107] As with Makar Ivanovich in *The Adolescent*, Zosima's reaction to this story provides insight into his religiosity. Like Makar Ivanovich, Zosima asks how Job could love and be happy with his new children, and answers: "But it is possible, it is possible: through the great mystery of human life old grief gradually passes into quiet tender joy" (265). In considering the story of Job, Zosima focuses on the divine mystery of his experience as well as on Job's ultimate acceptance of his fate. As one critic has commented, when Zosima speaks of Job, "Job's integrity and independence, his intellectual and spiritual energy . . . these are left out."[108] Instead, what moves Zosima to tears whenever he reads this biblical tale is the unquestioning humility that Job's story implicitly lauds, a humility that is the source of human happiness. Unceasing humility is also a hallmark of the two saints whose Lives Zosima mentions to his visitors as especially worth reading aloud to the peasants, Alexis, the Man of God, and Mary of Egypt.

Where Zosima's childhood departs from that of a conventional saint is in the fact that his intense appreciation of Job does not immediately result in a commitment to the religious life. Between the elder's childhood experiences and his decision to become a monk lies the life of a well-to-do young man, including the comparative debauchery of military service. This background is not without precedent. Among the famous nineteenth-century Russian monks who joined the military before entering a monastery were Ignatii Brianchaninov (1807–1867), a fellow student of Dostoevsky's at the Imperial School of Engineers, and Zosima of Tobol'sk. A military past characterizes both the fictional monk Pimen and Sergii in Tolstoy's story, "Father Sergii" ("Otets Sergii," 1890–1898).[109] This kind of background was not uncommon for Russian holy men. A pattern of profligacy followed by radical spiritual transformation is also typical of many saints' lives; the examples of Mary of Egypt, Francis of Assisi, and Augustine of Hippo are some of the most famous.

An encounter with his orderly Afanasii, who does not resist when

[107] On Dostoevsky's own childhood appreciation of Job, see Dmitry Felix Grigorieff, "Dostoevsky and the Russian Orthodox Church" (Ph.D. diss., University of Pennsylvania, 1958 [in Russian]), 7.

[108] Nathan Rosen, "Style and Structure in *The Brothers Karamazov* (The Grand Inquisitor and The Russian Monk)," *Russian Literature Triquarterly* 1 (1971): 357.

[109] Among the possible prototypes for Zosima, Al'tman also proposes Pimen. See Al'tman, "Iz arsenala imen i prototipov," 216.

Zosima (at this point a young officer) savagely beats him, succeeds in jolting Zosima out of his pointless and vicious existence. This spiritual resurrection is connected with Zosima's now long dead brother. Castigating himself for striking Afanasii, Zosima remembers Markel's words to his servants: "My darlings, dear ones, why do you serve me, why do you love me, and am I worth your serving me?" (270). Applying this idea to himself, Zosima also recalls Markel's assertion that everyone is responsible for everyone else and concludes: "in truth perhaps I am more responsible [*vinovnee*] than everyone for everyone, yes and am worse than all people in the world" (270). This observation marks the beginning of the kenotic route taken by Zosima. His new existential perception results initially in his begging forgiveness from Afanasii and from a man whom he had challenged to a duel.

In contrast to a conventional saint's Life, the account of Zosima's life supplies little information about the period between his decision to enter a monastery and the time of the novel, forty years later. The little one learns, however, attests to Zosima's kenotic spirit. In the early years of his monastic career, Zosima travels about Russia with his comrade Father Anfim, collecting alms for their monastery. Such activity itself bespeaks an attitude of humility, for wandering in search of alms is hardly the typical method of advancement within the ecclesiastical hierarchy. When, in the course of his wanderings, Zosima again encounters Afanasii, his behavior towards his former servant reveals how ingrained the habit of humility has become. When Afanasii asks him to pray for his children, Zosima responds: "Is it for me to bless them, . . . I am a simple and humble monk, I will pray to God about them" (287). This is a variant of a familiar topos: the insistence on God's power and denial of one's own.

Zosima's kenotic attitude does not prevent him from suggesting that it is monks who have embraced the way of humility who offer some hope of salvation for Russia. Recognizing that there are many venal monks, he also asserts that there are many who are "humble and meek," from whom may come "once again the salvation of the Russian land" (284). His detailed explanation of his views might serve as a fitting apologia for the kenotic way in any period of Russian history:

> The monastic path is a different matter. Obedience, fasting, and prayer are even laughed at, yet only in them is found the path to a real, true freedom: I cut off from myself superfluous and unnec-

> essary needs, I humble and castigate my vain and proud will with obedience, and thus I attain, with God's help, freedom of the spirit, and with it spiritual happiness! . . . from among us in the old days came popular leaders, why can't they now as well? The same humble and meek fasters and monks who have taken the vow of silence will rise up and set out for the great cause (285).[110]

In a sense, Zosima himself is one of these meek and humble monks who attempt to lead Russia to her salvation. In terms of his popularity, his methods of dealing with people, and his tremendous insight, his life as a renowned elder conforms to a centuries-old pattern. The observation has been made that his meeting with peasant women resembles a series of episodes from the Lives of the saints.[111] Indeed, his advice to the women is characterized by that tenderness devoid of condescension often ascribed to holy men. Moreover, Zosima will take no credit for his spiritual achievements. When a visiting monk asks him how he dares to do such things, having in mind specifically the purported healing of young Lisa Khokhlakova, the elder responds: "if there has been something, it is by no one's power except God's will. Everything is from God" (51). His statement again expresses the topos, mentioned above, of insistence on God's power and denigration of one's own.

In his remarkable insight into the psychology of the Karamazov family, Zosima evokes Tikhon's acute understanding of Stavrogin's complex motives. This ability to understand even the most tortured souls is one of the hallmarks of great kenotics. Zosima, like Tikhon, is also sometimes perceived as a kind of holy fool, although in his case the grounds for this perception are even more limited.[112] The reactions of his peers when he decides to become a monk are symptomatic; their attitude is indulgent, good-humored, but tinged with ridicule: they see his behavior as odd. Much later in his life, his bowing down to Dmitrii evokes this scornful observation from the seminarist Mikhail Rakitin: "With holy fools it's always like that: they cross themselves at

[110] In his study of Dostoevsky's youth, Joseph Frank asserts that "it was certainly of St. Sergey that Dostoevsky was thinking" when Zosima makes these comments. See Joseph Frank, *Dostoevsky: The Seeds of Revolt, 1821–1849* (Princeton, N.J., 1976), 47.

[111] Linnér, *Staretz Zosima*, 29.

[112] Linnér sees a major difference between Zosima and Tikhon in the comparative weakness that characterizes the latter (*Staretz Zosima*, 79–80). In terms of their hagiographical quality, this difference is of less significance than the similiarities between the two.

the tavern and throw stones at the temple. Like your elder: [he drives] away a just man with a stick, and [makes] a bow at the feet of a murderer" (73). Rakitin's comment demonstrates once again the fluid border between holy foolishness and saintly humility. Zosima later explains to Alesha that he bowed down to Dmitrii's "great future suffering" (258), thus manifesting a familiar combination of perception, humility, and compassion.

At the end of his life Zosima merges completely with the hagiographical tradition. As with his brother Markel, Zosima's peaceful and joyful demeanor immediately before his death calls to mind numerous saints, from the Venerable Bede (673–735), who died just after dictating the final sentence of a translation, to Serafim of Sarov, who was found praying before an icon; Zosima dies while praying and kissing the ground. Given his sanctity and the general expectation of miracles after his death, the "odor of corruption" that instead manifests itself comes as a rude shock. Yet even this scandalous development has links with hagiographical literature; Dostoevsky asserted that he had been influenced in the composition of this episode by a similar story told by Parfenii.[113]

Zosima is not a conventional saint, and his portrait is not conventionally drawn. Yet the topoi exploited in his portrayal and many of the attitudes he embraces link him to a major trend in Russian monasticism. Rather than a mere composite of details borrowed from a few recent historical monks, he represents a modern realization of the kenotic type. While idiosyncratic, his portrait may easily be added to those of Feodosii, Sergii, and their successors.

As another example of the type of the monastic saint, Alesha has not attracted as much attention as either Tikhon or Zosima. This may be partially because Alesha appears in *The Brothers Karamazov* only as a very young man, partially because, in comparison with traditional monastic behavior, his actions are even more unorthodox than those of Dostoevsky's elders. Moreover, he is not yet actually a monk and at the end of the novel it seems unlikely that he will ever become one.[114] Yet certain details tie the character of Alesha firmly to the hagiographical tradition.

[113] Letter to N. A. Liubimov of 16 September 1849. See Dostoevsky, *Pis'ma* 4: 117.

[114] The suggestion that Dostoevsky intended to make Alesha a revolutionary is based on comments made by Aleksei Suvorin in a diary entry of 1887. See *Dnevnik A. S. Suvorina*, ed. Mikh. Krichevskii (Moscow, 1923), 16. In her discussion of Alesha, V. E.

The foreword to *The Brothers Karamazov* opens with the words: "Beginning the life story [*zhizneopisanie*] of my hero, Aleksei Fedorovich Karamazov, I find myself in some perplexity" (5). It has been noted that the use of the term *zhizneopisanie* here is evocative of a hagiographical composition.[115] On one level *The Brothers Karamazov* may be read as an account of the life of Alesha, something obscured to some extent by the fact that Dostoevsky died before producing a sequel. More important in the present context is that the novel begins, as do many saints' Lives, with biographical sketches of the Karamazovs that give the most detailed attention to Alesha.

The description of Alesha's childhood exhibits many of the conventional elements typically associated with saints.[116] Thus, while Alesha loves people and they respond affectionately to him, he displays at the same time the slight reserve so typical of future saints:

> In childhood and youth he was not very effusive and not even very talkative, but not from distrust, shyness, or gloomy unsociability, but even quite the contrary, from something else, from some sort of seemingly inner care, strictly personal, that did not concern others, but was so important for him that because of it he would seem to forget others (18).

These solitary inclinations manifest themselves even in school, where Alesha prefers to read in a corner rather than play with his classmates, a familiar topos in the Lives of saints. As a boy, Alesha also resembles the saints in his "wild, ecstatic modesty and chastity" (19), which are reflected in his complete intolerance for smutty language and discussions, an intolerance supposedly shared, for example, by Joseph of Volokolamsk.[117] Alesha is also characterized by the indifference to material things especially common among kenotic saints:

Vetlovskaia expresses convincing criticisms of this idea. See V. E. Vetlovskaia, *Poetika romana "Brat'ia Karamazovy"* (Leningrad, 1977), 191.

[115] Vetlovskaia, *Poetika romana "Brat'ia Karamazovy*," 162–63. See also V. E. Vetlovskaia, "Literaturnye i fol'klornye istochniki 'Brat'ev Karamazovykh' (Zhitie Alekseia cheloveka bozhiia i dukhovnyi stikh o nem)," in V. Ia. Kirpotin, ed., *Dostoevskii i russkie pisateli* (Moscow, 1971), 326.

[116] Many of the topoi connected with Alesha's childhood and youth have also been discussed by Vetlovskaia in *Poetika*, 164–65, and "Istochniki," 327–28; and by Jostein Børtnes in "To Dostoevskijstudier," *Edda* 68 (1968): 8–11, and "The Function of Hagiography in Dostoevskij's Novels," *Scando-Slavica* 24 (1978): 28–29. The subject is also treated in Dostoevskii, *Pss* 15: 474–76.

[117] Cf. Fedotov, *Russian Religious Mind*, 2: 303.

> Aleksei was without fail one of those youths like the holy fools, who even if he suddenly wound up with an entire capital, would not hesitate to give it up, even at the first request, either for a good cause or perhaps even simply to a clever old fox, if he asked him. And generally speaking, he didn't seem to know the value of money at all (20).

This is the first of several times in the novel that Alesha is implicitly or explicitly considered a holy fool. This reaction is apparently evoked by his complete lack of self-serving pride, by his innate humility. During his school days this attitude is expressed in a characteristic unwillingness to draw attention to himself: "he never wanted to show off among his peers" (19). Alesha is even sometimes referred to as an angel by those around him, most notably by his father and brother Dmitrii, who tells him directly: "You are an angel on earth" (97). This calls to mind the formula borrowed from the Life of Sabas of Palestine and dear to Russian hagiography from the Life of Feodosii on, "an earthly angel and a heavenly man."[118]

Even his appearance may link Alesha to the saints. Scholars have commented upon the iconlike quality of the narrator's description of his face.[119] The narrator's eagerness to assure the reader that instead of being sickly and pale, Alesha is healthy and red-cheeked is in keeping with the Russian hagiographical tradition, which tends to portray its saints as physically strong, rather than as emaciated and weak.[120] For example, it was said of Sergii of Radonezh that "he was young and strong of body . . . [he] could do the work of two men."[121]

Like his beloved mentor Zosima, Alesha carries into adult life the memory of an intense childhood spiritual experience. His experience, connected with his long deceased mother, has assumed the quality of a vision. He vividly recalls his mother seizing him during a fit of hysteria and thrusting him towards the image of the Mother of God before which she is praying, "as if under the protection of the Mother of God" (18). Symbolically, this episode functions as a commitment of Alesha to the religious life. Analogous episodes may occur in the Lives of saints said to be the offspring of previously barren women who prayed for

[118] Cf. Fedotov, *Russian Religious Mind*, 1: 113.

[119] Børtnes, "Function of Hagiography," 28–29; and A. L. Wolynski, *Das Reich der Karamasoff*, trans. Alexander Eliasberg (Munich, 1920), 165.

[120] Fedotov, *Russian Religious Mind*, 2: 206.

[121] Cited in Fedotov, *Russian Religious Mind*, 2: 206.

divine aid in conceiving. In such instances, the child that is born is expected, either implicitly or explicitly, to live a life dedicated to God; this is suggested, for example, in the Lives of John the Baptist, the Virgin Mary, and Euthymius the Great (377–473). It has been suggested that this motif was adapted by Dostoevsky specifically from the Life of Alexis, the Man of God, with whom Alesha has strong connections.[122]

Unlike Zosima, Alesha follows an unswerving path of virtue that, from the point of view of hagiography, logically culminates in his desire to enter a monastery. As with Anthony of Egypt, his decision is based on the literal interpretation of Matthew 19:21. His actual entrance into the monastery is connected with another topos, that of the parent who does not wish his child to become a monk; this was supposedly true of many Russian monks, including Feodosii and Paisii Velichkovskii. When Alesha first asks his father's permission, Fedor willingly grants it. After his abortive visit to Zosima, however, Fedor announces his decision to take his son away from the monastery because of his purported suspicions of the monks. He reiterates this intention several times and tells Alesha to collect his pillow and mattress and come home. What is apparent here, as elsewhere in the neo-hagiography of Dostoevsky, is an unconventional realization of a typical component of saints' Lives. Fedor is far from the usual parent of hagiography, and his demand stems more than anything else from his inclination to buffoonery, yet nonetheless his instructions to Alesha serve as another link between the young man and the traditional monastic saint.

The reluctance of parents to see their son become a monk found expression in other Russian literary works of the period. A poem written just a few years after *The Brothers Karamazov* by a contemporary of Dostoevsky, Aleksei Apukhtin (1840–1893), contains a more conventional realization of this topos. In this poem, "A Year in a Monastery" ("God v monastyre," 1883), the narrator describes an incident in which the parents of the young monk Kirill attempt to convince him to return home and wait until their deaths to become a monk. Apukhtin had apparently witnessed such an incident at a monastery on the island of Valaam.[123] The sincerity of the tearful pleas of Kirill's parents is in marked contrast to Fedor Karamazov's clownishness.

[122] Vetlovskaia, *Poetika*, 170, and "Istochniki," 332.

[123] See A. N. Apukhtin, *Stikhotvoreniia* (Leningrad, 1961), 352.

Unlike Tikhon and Zosima, Alesha cannot be neatly linked to particular eighteenth- and nineteenth-century Russian monks. Yet he is associated with a specific saint, one of the two singled out by Zosima and one of the most popular saints among nineteenth-century Russians: Alexis, the Man of God, whose Life was discussed in the preceding chapter. Like Tikhon in *The Possessed*, Alesha is the namesake of the holy man on whom he is to a certain extent modelled.

Alexis, the Man of God, is mentioned several times in *The Brothers Karamazov*. Early in the novel Zosima speaks to a peasant woman who has lost her young son, also named Aleksei. Zosima comments on the name and asks the woman if her son was named after Alexis. When she replies in the affirmative, Zosima exclaims enthusiastically: "What a saint" (47). Thus, early on, an implicit association based on their shared name is made between Alesha and St. Alexis. This association is then made explicit, first by Rakitin, who jeeringly calls him "Aleshen'ka, you little man of God" (321). Much later Dmitrii tells Alesha: "I am lost, Aleksei, I am, you man of God!" (15: 27).[124]

In the details of his life Alesha little resembles the saint who stole away from his home on his wedding night, lived as a beggar for many years, and finally returned incognito to the home of his parents, disclosing his identity only at his death. Symbolically and philosophically, however, the two have much in common. Alexis, the Man of God, personifies the realization of virtue in the world. Instead of pursuing his ascetic path in a traditional monastic context, he remains in a secular environment, even to the extreme of living among his family. Yet he succeeds in achieving sanctity. By suggesting a comparison between Alesha and this saint, Dostoevsky provides a religious model for the assertion that his hero belongs in the world. Moreover, Valentina Vetlovskaia, a Soviet scholar who has devoted much attention to points of similarity in the lives of Alexis and Alesha, notes that the latter is also implicitly sent back to his family by divine instruction.[125] In voluntarily assuming the lowly role of beggar for his entire life, Alexis epitomizes kenotic humility. Alesha is his spiritual brother in this sense as well. As mentioned above, from his childhood on Alesha is free of vanity, and his innate humility early takes the form of a refusal to judge

[124] Dostoevskii, *Pss* 15.

[125] Vetlovskaia, *Poetika*, 171. For her complete discussion of the Life of Alexis, see 168–83. See also her earlier article on the subject, "Istochniki."

others.[126] It is this trait that enables him to become the confidant of his father and brothers.

The scandal surrounding the aftermath of Zosima's death affects Alesha especially strongly. Yet his crisis of faith culminates in his vision of Zosima at the biblical feast in Cana of Galilee. In hagiographical terms, the events of these few days are a test that results in Alesha's renewed and strengthened commitment to the path outlined by Zosima, God's messenger. Significantly, his spiritual awakening is couched explicitly in terms suggestive of the Resurrection: "Three days later he left the monastery, which was in accordance with the word of his deceased elder, who had ordered him to abide in the world" (328).

That Alesha may be expected to reveal in the world the insight and prescience characteristic of monastic saints is made clear in his encounters with his brother Ivan. Here Alesha acts, as saints often claim they do, as the inspired instrument of God. When he assures Ivan that he is not his father's murderer, the narrator comments that he speaks "as though outside of himself, as though not by his own will, obeying some sort of irresistible command" (40).[127] Twice Alesha asserts that he has been sent by God to tell Ivan this. Ivan's reaction confirms the hagiographical nuances of his brother's behavior, for he tells Alesha he dislikes prophets, epileptics, and messengers of God. Yet he is sufficiently undone by Alesha's insight to accuse him of having been there when "he" came, "he" meaning Ivan's devil. This calls to mind Stavrogin's reaction of combined anger and amazement at Tikhon's insight. Clearly Alesha has the potential for becoming as charismatic a figure as Zosima, an agent of humility, perception, and love. As a transmuted saintly kenotic monk, he differs from his mentor primarily in his youth. *The Brothers Karamazov* ends with a scene in which he succeeds in inspiring a group of schoolboys to an affirmation of love and eternal life. Presumably Alesha's future would have held more examples of his emulation of those meek and humble monks whom Zosima claims to be the source of Russia's salvation.

From Myshkin to Alesha, many of Dostoevsky's characters have features borrowed from holy fools and/or saintly monks. The majority of these characters share a profoundly kenotic approach to existence. Often

[126] Cf. Guardini, "Dostoevsky's Idiot," 362; and Gorodetzky, *The Humiliated Christ*, 65.

[127] Dostoevskii, *Pss* 15.

regarded as slightly or extremely eccentric by those around them, they are totally lacking in any vanity or self-serving tendencies. Their pervasive humility is expressed in a gentle compassion for and refusal to condemn others. The spiritual reward such characters apparently receive for their selflessness is their remarkable insight into the complex motives behind human behavior.

There are many similarities between Dostoevsky's characters and the types of the holy fool and the kenotic monk. Differences from tradition arise, however, in the depiction of the effect Dostoevsky's saintly characters have on those around them. Within Dostoevsky's depiction of contemporary life, those characters most strongly modelled on kenotic monks appear to exemplify the most viable form of spirituality. Characters like Myshkin, or even to a certain extent Tikhon, suffer from a peculiar spiritual impotence; their goodness is admirable, but largely unproductive. It is instead characters of the type of Zosima and Alesha who seem most capable of positive, constructive action, who indeed seem to contain the potential for acting as agents of Russia's salvation.

Later Russian writers did not always perceive kenotic monks as possessing such capabilities. A sharp contrast to Dostoevsky's portrayal of contemporary saintly monks is provided by Kallinikov in *Women and Monks*. Against a general background of vice and corruption, the figure of the elder Akaky stands out as a shining exception. Nothing is known about Akaky's past or entrance into the monastery by those still alive at the time the novel opens, and all the narrator contributes is the information that the elder sought to forget a wife who deserted him. Now an old man, Akaky adheres precisely, if somewhat unexcitingly, to the ideal of the kenotic monk. Characteristically, he is endowed with a great sense of humility and of his own unworthiness. This becomes especially apparent when he is coerced into becoming a *skhimnik*, the highest and most demanding degree of monastic life. Akaky tries to avoid this honor, saying: "To be ordained a skhimnik is bound up with a hard and mighty vow. And even now when I am an old man I am not worthy to take this vow upon me, for I am a sinful creature and weak" (613).[128]

Akaky lives in a forest hut near where the cell of the recluse Simeon,

[128] Joseph Kallinikov, *Women and Monks*, trans. Patrick Kirwan (New York, 1930). First (incomplete) Russian edition published under the title *The Sacred Relics* (*Moshchi*). First complete authorized edition published under the title *Frauen und Mönche* (Leipzig, 1928).

the founder of the monastery, formerly stood. He has many visitors, particularly peasants, whose company, like Tikhon of Zadonsk, he especially welcomes. The peasants love him because of his power of healing spiritual ills, which stems from his forgiving nature: "He never condemned a sinner nor those who had acted in conscienceless ways; he had sympathy with all those who had strayed" (358). In addition to his all-embracing spirit of forgiveness, Akaky also shares with the great Russian monks the gift of insight into both the striving and the fallen. The narrator asserts that such a sensibility is essential for an elder and says that Akaky is able to diagnose the suffering of his visitors "more surely than any physician" (358). Throughout the novel many examples are given of his power, one of which involves the student Boris Smolyaninov, who decides to becomes a novice in sorrow over the death of his fiancée and his subsequent sexual betrayal of her. Akaky understands immediately that she, not God, is the reason that Boris wants to become a monk, and he encourages the young man to remain in the world. "It was as though the old man's kindly eyes pierced his soul and saw everything" (273), observes the narrator.

In spite of his saintly character, however, Akaky is neither respected nor loved within the monastic community. The only merit most of the other monks see in him is his usefulness in attracting visitors. Regarding his obvious holiness, they are scornful and envious. When the elder gradually trains a stork to follow him and eat from his hand, the monks are so vicious in their jealousy that, like the monks who killed the tame bear of St. Florentius of Foligno (d. 540), they finally destroy the bird. Unlike Zosima, Akaky is truly a candle shining under a bushel.

Kenotic Characters in the Stories of Leskov and Uspenskii

Many of Dostoevsky's characters provide clearcut examples of the use of hagiographical topoi and traditional features of saintly personality in the creation of new hagiography. Several other nineteenth-century writers made similar, albeit less fully developed, use of such techniques. Adaptation of hagiographical techniques is by no means limited to writers as intensely (if idiosyncratically) Orthodox as Dostoevsky. In fact, in stories by writers like Nikolai Leskov and Gleb Uspenskii, the tensions between traditional and liberal, or even radical, thinking make their use of hagiography most interesting.

As noted in the previous discussion of hagiographical adaptation, Leskov prided himself on being well versed in Russian and Byzantine hagiography. At the same time, his attitude toward such works was curiously ambivalent. He wrote in regard to saints' Lives: "the characters of the persons about whom these hagiographical narratives were composed constitute . . . the 'spiritual beauty' of our people. And art must and is even obligated to preserve insofar as it is possible all the features of this national 'beauty'."[129] Elsewhere he defined saints' Lives as "sacred sagas, which the memory of the people reverently preserves and honors."[130] Yet his approval was not unqualified. While admiring their spiritual content, Leskov was critical of formalization in hagiographical compositions. He complained about appraisals of prominent ecclesiastical figures thus:

> Their necrologies . . . constitute either a dry and sorry paraphrase of their official service records, or—what is even worse—provide a sorry collection of general phrases, in which one may perhaps notice much zeal by the panegyrists, but nevertheless also the complete absence of the power of observation and understanding of what in the life of a man, which is woven of everyday trifles, can represent his mind, character, view, and way of thinking,—in a word, that can show a man from his most interesting, internal spiritual side, in simple everyday manifestations.[131]

While Leskov is concerned here with more contemporary accounts, his objection to the tendency towards abstraction might apply equally well to medieval hagiography. Certainly the intention of most hagiographers was to tailor their subjects' lives to an archetypal pattern. With his far different attitude, Leskov returns time and again to the importance of trifles, of those revealing little details he believes give important insights into personality.[132] In this context, the title, "The Little Things in a Bishop's Life" ("Melochi arkhiereiskoi zhizni," 1878–1879), is indicative. In this work, as well as in "Episcopal Justice" ("Vladychnyi sud," 1877), Leskov tries to fulfill the aim of providing

[129] "Zhitiia kak literaturnyi istochnik," *Novoe vremia*, 17 August 1882.

[130] N. S. Leskov, *Ss*, 11 vols. (Moscow, 1956–1958), 6: 465.

[131] Leskov, *Ss* 6: 129.

[132] See, for example, Leskov, *Ss* 6: 534–35, 536, 502.

revelation through detail. Yet at the same time, his good bishops retain traditional features.

Both "Episcopal Justice" and "The Little Things in a Bishop's Life" revolve around actual historical figures. A major character in each is Metropolitan Filaret (Amfiteatrov) of Kiev (1779–1857), whom Georges Florovsky describes as "a man of warm piety, great tenderness, and true spiritual life, a just and saintly man."[133] "Episcopal Justice" touches upon one of the more lamentable chapters of Russian history under Nicholas I, the forcible conscription of young Jewish boys into the army, in which Leskov himself, as an army recruiting clerk in the 1850s, had indirectly participated. Yet the story has an atypically happy outcome, for it concerns the intercession of Filaret on behalf of a particular boy. The story is thus intended less as social criticism than as a demonstration of the prelate's saintliness. Leskov describes the rescue of the Jewish boy as a miracle, commenting that many in Kiev consider Filaret a meek "earthly angel" (97). As has been noted, this formula is borrowed directly from the hagiographical tradition.[134]

In keeping with his belief that trifles serve as a key to the larger personality, Leskov provides many informal glimpses into Filaret's life. The portrait that emerges has much in common with the kenotic monastic saints of earlier centuries. Filaret's humility manifests itself most noticeably in his characteristic refusal to judge other religions in a narrow-minded and dogmatic fashion. On one occasion he shows himself willing to bless a Protestant. This generosity has positive repercussions: this young woman later becomes a devout member of the Orthodox Church. Similarly, when the police refuse to permit a woman to be buried in consecrated ground because her doctor claims that she committed suicide in full control of her faculties, Filaret questions the infallibility of the doctor, shows greater compassion, and orders that she be buried where her relations wish. This spiritual tolerance is one of the distinguishing characteristics of the kenotic saints.

Filaret also exhibits a resemblance to the stereotype of the holy fool. The narrator of "Episcopal Justice" observes that when he first met the metropolitan, the latter seemed to him both very good and somewhat coarse. This reaction derives to some extent from Filaret's habit of

[133] Florovskii, *Puti russkoi bogosloviia*, 192.

[134] The text of "Episcopal Justice" ("Vladychnyi sud") is found in Leskov, *Ss* 6: 88–145.

expressing his insight into shallow personalities in a less than tactful fashion. When a silly elderly woman who is attempting to engage him in social chit-chat asks whether he finds Kiev boring after Petersburg, he replies: "What's that? . . . what's Petersburg to me?," adding quite audibly, "stupid [woman],—truly stupid" (132). Similarly, when some society ladies encounter Filaret in his summer retreat, he responds to their demands for some significant statement with the command: "What do you want, little fools? Ekh, you're stupid, stupid—be off to your own place" (135). This eccentric behavior, which Leskov adored, links Filaret to the broader Russian spiritual tradition.

Filaret Amfiteatrov also appears in "The Little Things in a Bishop's Life," Leskov's rambling catalogue of good and bad bishops.[135] He prefaces his discussion of Filaret with a short discourse on the people's love of simplicity in its holy men:

> Popular memory preserves the names of "simple and very simple" prelates and not of the magnificent and important. In general our people never consider the "unsimple" [*neprostykh*] either righteous or God-pleasing. The Russian people like to look at splendor, but they respect simplicity (448).[136]

Earlier in the work, Leskov characterizes such simplicity as a specifically Russian trait, contrasting it with "cultivated . . . Byzantine etiquette" (439). While he avoids precise definition of this desirable quality, he clearly suggests a simplicity that stems from humility and shuns self-aggrandisement. Thus he specifically mentions the veneration of Tikhon of Zadonsk as an example of popular approbation of this type of simplicity.

According to Leskov, a winning simplicity was characteristic of Filaret as well. Describing the metropolitan as "childishly pure and simple" (457), the narrator adds that it would be impossible to find anyone so "submissive to a meek love of goodness, not in theory, not because of the ethics of his education . . . he submitted to this demand organically in the strongest way" (457–458). This description could easily be applied to many kenotic saints.

[135] It is interesting to note that in early Soviet editions the chapters on good bishops were omitted. See Hugh McLean, *Nikolai Leskov: The Man and His Art* (Cambridge, Mass., 1977), 349.

[136] The text of "The Little Things in a Bishop's Life" ("Melochi arkhiereiskoi zhizni") is found in Leskov, *Ss* 6: 398–538.

The picture of Filaret provided in "Episcopal Justice" and "The Little Things in a Bishop's Life" is far from thorough. More comprehensive portrayals of monks and other churchmen are found in Leskov's purely fictional stories, in which sanctity often manifests itself in a similar simplicity bordering on simplemindedness. The portrait of the hermit Pamva in "The Sealed Angel" ("Zapechatlennyi angel," 1873), Leskov's adventure tale about a group of Old Believers who seek to rescue a beloved icon from Orthodox captivity, is especially significant. The narrator of the story, a former Old Believer, describes how he and his young companion Levontii searched for a painter to make a copy of their treasured ancient icon. In the course of their journeying, Levontii becomes curious to set eyes on Pamva, though the latter is Orthodox, because he has heard that the monk is an "anchorite completely without envy and without anger" (357).[137] The fulfillment of his wish comes about in an unexpected fashion, when Levontii is critically ill.

Pamva's sudden apparition in the forest before the narrator Mark and the sick Levontii has the aura of a miracle; indeed, Mark describes what happens as a "marvel" (361). Pamva, whose appearance has been compared to iconic representations of Serafim of Sarov, approaches carrying a load of wood.[138] When he catches sight of the sick youth lying on the ground, he orders him to stand and carry the wood for him. Levontii obeys as if in a trance. Mark follows them in hot pursuit and asks where Pamva is leading them, to which the monk enigmatically responds: "I am not leading anyone anywhere, the Lord leads everyone" (361). This statement reflects the refusal to assume personal responsibility for positive actions so characteristic of the kenotic monk.

When the three reach Pamva's quarters, which he shares with the monk Miron, the elder has another opportunity to display his humility. Miron reacts to Pamva's appearance by pushing him so hard that he almost falls. Yet Pamva does not lose his temper, and instead says: "May God save you, my brother, for your service" (361). The Lives of the kenotic saints are filled with many such instances of gratitude where anger would be expected. When Mark later asks the elder who it is who threatens him so coarsely, Pamva responds: "It's my lay brother Miron . . . a good man, he looks after me" (363). Such a generous interpre-

[137] The text of "The Sealed Angel" ("Zapechatlennyi angel") is found in Leskov, *Ss* 4: 320–84.

[138] Nadejda Gorodetzky, *The Humiliated Christ in Modern Russian Thought*, 73.

tation of Miron's rudeness convinces Mark that they are indeed dealing with Pamva, the anchorite without envy or anger.

Pamva also proves to have the religious tolerance typical of kenotics and especially characteristic of Leskov's saints. When Mark asks him if he and Levontii may remain overnight, he feels compelled to mention that they are Old Believers, to which Pamva responds: "All are limbs of the one body of Christ. He will gather everyone together" (362). Mark is not impressed by this thinking, however. In fact, when shortly afterwards he decides the old man must be Pamva, he is anxious to leave as quickly as possible before Levontii realizes they are in the company of the famed anchorite and is corrupted.

But Levontii is already firmly under Pamva's spiritual sway. During the night Mark seems to see the two of them engaged in mysterious wordless communication. Gazing at the elder in the morning, even such a sceptic concerning Orthodoxy is forced to admit that he makes a profound spiritual impression: "Ah, how good he is! How spiritual! As if it were an angel sitting before me and weaving bast sandals" (363). In the course of the ensuing enigmatic conversation between the two, Pamva makes reference to Mark's humility, but Mark insists that it is Pamva who is humble, not he. The elder disagrees, saying: "Ah, no, brother, I am not humble. I am a great insolent fellow, I desire a part in the heavenly kingdom for myself" (364). Bursting into tears, he continues: "Lord, do not be angry with me for this fickleness [*volevrashchnost'*]: send me to the nethermost regions of hell and order the demons to torment me, as I am deserving of that" (364). Ironically, this supremely kenotic display of self-abnegation makes Mark doubt the identity of the elder: Mark concludes that such self-castigation can only result from mental derangement. At the same time, however, the bewildered Old Believer does recognize the indomitability and fearlessness of Pamva's attitude. He is also astute enough to perceive that love is the motivating force behind the elder's behavior, and decides: "If there are only two such persons in the [Orthodox] church, then we are lost, for this one is entirely inspired by love" (365).

The events surrounding the death of Levontii frighten Mark and drive him to accuse Pamva of killing the youth. Immediately before his death, Levontii enters, bows before the elder, tells him he has accomplished everything, and asks for his blessing, whereupon the old man answers: "Peace to you: take your rest" (364). When Mark looks for Levontii a short time later, he is dead. With its suggestion of a miraculously programmed death, this episode is reminiscent of stories from the Kiev Cave Paterikon, those about the sexton Marko, for example; in one of these stories the gravedigger convinces a dying monk to postpone his death until he has finished preparing his grave.

At the very last Mark cannot control his instinctive recognition of Pamva's sanctity and bows to the ground as the elder walks away from him. When he raises his head, Pamva has mysteriously disappeared. His departure from "The Sealed Angel" is thus as enigmatic as his appearance.

Pamva's milieu, the isolated anchoretic existence amidst the peaceful forest, evokes a romanticized medieval monasticism. In a story written not long afterwards, "At the Edge of the World" ("Na kraiu sveta," 1875), which concerns missionary work among Siberian tribesmen, Leskov portrays a wilder, more exotic world. Yet the religious values that inspire the saintly hero of the story resemble those practiced by Filaret and Pamva. Like them, the monk Kiriak exhibits a great religious tolerance that derives from an unwillingness to judge and harry others. Having seen how the process of conversion may be corrupted by the overzealousness of missionaries and the ignorance of converts, Kiriak refuses to proselytize.

The bishop who tells the story of Kiriak is impressed by the simplicity of his faith.[139] The bishop reiterates Leskov's opposition between Russian Christianity and "magnificent Byzantinism" (465).[140] His appreciation of this aspect of Kiriak's personality does not, however, entail an understanding of the monk's refusal to engage in conversion work. This he understands only after a harrowing adventure in the snowy wilderness, where events convince him that Kiriak is right in believing that a superficial Christianity may be worse than the lack of Christianity. This episode also provides an opportunity for Kiriak to display his profound spiritual insight. When he and the bishop set out, Kiriak assigns a pagan driver to the bishop, a Christian to himself. While the pagan remains faithful to the end, the Christian steals all their ecclesiastical property and abandons Kiriak. Lengthy exposure to the winter cold causes the old monk's death. Characteristically, Kiriak

[139] "At the Edge of the World" is based on an actual episode in the missionary activity of the bishop of Irkutsk and later Iaroslavl', Nil (Isakovich) (1799–1874). See Leskov, *Ss* 5: 618.

[140] The text of "At the Edge of the World" ("Na kraiu sveta") is found in Leskov, *Ss* 5: 451–517.

wishes no harm to come to the driver and instead desires that he be forgiven.

As Kiriak lies dying, he prays for God's blessing on all, Christian and pagan alike. The bishop is again impressed by the saintly simplicity of his faith, which he now better understands. After his death Kiriak achieves in a meaningful fashion what he had been unwilling while alive to perform in a hasty and meaningless way, for many of the Siberians, impressed by Kiriak's goodness, decide to convert to his God. In this way Leskov, who never likes to see virtue go unrewarded, shows that a kenotic approach to missionary activity may ultimately be the most successful.

Leskov's gallery of hagiographically-influenced characters also includes some non-ecclesiastical figures. A transitional type appears in "The Enchanted Wanderer" ("Ocharovannyi strannik," 1873), which traces the history of a peasant and one-time soldier who eventually becomes a lay brother in a Ladoga monastery. Ivan Sever'ianych, or Father Izmail, believes that he has been destined since birth to enter a monastery. Like many saints, he was, to borrow his terminology, a "prayed-for son" (396), produced after many years of infertility.[141] When he is eleven years old, the wanderer accidentally kills an old monk. In a dream the deceased informs him that he is also a "promised son" (399), that his mother promised he would dedicate his life to God. Ivan regards all of his subsequent adventures as a futile attempt to escape his true destiny.

Ivan does not conform to the traditional image of a monastic saint, nor is he in any conventional sense saintly. He is rather a picaresque hero with strong legendary overtones; this is symbolically underscored by the narrator's observation that his physique and personality are reminiscent of the epic hero Ilya Muromets as portrayed by the artist Vasilii Vereshchagin and the writer Aleksei K. Tolstoi.[142] Yet his spirituality is not devoid of a basic humility. When he comes upon a slain missionary who had earlier refused to help him escape from Tartar captivity, Ivan asks his forgiveness for having blamed him for his refusal and buries him with appropriate ritual. Later he tells his listeners that

[141] The text of "The Enchanted Wanderer" ("Ocharovannyi strannik") is found in Leskov, *Ss* 4: 385–513.

[142] The works referred to here are Vereshchagin's painting "Ilya Muromets at the Feast of Prince Vladimir" (1871) and Tolstoy's "Ilya Muromets" (1871). See Leskov, *Ss* 4: 554.

he does not consider himself worthy to take monastic vows and is content to remain a lay brother.

As a lay brother, Ivan claims he is tormented by devils. The naiveté of his stories about the imps who persecute him is reminiscent of stories found in various paterika. His experiences with the purported devils finally drive the monastic authorities to seclude him in an empty cellar. There Ivan ponders the lamentable state of his soul. He attempts to amend his nature with a program of prayer and reading. His reading material includes newspapers and, significantly, the Life of Tikhon of Zadonsk. These activities culminate in his acquiring the gift of tears and beginning to make prophecies regarding war. Although Leskov's portrayal does not suggest complete confidence in the validity of these developments, as motifs they conform to tradition. The narrator's ambiguous conclusion reflects this ambivalence: "he confessed the tales of his past with all the frankness of his simple soul, and his prophecies remain for the time being in the hands of the one who hides his destinies from the clever and the wise and only sometimes discloses them to babes" (513).

In spite of its occasional use of hagiographical motifs, "The Enchanted Wanderer" is much more an adventure story than a portrayal of sanctity. Yet Leskov did later include it in his cycle, "Righteous Men" ("Pravedniki").[143] The protagonists of some of these stories are more thoroughly saintly and, in turn, more hagiographically influenced than Ivan. The heroes of "The Monognome" ("Odnodum," 1879) and "Deathless Golovan" ("Nesmertel'nyi Golovan," 1880) are particularly interesting.

Aleksandr Ryzhov and Golovan, the heroes of "The Monognome" and "Deathless Golovan," do not operate in a formal religious context at all, but rather manifest their virtue in the secular sphere. Ryzhov works as a rural postman and later as a village policeman. He differs from his peers in the depth of his religious concern, which is nourished by his constant reading of the Bible. According to the narrator, this causes him to become "half a mystic, half a propagandist in a biblical spirit" (215).[144] This development does not seem entirely positive to those around him. Even the local priest believes that Ryzhov has read

[143] The cycle was found in vol. 2 of Leskov's collected works published in 1889. See Leskov, *Ss* 6: 639–40.

[144] The text of "The Monognome" ("Odnodum") is found in Leskov, *Ss* 6: 211–43. On a possible historical prototype for Ryzhov, see Leskov, *Ss* 6: 640.

the Bible excessively, and the narrator observes: "In Rus' all the Orthodox know that reasonable actions cannot strictly be asked from anyone who has read through the Bible and 'read as far as Christ'; but rather, such people are like holy fools,—they behave oddly, but are harmful to no one, and are not feared" (222). This comment provides an excellent key to the portrayal of Ryzhov's character. In its humorless excessiveness, his dedication to his own interpretation of biblical teachings does call to mind a holy fool. The townspeople consider him strange because of his total honesty, which is constantly on display because of his unheard-of refusal to take bribes or abuse his official position in any way. In its own fashion, such behavior constitutes a commitment to poverty. The priest's wife is so impressed by Ryzhov's insistence on living simply, with the bare minimum of creature comforts, that she maliciously tells her husband: "Here's who should stand at the altar, not you" (221).

As does a traditional holy fool, Ryzhov comments on the actions of others without regard for social conventions or secular authority. The most striking example of this involves the visit of the governor of the province, Sergei Lanskoi, an actual historical figure. The latter irritates Ryzhov by his insufficient display of piety inside a church, to which the policeman reacts by forcing him into a bow and loudly declaring: "God's slave Sergii! Enter the Lord's temple not haughtily, but humbly, presenting yourself as the greatest sinner" (237). The great emphasis on humility as well as this fearlessness before authority are equally typical of the kenotic saint. In true Leskovian fashion, Ryzhov is not punished for his brash behavior, but is instead nominated by the governor for a Vladimir cross. Characteristically, however, he owns nothing appropriate on which to wear the order.

Julia Alissandratos, who has analyzed in detail the parallels between "The Monognome" and a typical saint's Life, observes that while Ryzhov resembles a kenotic saint in his poverty and humility, he does not exhibit the general love for humanity characteristic of the type.[145] Alissandratos sees many points of similarity between Ryzhov and Feodosii of the Kievan Cave Monastery, in particular the emphasis on wretched attire.[146] Because of the prevalence of this topos, however, one cannot be certain that Leskov adopted it from the Life of Feodosii.

[145] Julia Alissandratos, "A Stylization of Hagiographical Composition in Nikolaj Leskov's 'Singlethought' [*Odnodum*]," *SEEJ* 27 (1983): 427.

[146] Alissandratos, "Stylization of Hagiographical Composition," 427.

Though regarded as eccentric by his neighbors, Ryzhov possesses a sufficiently commanding personality to leave behind him a "heroic and almost legendary memory" (228). This quality of appearing larger than life to those around him is equally true of the hero of "Deathless Golovan," of whom the narrator observes: "He himself is almost a myth, and his story—a legend" (351).[147] And at the end of the story, the narrator generalizes about Golovan's type:

> They are unbelievable, while a legendary fiction surrounds them, and they become even more unbelievable, when one manages to remove this veneer from them and see them in all their sacred simplicity. Only the perfect love that inspired them placed them higher than all fears and even subordinated nature to them, and did not induce them to bury themselves in the earth or to struggle with the visions that tormented St. Anthony (397).

This statement is noteworthy both for its familiar insistence on simplicity—in Leskov's eyes, an essential and quintessentially Russian ingredient for sanctity—as well as for the opposition it draws between extreme asceticism and virtue motivated by love. As will be seen, in the case of Uspenskii's heroes this opposition becomes even more pronounced.

By his simplicity and self-sacrificing love of his fellow man, Golovan admirably meets the narrator's specifications. His selfless behavior results in his being nicknamed "deathless," for during a plague he fearlessly attends to the sick and dying, offering them both spiritual and medical comfort, and yet himself remains unscathed. Many consider this nothing short of supernatural. In less tumultuous times Golovan shows his love of his neighbors by giving good advice on a variety of topics. He also displays great religious tolerance, which, as noted earlier, is a frequent component of both Leskovian and kenotic goodness. Many of his acquaintances believe that Golovan is a sectarian, but the narrator suggests that this is unlikely precisely because such people are usually bigoted, whereas Golovan appears oblivious to religious differences; this even extends to his giving a Jew milk for his children, an astounding act in the eyes of his neighbors. Finally, Golovan's self-sacrificing death is truly that of a committed believer: during a great

[147] The text of "Deathless Golovan" ("Nesmertel'nyi Golovan" [iz rasskazov o trekh pravednikakh]) is found in Leskov, *Ss* 6: 351–97.

fire in Orel, he falls into a boiling pit while trying to rescue some person or his belongings and drowns.

But Golovan's saintliness extends beyond his practice of the command to love one's neighbor. The local priest declares that "his conscience is whiter than snow" (375), and the narrator's grandmother later asserts that he lived "angelically" (396). His angelic existence derives largely from his virginity, about which the grandmother learns from the priest. General ignorance about Golovan's virginity permits him to engage in an unusual form of kenotic humiliation. While practicing chastity, he also has under his roof Pavla, who has been deserted by her husband and whom everyone refers to as "Golovan's sin" (357), assuming an illicit liaison between the two. Golovan does not attempt to convince anyone otherwise. Nor is his self-denial limited to tolerating this assumption. He also endures the periodic abuse of the itinerant and supposedly holy fool Fotei, which naturally titillates the curious. Later it transpires that Fotei is actually Pavla's husband and that, in their goodness, Golovan and Pavla wish neither to reveal his identity nor to pretend that they do not know he is alive. Golovan's unceasing patience in dealing with this scoundrel reflects true humility.

The characterization of both ecclesiastical and secular virtuous men throughout Leskov's stories is influenced by spiritual values associated with Russian kenoticism. In a monastic figure like Pamva an overt commitment to humility is readily apparent; he is indeed "irresistible in his humility."[148] In other characters humility expresses itself indirectly, but no less forcefully. Selfless charitableness, in conjunction with an unusual religious tolerance, are the kenotic virtues most emphasized by Leskov. The one character discussed above who deviates somewhat from the kenotic ideal, largely because of his rigidity and self-centeredness, is Ryzhov, the hero of "The Monognome." Yet Ryzhov manifests in an extreme form a general tendency of Leskov's hagiographical technique, a technique influenced at least in part by the Russian hagiographical tradition. In Leskov's hands, one of the dominant characteristics of saintliness becomes eccentricity. His characters reflect a belief that true spirituality may express itself in behavior often deemed odd by those of more humdrum ethical convictions. Such an attitude on the part of the quirk-loving writer is but an extreme instance of the weakness for

[148] A. L. Volynskii, *N. S. Leskov: Kriticheskii ocherk* (St. Petersburg, 1898), 41.

unconventionality indicated by the general Russian regard for kenotic monks and holy fools.

Leskov prided himself on his critical attitude towards Russian Orthodoxy and, as noted in the preceding chapter, this attitude became increasingly marked in his later years. Questioning the validity of a formalistic hagiographical approach, he attempted to emend such an approach through the use of his much-vaunted trifles. Yet ironically, in creating his gallery of eccentric but saintly characters, Leskov departed from the hagiographical tradition only superficially. The spiritual values his saints display through "trifles" are often recognizably kenotic.

Moving beyond Leskov, one finds completely secular characters in nineteenth-century Russian fiction who are kenotic without being considered eccentric. In a short sketch entitled "The Monk" ("Monakh," 1879), one of a cycle of poems in prose written in the late 1870s and early 1880s, Ivan Turgenev describes a hermit and saint who "achieved annihilation of himself, of his hateful 'I' " (196).[149] This appraisal might serve as a definition of kenoticism. Such intense humility, a near-total abnegation of self, is characteristic to one extent or another of many of Turgenev's peasant characters. Perhaps the most extreme example is that of Luker'ia, the protagonist of "Living Relics" ("Zhivye moshchi," 1874). The narrator of this story, which is included in the collection *A Sportsman's Notes* (*Zapiski okhotnika*, 1847–1874), encounters Luker'ia during one of his hunting trips. Luker'ia's story is simple and tragic. A former servant of the narrator's mother, she succumbed during her youth to a disease that caused her literally to waste away. Now she lies in a hut in the summertime, a bathhouse in the wintertime, in pain and almost totally paralyzed. The title of the story refers to the nickname the local peasants have given her and reflects their perception of her as saintly.

Luker'ia's kenoticism expresses itself primarily through her unassuming resignation to her ugly fate. She tells the narrator her story with no trace of self-pity, and when he marvels at her patience, she demurs: "What do you mean? What sort of patiece is this? Now the patience of Simeon the Stylite was indeed great: he stood for thirty years on a

[149] The text of "The Monk" ("Monakh") is found in I. S. Turgenev, *Pss*, vol. 13 (Moscow, 1963), 196.

column!" (364).[150] Such belittling of one's own virtue is distinctly kenotic. Similarly, Luker'ia gives little weight to her own troubles, but does ask the narrator to request his mother to lower the rent for the local peasants because of their poverty. This selfless concern for others is also typical. These qualities endow Luker'ia with the aura of a peasant saint, chaste, meek, and good.

Among the writers who made use of the hagiographical tradition in their own writings were not only conservatives and liberals like Dostoevsky, Leskov, and Turgenev, but radicals as well. The conception of sanctity held by Gleb Uspenskii (1843–1902), while differing significantly from that of the other writers discussed thus far, nonetheless reveals links to the kenotic way. As a writer with Populist sympathies and strong civic concerns, Uspenskii tended to focus on the benefits of sanctity to others rather than on the saint's own spiritual gains.[151] Yet the wellspring of his characters' virtuous actions is often consistent with the values that inspire the characters of more traditional writers.

In "Rodion the Concerned" (Rodion radetel'," 1889), which first appeared in 1889 and was later made one of a cycle of stories devoted to positive individuals, Uspenskii provided his own definition of sanctity:

> A man who does not pity his flesh, goes barefoot in severe cold, or puts himself in chains, in order to preserve his own soul in purity by emaciating his flesh, is not a saint, but a holy fool, a man of God. A saint is someone who works tirelessly for the poor, dark, and unfortunate people (457).[152]

In an essay on "A Good Russian Type" ("Khoroshii russkii tip," 1885) written a few years earlier, Uspenskii had expressed similar reservations about the connection between asceticism and sanctity:

> The Russian holy man is a highly remarkable type. Stereotyped Lives usually do all they can to drive his biography into the ster-

[150] The text of "Living Relics" ("Zhivye moshchi") is found in Turgenev, *Pss*, vol. 4 (Moscow, 1963), 352–65.

[151] On Uspenskii's relationship to Populism, see Nikita I. Prutskov, *Gleb Uspensky* (New York, 1972), 61–67, especially.

[152] The text of "Rodion the Concerned" ("Rodion radetel' ") is found in Uspenskii, *Ss* 8: 446–66. The "*nevidimki*" cycle was first compiled by Uspenskii for vol. 3 of his *Sochineniia* (St. Petersburg, 1891) from works previously published in other cycles. See Uspenskii, *Ss* 8: 673.

> eotyped limits of a "saint's Life," thinking that the less space is allotted in this biography to the practical, real business on earth done by the holy man and, on the other hand, the more that is said about fasting food, nocturnal vigils, and the temptation of the devil, the more holy will be the life of the revered person to the common reader and the more he will feel spiritual tenderness on reading the biography (259).[153]

According to Uspenskii, this approach is flawed. Instead, he suggests, "practical benefit, clear, visible, tangible good and useful work always constituted the distinctive trait of the holy man, always constituted the very chief feature of his personal desire to be 'pleasing to God' " (259). Such a desire, Uspenskii claims, would express itself in labor on behalf of one's poor and ignorant neighbor, and as evidence he cites the examples of the missionaries to the Slavs Cyril and Methodius, Tikhon of Zadonsk, and the Russian missionary Stefan of Perm'. What is particularly interesting about Uspenskii's observations here and in "Rodion the Concerned" is that, in marked contrast to many of the other works discussed in this chapter, the often fluid boundary between holy foolishness and some other types of kenotic behavior becomes an impregnable barrier. The bizarre asceticism adopted by holy fools, as well as ascetic habits in general, held little appeal for Uspenskii. Yet his ideal of sanctity, with its implicit call for radical self-abnegation for the sake of the good of others, is essentially kenotic and completely in keeping with the sentiments expressed in Paul's letter to the Philippians. The difference is that the focus of Uspenskii's program is primarily social rather than ethical.

The hero of "Rodion the Concerned," a reworking of a late seventeenth-century legend about a wonder-working icon, provides an excellent example of this kind of saintly behavior. In Uspenskii's version, Rodion claims to have had a series of visions in which he has seen both frightening idols representing the sinful life led by his fellow villagers and an angel who instructs him on bringing the people back to the path of true faith and piety. Rodion asserts that the ultimate author of his message is the Mother of God, whose icon then proves to be a rallying point for his crusade. His forceful and charismatic account achieves the

[153] The text of "A Good Russian Type" ("Khoroshii russkii tip") is found in Uspenskii, *Ss* 6: 244–64.

desired effect, and the people enthusiastically follow all his instructions for reform.

In typically kenotic fashion, Rodion insists that he is merely a mouthpiece for divine orders. But Uspenskii is not content to regard his hero merely as a pious instrument. Instead, he emphasizes the intentionality of Rodion's behavior:

> Rodion could have seen with his own eyes everything that he saw, and heard everything that he heard; he could in fact have lain for two days in a faint, but for all these visions, all these hallucinations to possess such a very defined content, it was necessary for Rodion himself to have suffered about the people's disorderliness, to have been tormented by this, to have thought about how to free the people from sin, to have thought to the point of nervous disorder, of hallucination (456).

As a contemporary analogue to Rodion, Uspenskii mentions Father Stefan, a former schoolteacher who left his monastery to live as a hermit near his native village. There he taught the peasants and wrote books in an accessible style on useful subjects. In each instance a willingness to subordinate oneself to a positive aim, to become a humble agent of good, is apparent. The lives of Stefan and Rodion do retain external similarities to the Lives of traditional saints. On one level, Stefan is a virtuous, though idiosyncratic, anchorite, while Rodion's personal goodness is such that he is granted a divine vision. The major link between such types and the saints, however, lies in their selflessness, in their willingness to do whatever is necessary for the salvation of others, even if that involves denigrating one's own personality and background.

Some of Uspenskii's saints manifest this essentially kenotic tendency even more overtly. In two stories in the cycle, "The Blind Singer" ("Slepoi pevets," 1888) and "Invisible Avdot'ia" ("Nevidimka Avdot'ia," 1880), Uspenskii develops the image of the "invisible being" who serves others with no thought of recompense, even to the point of social or psychological self-humiliation. A mysterious blind singer movingly performs religious songs for the common people, songs he learned from a monk in a Kievan monastery. A former lawyer abandoned by his wife, this lover of the people once divided his time between psalm-singing and legal practice, but now can only sing. The narrator notes that the singer, Semen Vasil'evich, could earn a great deal more if he chose to play for other types of audiences, but apparently prefers to touch the soul of the common people. As emphasized above, this willingness to relinquish social status is typically kenotic. The narrator concludes his comments with a general observation: "It is impossible not to esteem him side by side with those 'invisible beings' who look after the people's conscience, who, invisibly and incomprehensibly for us, do among the people good deeds of an incomparably greater degree" (446).[154] The first description of the singer best illustrates the joy in doing for others that appears to inspire him:

> In spite of his sunken, dead eyes, his face did not bear the imprint of grief or misfortune, but was the most good-natured and cheerful, cheerful even to the extent that it weakened the impressions of sorrow that reached one's ears from the place where the blind singer and his harmonium were (435).

His enjoyment of the company of common people and his self-effacement unite the blind singer with historical kenotic saints like Tikhon of Zadonsk, as well as fictional characters like Father Zosima.

The heroine of "Invisible Avdot'ia," an ill-treated servant and former serf, also embodies the ideal of unselfish love of one's neighbors. Avdot'ia's existence is a constant round of small tasks performed for others. Many of her thoughtful gestures are totally unsolicited. For example, in the middle of the night the narrator catches sight of her taking his shoes to clean. Avdot'ia's lifelong and absolute commitment to others is so extreme that the narrator describes her as "belonging entirely to others" (499); like Turgenev's monk, she has succeeded in annihilating her ego.[155] Avdot'ia emphasizes her own lack of self-interest when she tells the narrator: "Do you think I'm worried about myself? . . . Put a thousand rubles there on the table, give it to me, but I won't take it, what's it to me?" (499). In Avdot'ia's mouth, this claim rings true. The absence of materialistic tendencies is only one indication of her self-abnegation.

The protagonist of the other story in the "Invisible Beings" cycle, "A Sensitive Heart" ("Chutkoe serdtse," 1889), is another Good Samaritan, the midwife Anna Petrovna Ivanova. Anna Petrovna's character is expressively conveyed by her luggage, which contains, in addition to

[154] The text of "The Blind Singer" ("Slepoi pevets") is found in Uspenskii, *Ss* 8: 429–46.

[155] The text of "Invisible Avdot'ia" ("Nevidimka Avdot'ia") is found in Uspenskii, *Ss* 8: 487–506.

the instruments necessary for her profession, booklets for the popular instruction of reading, healing manuals, calendars, and articles of children's clothing. All of these items point to her desire to help others, a desire apparent even to casual observers. When Anna Petrovna visits her aging mother, her driver immediately recognizes her as a good, simple person, someone who has "a pure conscience, a childlike soul, but an ardent heart" (468).[156] The vacationing midwife confirms this by immediately becoming involved in local issues, helping peasants save land from the rapacious grasp of a greedy merchant.

Anna Petrovna seeks no credit for her actions, and thus her behavior echoes the kenotic tradition. This is brought out at the conclusion of "A Sensitive Heart" when the tax assessor Gavrilov uses the example of Anna Petrovna to inspire an after-theater gathering of old friends, discouraged liberals of the sixties. He calls her a good, simple type of person who loves her neighbor as much as herself, the kind of person who doubtless is responsible, in a self-effacing way, for positive accomplishments for the general good of the kind reported in the newspapers. Gavrilov's story heartens his listeners and renews their belief in the ideals of their youth.

Uspenskii's saints are portrayed most forcefully as active agents of good. In their doggedly practical orientation, they have little in common with Dostoevsky's more mystical characters. They are also noticeably lacking in that air of eccentricity typically associated with the saintly characters of Leskov; Uspenskii has little real regard for anything that smacks of holy foolishness. Nonetheless his "invisible beings" are to some extent inspired by kenotic values. As their very name suggests, they subordinate their own personalities to the common weal, even if that involves humiliation. The difference is that their kenosis has been secularized to the point that, while some of Uspenskii's characters manifest a certain piety, their formal religious commitment is less significant than their social dedication.

In an article on the religious sources of Russian Populism, Fedotov persuasively argues that the "millenarium ethical ideal of the Russian people," the kenotic dream of self-abnegation, influenced the Populists in their desire to devote themselves to social service.[157] Certainly

[156] The text of "A Sensitive Heart" ("Chutkoe serdtse") is found in Uspenskii, *Ss* 8: 467–86.

[157] G. P. Fedotov, "The Religious Sources of Russian Populism," *Russian Review* 1 (1942): 39. On similarities between the Populists and monks in regard to humility, see

Uspenskii's saintly heroes and heroines bear out the validity of this hypothesis. This is doubtless also one reason why Soviet critics are uncomfortable with Uspenskii's extreme idealization of his "invisible beings."[158] While they operate in a secular context, the social commitment exhibited by these paragons of virtue has a distinctly religious cast. In a transmuted fashion, they uphold the kenotic tradition no less than many more traditional exponents of this most Russian of existential approaches.

THROUGHOUT the nineteenth century, Russian literature experienced the impact of treasured spiritual values of preceding centuries. The figures of the holy fool and the kenotic monk appear transformed in many neo-hagiographical works by a variety of authors. As will be seen in the following chapter, the type of the Josephite monk also found admirers. The choice of saintly models for emulation depended largely on the given author's politics. Kenotic features found their most enthusiastic adapters among conservative and liberal writers. For writers like Dostoevsky, Leskov, and to some extent even Turgenev and Uspenskii, a strength derived from self-abnegation, an insight accompanied by compassion and tolerance: these were the desirable spiritual traits. The precise mixture of these elements varies greatly from author to author. While Dostoevsky gives particular emphasis to the kenotic gift of perspicacity, Leskov stresses humility as apparent eccentricity and Uspenskii humility as service to others. Of all these, Dostoevsky remains most faithful to the ideal of kenoticism as it was portrayed in Orthodox hagiographical literature.

With great justification Fedotov called kenoticism "the dominant motif in Russian spirituality."[159] Moreover, although it is not supported by official Soviet literary practice, kenoticism has not vanished entirely from the Soviet scene. Mary and Paul Rowland have shown that the character of Iurii Zhivago, of Boris Pasternak's *Doctor Zhivago* (*Doktor Zhivago*, 1957), reveals the impact of kenotic thinking.[160] Zhivago adopts the kenotic way at the end of the novel, when he returns to

---

also James H. Billington, *The Icon and the Axe: An Interpretive History of Russian Culture* (New York, 1970), 204.

[158] Cf. N. I. Prutskov, *Tvorcheskii put' Gleba Uspenskogo* (Moscow, 1958). 93.

[159] Fedotov, *Treasury of Russian Spirituality*, 14.

[160] Mary F. and Paul Rowland, *Pasternak's Doctor Zhivago* (Carbondale, Ill., 1967), 173–82, especially.

Moscow from Siberia. He arrives dressed in rags, looking like a "seeker of truth from the common people" (478).[161] According to the narrator, during the last few years of his life, Zhivago goes "more and more to seed" (477). He ceases practicing medicine, ceases writing, and instead lives in great poverty, doing odd jobs to support himself and his common-law wife, the daughter of a former porter at his first wife's house. All of these actions reflect a voluntary striving for self-humiliation and easily conform to the kenotic model.[162]

The persistent appeal of kenotic features is also demonstrated by Matrena in Alexander Solzhenitsyn's "Matrena's House" ("Matrenin dvor," 1963). Matrena exhibits traits associated with both the holy fool and the kenotic monk. Free from vanity and materialistic tendencies, she is willing to help anyone who asks her. She has been called an example of "people whose reliability rests on their complete freedom from any kind of self-interest or opportunism."[163] As a result, her neighbors and relatives callously exploit her good nature, while simultaneously finding her laughable. She meets her death during a final act of self-abnegation: she is struck by a train while helping her relatives to carry off dismantled planks from her own house. Matrena's essentially kenotic spirituality is not linked to a formal religious commitment, but she is a model of self-sacrificing service to one's neighbors without expectation of recompense or even gratitude. The narrator concludes his account of Matrena with a general observation:

> We all lived side by side with her and did not understand that she was that very righteous person without whom, according to the saying, no village can stand.
>
> Nor city.
>
> Nor our entire world (231).[164]

This is a fitting epitaph on the kenotic personality in a secularized world.

[161] The text of *Doctor Zhivago* (*Doktor Zhivago*) is found in *Doktor Zhivago* (Ann Arbor, Mich., 1967).

[162] Cf. Rowland, *Pasternak's Doctor Zhivago*, 179.

[163] Robert Louis Jackson, " 'Matryona's Home': The Making of a Russian Icon," in Kathryn Feuer, ed., *Solzhenitsyn: A Collection of Critical Essays* (Englewood Cliffs, N.J., 1976), 65.

[164] The text of "Matrena's House" ("Matrenin dvor") is found in A. Solzhenitsyn, *Sochineniia*, 2d ed. (Frankfurt, 1968), 195–231.

CHAPTER FIVE

Hagiography and the Rigorous Hero: The Josephite Type in Later Russian Literature

> We can define the classic Russian *intelligent* as a militant monk of the nihilistic religion of earthly well-being . . . . The intelligentsia is a kind of independent state, . . . nowhere in Russia are there such unshakeably firm traditions, such definiteness and severity in the regulation of life, such categoricalness in the valuation of people and conditions, such loyalty to the corporative spirit, as in that all-Russian spiritual monastery that the Russian intelligentsia makes up.
>
> Semen Frank, "The Ethics of Nihilism"

THE DISCUSSION of neo-hagiography in the preceding chapter shows how writers of a conservative, liberal, or mildly radical stamp, like Fedor Dostoevsky, Nikolai Leskov, Ivan Turgenev, and Gleb Uspenskii, were consistently attracted to the kenotic brand of Russian saintliness. As for the Josephite type of goodness, with its severity and insistence on strict regulation, if treated at all in their fictional works, it was only criticized. For example, the figure of Ferapont in *The Brothers Karamazov* exemplifies a highly jaundiced view of traditional Josephite characteristics.[1] Contemptuous and suspicious of the institution of elders, Ferapont observes an idiorhythmic but severe manner of existence; he frequently practices silence and engages in strict fasting, consuming only a small amount of bread and water. With the demono-

[1] Linda J. Ivanits points to the polarization of Russian saintly types as reflected in *The Brothers Karamazov*, when she comments that, though both Ferapont and Zosima resemble the saints of the Lives, "Ferapont's fasting and silence are stressed, while Zosima exhibits such interior qualities as humility, insight, and tenderness (*umilenie*)." See Linda J. Ivanits, "Hagiography in *Brat'ja Karamazovy*: Zosima, Ferapont, and the Russian Monastic Saint," *Russian Language Journal* 34 (1980): 116.

logical and fantastic bent frequent in monks of such habits, he claims to see devils and to communicate with the Holy Spirit in the form of a bird. He is an ignorant and narrow-minded peasant, incapable of conceiving of spirituality devoid of ritualism. When the petty-minded monk from Obdorsk visits him, Ferapont expresses an exclusive interest in the details of how the monk's home monastery keeps the fasts; the monk from Obdorsk, whose concerns are equally narrow, responds in loving detail. The picture emerges of an unproductive, essentially unspiritual formalism. This is asceticism at its worst, where it has become nothing more than an end in itself.

Not everyone, however, found the Josephite trend in Russian monasticism as uncongenial as did Dostoevsky. Among more radical writers the severity and dogmatism of the Josephites seem to have struck a responsive chord. These writers must have equated a kenotic approach with submissiveness, while discipline and firm dedication to highly systematized behavior would undoubtedly have proved appealing. Such virtues would have seemed desirable to those wishing to make drastic changes in the world around them.

The Josephite type has found expression in modern Russian literature both in the form of neo-hagiography, in the stern heroes of radical writers, and in adaptations of an important work by a religious personage of decidedly Josephite tendencies, the seventeenth-century sectarian leader Archpriest Avvakum Petrovich. Avvakum was greatly admired by many radicals, including some of the very same writers who endowed their own characters with Josephite virtues. These two very different ways in which a religious tradition wholly at odds with the kenotic mode had an impact on later Russian literature are the subject of this chapter.

The Josephite Monk and the Radical Hero

Two writers who profoundly affected the development of what would eventually evolve as the socialist realist hero were Nikolai Chernyshevskii (1829–1889) and Maxim Gorky (1868–1936). Both came from backgrounds saturated with religion: Chernyshevskii was the son of a priest, while Gorky came from a provincial middle-class milieu distinguished by its devotion to hagiographical legends and tales, particularly those of a more spectacular nature. In his autobiography, Gorky specifically mentions being enraptured as a child by the Lives of the popular saints Alexis, the Man of God, and Mary of Egypt, among others—the same saints beloved by Dostoevsky's Zosima.[2] Other Lives he mentions include those of the early Christian martyrs Cyricus, Julitta, Barbara, and Pantaleon.[3] Both Chernyshevskii and Gorky made radical breaks with their pasts: Chernyshevskii became a fervent revolutionary and was arrested and exiled to Siberia; Gorky became a convinced Marxist, the friend of Lenin and supposed father of Soviet literature. Yet neither of these would-be iconoclasts escaped the impact of their childhood exposure to Orthodoxy. In the literary heroes of Chernyshevskii and Gorky traces of the Josephite tradition are clear. The examples of Rakhmetov in *What is to be Done?* (*Chto delat'?*, 1863) and Pavel Vlasov in *Mother* (*Mat'*, 1906) are indicative.[4]

Rakhmetov occupies a special place in the tendentious world of *What is to be Done?*, Chernyshevskii's tedious blueprint for positive revolutionary activity said to have "served as a bible for two generations of Russian radicals and revolutionaries."[5] Faithful to the Old Russian literary tradition, the narrator of the novel indulges in the modesty topos at the very beginning of his narrative: "I don't have a trace of artistic talent. I even have a poor command of the language" (14).[6] He also adheres to time-honored technique in leaving nothing to chance in the reader's interpretation of characters and events. Thus he explains that he has introduced the figure of Rakhmetov, who appears relatively briefly in the novel, in order to throw into relief his more ordinary positive heroes:

[2] M. Gor'kii, *Ss*, 30 vols. (Moscow, 1949–1956), 13: 54, 138, 180. On Gorky's admiration of saints' Lives, see Irwin Weil, *Gorky: His Literary Development and Influence on Soviet Intellectual Life* (New York, 1966), 54; and Katerina Clark, *The Soviet Novel: History as Ritual* (Chicago, 1981), 50.

[3] Gorky, *Ss* 13: 138.

[4] On the rationale in general for comparing Old Russian saints to the revolutionary heroes of Chernyshevskii, cf. Iu. M. Lotman, "O tipologicheskom izuchenii literatury," in N. L. Stepanov and U. R. Fokht, eds., *Problemy tipologii russkogo realizma* (Moscow, 1969), 129.

[5] E. H. Carr, *1917: Before and After* (London, 1969), 61. On the tremendous influence of *What is to be Done?* on radical circles, see also Adam B. Ulam, *The Bolsheviks* (New York, 1965), 54.

[6] The text of *What is to be Done?* (*Chto delat'?*) is found in N. G. Chernyshevskii, *Chto delat'? iz rasskazov o novykh liudiakh* (Leningrad, 1948). On the similarity between Chernyshevskii's statement and commonplaces found in saints' Lives, cf. Julia Alissandratos, "Hagiographical Commonplaces and Medieval Prototypes in N. G. Chernyshevsky's *What is to be Done?*," *St. Vladimir's Theological Quarterly* 26 (1982): 106–7.

> If I had not shown the figure of Rakhmetov, the majority of readers would have been confused about the main characters of my story. I bet that up to the last sections of this chapter Vera Pavlovna, Kirsanov, and Lopukhov seemed to the majority of the public to be heroes, persons of a superior nature, perhaps even idealized persons, perhaps even persons impossible in reality because of their excessively lofty nobility . . . superior natures are not like these. I have shown you the faint outline of the profile of one of them; the features are not the same, as you see (359–60).

Rakhmetov differs from the other positive characters in *What is to be Done?* in that (with the exception of a fondness for cigars) he succeeds in ridding himself of all human weaknesses.[7] He adopts at an early age special rules regarding his physical, moral, and intellectual life. Later these are integrated into a complete system, to which he always adheres. These rules include sexual abstinence, temperance, and the consumption of the cheapest of food, primarily black bread; the only exception to this diet is the high-quality meat Rakhmetov eats in order to preserve his epic physical strength. His vow of chastity is as sincere as a monk's, and he informs a young widow who loves him, and to whom he is far from indifferent, that he cannot marry because people like him "do not have the right to bind anyone's destiny with their own" (328). Impressed by Rakhmetov's virtuous character, the widow tells his friend Aleksandr Kirsanov: "I see him in my dreams surrounded by a halo" (337). The serious-minded heroine of *What is to be Done?*, Vera Pavlovna, refers to Rakhmetov as her "good angel" (340). Such less than subtle comments reinforce the impression of the young radical's saintliness.

His chastity and other abstemious habits link Rakhmetov to the ascetic saint.[8] His self-inflicted physical trials are analogous to the labors of the saints. On one occasion the parallel is made particularly clear. Summoned by his friend's landlady, who is distraught because through a crack in his door she has caught sight of him covered with

[7] On possible similarities between the major protagonists of *What is to be Done?* and traditional saints, see Alissandratos, "Hagiographical Commonplaces," 108–12. Alissandratos also discusses Rakhmetov as a saintly figure (112–16).

[8] Nicholas Zernov observes of Rakhmetov: "The behavior of this hero resembled in some respects monastic asceticism." See *The Russian Religious Renaissance of the Twentieth Century* (London, 1963), 22.

blood, Kirsanov discovers the explanation: Rakhmetov has been testing himself by sleeping on a bed of nails. Earlier he reacts to a reading list Kirsanov gives him by reading for eighty-two hours straight until he collapses from exhaustion. Not for nothing do his friends refer to him as "the rigorist" (313).

Rakhmetov is also saintlike in his charity, which most often assumes the form of supporting students. He also offers a large sum of money to a German philosopher for the publication of his works. Yet it is worth noting that Rakhmetov prefers to retain control over his money. It will be recalled that a proprietary approach to the caritative ideal is typical of the Josephite orientation.

In his dedication to his system and in his commitment to ascetic rigors, Rakhmetov reveals a kinship with the Josephites. The similarity goes further, however. Rakhmetov has been compared to Alexis, the Man of God, because of the radical conversion he undergoes, his intense faith, and his extreme asceticism.[9] Yet Chernyshevskii's hero exhibits none of the self-effacing humility so characteristic of that preeminently kenotic saint. Instead, he does not hesitate to judge others in a remarkably dispassionate way. The narrator compares him to a "historian who judges coldly" (323), and Vera Pavlovna's first husband, Dmitrii Lopukhov, sends him to speak to his wife about his disappearance because he knows that her sorrow will not weaken Rakhmetov. Indeed, "the rigorist" does not hesitate to criticize both Vera Pavlovna and her husband with unconcealed gusto. This absence of reluctance to pass judgment on others links him to the Josephite tradition. It is undoubtedly this ruthlessness of spirit that inspires fear in many of his peers.

Rakhmetov's behavior is in no way evocative of kenoticism. Humility is completely alien to this self-styled superman. Willing to spend time only on those he deems important and influential, he perceives himself and his comrades as shining exemplars:

> we demand for people the full enjoyment of their life,—we must bear witness by our lives that we demand this, not for the satisfaction of our personal passions, not for ourselves personally, but for mankind in general,—that we speak only according to principle, and not from prejudice, according to conviction, and not personal necessity (317).

[9] Clark, *Soviet Novel*, 50.

Rakhmetov not only lacks a sense of humility, he also is noticeably unburdened by the sensitive compassion so often characteristic of the kenotic type. His unequivocal attitude towards suicide, except in cases of incurable disease or inevitable death, is revealing: "It's madness" (333).

The narrator believes that some readers may find Rakhmetov droll, and it has been suggested that this may link him to the holy fools.[10] The similarity is very superficial, however; while often unusual, Rakhmetov's behavior is rarely overtly ridiculous. Most importantly, his strangeness has little in common with the holy fool's spirit of radical self-humiliation. The essential similarity between this idealized revolutionary and the hagiographical tradition lies with the Josephites. In his untempered severity and unyielding inclination to pass judgment, Rakhmetov embodies the Josephite ideal in a secular, politically radical context.

Pavel Vlasov, the paragon of socialist virtue and central hero of *Mother*, resembles Rakhmetov in his ideological probity. Pavel's commitment to political beliefs is as complete and uncompromising as that of a saint to religious beliefs. It has been noted that the first external sign of Pavel's political transformation is a religious one; he hangs up a picture of the resurrected Christ.[11] Moreover, the precise ways in which his involvement in socialist circles expresses itself evoke the saints. For example, his newfound faith leads him to abandon the amusements of his peers and to return home sober on holidays. His former companions cease visiting him, and, instead, Pavel often sits carefully reading and taking notes.

As a hagiographically influenced figure, Pavel has been compared to the type of the saintly prince.[12] His courage and his struggle to free his "people" from the enemy do indeed call to mind many a medieval hero. Yet there is a great affinity between Pavel and a saintly monk as well. When his mother thinks about all the changes that have taken place in him, she observes: "he's like a monk. He's really very severe. It's beyond his years" (202).[13] Later the narrator comments that the "monastic severity of Pavel bewildered her" (225). Even local gossip perceives Pavel's new activities in religious terms. Thus Mar'ia Korsu-

[10] Alissandratos, "Hagiographical Commonplaces," 113.

[11] F. M. Borras, *Maxim Gorky the Writer: An Interpretation* (Oxford, 1967), 111.

[12] Clark, *Soviet Novel*, 58–59.

[13] The text of *Mother* (*Mat'*) is found in Gor'kii, *Ss* 7: 193–516.

nova, the Vlasovs' neighbor, tells Pavel's mother she should keep an eye on him and warns her: "There's a rumor going around . . . that he's setting up a sort of *artel*, like the Khlysty. Sects, this is called. They're going to whip each other like the Khlysty" (225).[14]

While Pavel abstains from alcohol, there is no evidence to suggest that he denies himself food as does Rakhmetov. As with Rakhmetov, however, Pavel's monk-like dedication to the cause extends to a belief that conventional relations between men and women are not for him. When his comrade Andrei speaks of love for a woman, Pavel tells him that it would be more honorable for him to be silent and points out that if he married, he would be so occupied with the struggle to support a family that he would have no time for the political struggle. "Both cannot be" (226), asserts Pavel in no uncertain terms, although he himself is not oblivious to the charms of the opposite sex. (This uncompromising attitude was actually shared by some of Russia's radical workers.[15])

The absolute self-control that Pavel exhibits in regard to women is typical of his behavior. He thus resembles a monk who has successfully passed through trials and temptations. Andrei calls him a "rare person . . . an iron person" (270). This self-discipline is reflected in his manner, which is always "even and calm" (417), while his smile is described as "calm and firm" (463). At his trial he manifests that same calm severity, and, listening to him, his mother senses "the strange, captivating power of his faith" (488).

Pavel clearly has much in common with a committed monk. As repeated references to his severity and iron-like personality indicate, he is most similar to a Josephite monk. Like Rakhmetov, Pavel Vlasov shows no traces of kenotic humility. There is also little sign of the unusual tolerance and compassion often associated with kenotic monks. An excellent example of this is provided when his mother voices her fear that he will be arrested and Pavel, making no attempt to soften the blow, agrees without qualification. His mother reacts with understandable dismay: "How severe you are, Pasha! If you would only comfort me sometime! But instead—I say something terrible, and you say

[14] The Khlysty are a radically ascetic peasant sect which arose in the seventeenth century.

[15] Cf. Reginald E. Zelnik, "Russian Rebels: An Introduction to the Memoirs of the Russian Workers Semen Kanatchikov and Matvei Fisher," *Russian Review* 35 (1976): 277–78.

something even more terrible" (237). Pavel's response is in keeping with the unrelenting nature of his virtue: "I cannot, Mama! You have to get used to it" (237). He is right, but he is not kind. Like Rakhmetov and the Josephites, his harsh standards permit no exceptions.

As the resurgence of Josephite traits in the characters of Chernyshevskii and Gorky shows, not only the kenotic monk, but also the austere, unyielding monk appealed to nineteenth-century Russian writers. In the writings of Chernyshevskii and Gorky Josephite features are stripped of their specifically religious meaning and adapted to a political credo. But the essential characteristics remain the same. Thus one can visualize Pavel Vlasov in a different era as a follower of Joseph of Volokolamsk but never of Sergii of Radonezh. Moreover, the impact of such characters, and through them of Josephite values, has persisted to the present: the protagonists of the novels of Chernyshevskii and Gorky played a decisive role in the creation of the socialist realist hero. In the grim heroes of novels like Fedor Gladkov's *Cement* (*Tsement*, 1925) and Nikolai Ostrovskii's *How the Steel was Tempered* (*Kak zakalialas' stal'*, 1934) may be distinguished the shadow of the Josephites, who, *mutatis mutandis*, eventually dedicated themselves to service of the state, much as would their socialist realist descendants. There was little place in either world for kenoticism.

Auto-hagiography: Avvakum in Later Russian Literature

Whatever the differences in their religious perspectives, the original hagiographical works mentioned thus far, both Orthodox and apocryphal, share an important compositional feature: they are all narrated in the third person. While a becoming diffidence regarding his or her own sanctity might seem an essential characteristic of even the most self-confident holy man or woman, thus precluding any other kind of hagiographical narrative, this is not actually the case. There is another kind of literary work that may be termed auto-hagiography, of which the *Life of the Archpriest Avvakum, Written by Himself* (*Zhitie protopopa Avvakuma im samim napisannoe*, 1672–1675) is the outstanding example.[16] Long an underground classic among Russian schismatics, this

[16] In composing his *Life*, Avvakum was to some extent influenced by the example of the sixth-century Syrian monk Dorotheos of Gaza, whose autobiographically-slanted writings were published in Moscow in 1652. He also had in mind the example of the Acts and Epistles of the apostles. Cf. *Archpriest Avvakum: The Life written by Himself*,

tendentious autobiography attracted much attention among Russian intellectuals of various religious and political persuasions after its publication in 1861.[17] Literary interest in it has persisted to the present day.

Archpriest Avvakum Petrovich (1620?–1682) was a provincial Russian cleric who became an outspoken opponent of the mid-seventeenth century ecclesiastical reforms initiated by Patriarch Nikon of Moscow. These reforms were intended to bring Russian practices into conformity with those of the Greek Church and included making the sign of the cross with three fingers instead of two, bowing to the girdle rather than the knee, and a host of orthographic, syntactic, and other changes in the liturgy and other religious texts. Intransigent in opposing such departures from tradition, Avvakum, together with his family, was for many years exiled to remote areas of Siberia. Condemned and anathematized by a Church council, he was imprisoned in the far north under wretched conditions. In 1682 Avvakum's refusal to exercise the least verbal restraint, coupled with his growing influence, resulted in his being burned at the stake. The martyred archpriest was deemed a saint by subsequent generations of schismatics, and his *Life* was regarded as a sacred book.

The reasons for the magnitude and violence of the schism in the Russian Orthodox Church are a matter of continuing controversy. Many complex religious, political and social forces, discussion of which is beyond the scope of this study, came into play.[18] Important in the present context, however, is the suggestion that one factor contributing to the troubles of this period may have been the Josephite tradition, with its overweening regard for externals which had persisted among both the Old Believers and their opponents.[19] Avvakum himself per-

---

trans. and ed. Kenneth N. Brostrum (Ann Arbor, Mich., 1979), 207–8; and *Zhitie protopopa Avvakuma, im samim napisannoe*, ed. N. K. Gudzii, with an introduction by V. E. Gusev (Moscow, 1960), 34. For a detailed discussion of earlier examples of the autobiographical genre in medieval Russian literature, see especially Serge A. Zenkovsky, "The Old Believer Avvakum: His Role in Russian Literature," *Indiana Slavic Studies* 1 (1956): 7–12. I recall seeing the term *auto-hagiography* used in reference to the Life years ago, but have unfortunately not been able to relocate its source.

[17] The *Life* was first published by N. S. Tikhonravov in *Letopisi russkoi literatury i drevnosti*, vol. 3, bk. 6, pt. 2 (Moscow, 1861), 117–73. Tikhonravov's edition of the text was also published separately in St. Petersburg in 1862.

[18] On the role played by Avvakum in the schism, see especially Pierre Pascal, *Avvakum et les débuts du Raskol: la crise religieuse au XVIIe siècle en Russie* (Paris, 1938).

[19] Timothy Ware, *The Orthodox Church* (Baltimore, Md., 1963), 124; and G. P. Fedotov, *A Treasury of Russian Spirituality* (Belmont, Mass., 1975), 134.

fectly exemplified the Josephite approach to religion. Of irreproachable integrity, he displayed an extraordinary concern for absolute adherence to proper rituals and customs. Fiercely loyal to his coreligionists, he had nothing but vituperative scorn for his enemies. It has been observed that "the feeling which he can best express [in his *Life*] is hatred."[20] His lack of compassion extended to a temporary refusal to pray for a sick child because the mother had dared to enlist the services of a sorcerer. According to his own testimony Avvakum was occasionally subject to religious visions; these were, however, subordinated to his struggle with Nikon and other reformers. The notion of a mysticism detached from immediate worldly concerns was alien to the archpriest. His was a life of action, a life dedicated to unyielding assault on the sinful behavior of himself and others.

Avvakum was the author of numerous works ranging from biblical commentaries to letters.[21] His autobiographical Life is his most unusual achievement. In it he discusses his background and early experience as a village priest, his conflicts with the ecclesiastical hierarchy in Moscow, and his family's misadventures in Siberia and the far north. An unvarnished portrayal of a violent age, the Life provides a realistic account of the sometimes brutal treatment meted out to a strict priest by his unappreciative parishioners and the sufferings inflicted on the schismatics by their opponents. Linguistically, the Life represents a significant departure from Old Russian literary norms: Avvakum does not hesitate to employ an earthy vernacular in the description of his travails. The often mundane subject matter is thus matched by an unadorned style.

For all its realism of incident and tone, the links between Avvakum's autobiography and hagiography remain strong. At the end of his narrative, the archpriest makes reference to the Apostles' accounts of their achievements. The tacit conviction that this provides a precedent for his own work is suggestive. For all his stereotyped protestations of humility, Avvakum doubtless believed that he was an agent of God and that "his life, like an apostle's life, deserved description as the result of the 'divine' will that had manifested itself in it."[22] His religious self-

[20] Dmitrij Čiževskij, *History of Russian Literature from the Eleventh Century to the End of the Baroque* ('s-Gravenhage, 1962), 371.

[21] The standard editions of Avvakum's works include Gudzii, *Zhitie protopopa Avvakuma*; and A. N. Robinson, ed., *Zhizneopisania Avvakuma i Epifaniia: issledovanie i teksty* (Moscow, 1963).

[22] A. N. Robinson, "Tvorchestvo Avvakuma v istoriko-funktsional'nom osve-

confidence is expressed not only in the assumption that right is on his side ("I am not afraid of them, living with Christ" [85]), but in the implicit assertion that he is both the recipient and the performer of miracles. In addition to the visions described in the Life, divine interest takes a more concrete form. When an angry parishioner attempts to shoot the archpriest, both his pistols misfire. Avvakum assures the reader that this was God's will. Elsewhere he relates how he cured two women who were possessed and a little boy whose hand and foot had dried up. In true hagiographical fashion, such apparent miracles are also attributed to God.

Not only is Avvakum's existence characterized by manifestations of the miraculous typical of a saint's Life, but he also undergoes and triumphs over temptation in a manner familiar to hagiography. When a dissolute young woman inflames his imagination during her confession, he regains control by holding his hand in a candle flame. As will be seen in the following chapter, a similar episode is described in the *Menaea* Life of Iakov the Faster. Avvakum's victory over temptation thus evokes hagiography in specific as well as general terms.

Avvakum's autobiography is replete with the hagiographical stylization of his own existence. Moreover, evidence provided by recent Soviet scholarship suggests that this process was unquestionably deliberate. N. Demkova's close study of the extant manuscripts of the Life has revealed that as Avvakum revised his work, the hagiographical element became more pronounced.[23] In addition, analysis by Viktor Vinogradov in the 1920s and further research by the Norwegian scholar Jostein Børtnes suggest that Avvakum used mythical patterns associated with the life of Christ as analogues for events in his own life.[24] Thus the archpriest couches the description of his hearing in terms of the trial of Christ.[25] Surely the desire to portray oneself as a saint could express itself no more forcefully (and arrogantly!) than this.

shchenii," in N. V. Osmakov, ed., *Russkaia literatura v istoriko-funktsional'nom osveshchenii* (Moscow, 1979), 147–48.

[23] N. S. Demkova, *Zhitie protopopa Avvakuma (tvorcheskaia istoriia proizvedeniia)* (Leningrad, 1974), 93–95, especially.

[24] V. V. Vinogradov, "On the Tasks of Stylistics: Observations Regarding the Style of *The Life of the Archpriest Avvakum*," in Brostrum, *Archpriest Avvakum: The Life written by Himself*, 122; and Jostein Børtnes, "Dissimilar Similarities: *Imitatio Christi* in the *Life* of Archpriest Avvakum," *Canadian-American Slavic Studies* 13 (1979): 226.

[25] Vinogradov, "On the Tasks of Stylistics," 122.

Until its publication in 1861 by the noted scholar Nikolai Tikhonravov, the reading of the Life of Avvakum was limited to merchant and peasant Old Believers, among whom it circulated illegally.[26] After 1861, however, the *Life* acquired many readers in intelligentsia circles, primarily among the gentry and the *raznochintsy*.[27] The readership of the Life became remarkably diverse. Many were captivated by its style and language, which were perceived as quintessentially Russian. "The living speech of Moscow," Ivan Turgenev called it.[28] Leo Tolstoy was similarly entranced, praising Avvakum as a "magnificent stylist" and jotting down words and phrases from the archpriest's writings in his notebooks.[29] In later years he would read the Life aloud to his family.[30] A contemporary of Tolstoy who also admired Avvakum's style was Nikolai Leskov. In an early redaction of *Cathedral Folk*, he imitated the archpriest's style: Avvakum appears in a vision to the priestly hero, Savelii Tuberozov.[31] Avvakum's language continued to provide Leskov with a source for words and expressions, particularly in his stories about Old Believers.[32]

For many Russian intellectuals of a liberal, but not radical stamp, it was Avvakum's style, rather than his personality, that appealed.[33] Turgenev's appraisal is indicative: "Avvakum was coarse and stupid . . .

[26] Robinson, "Tvorchestvo Avvakuma," 104.

[27] Robinson, "Tvorchestvo Avvakuma," 104–05.

[28] A. L. Lukonina, "Moe znakomstvo s I. S. Turgenevym," *Severnyi vestnik*, 1879, no. 2: 55–56. Cited in Robinson, "Tvorchestvo Avvakuma," 122. I am indebted to Robinson's study for acquainting me with many observations made by nineteenth-century Russian intellectuals on Avvakum and his Life. A compilation of such comments is also provided by V. I. Malyshev, "Russkie pisateli o 'Zhitii' protopopa Avvakuma," in his "Zametki o zhitii Avvakuma," *TOdl* 8 (1951): 388–91; and his "Neizvestnye spiski 'Zhitiia' Avvakuma i vyskazyvaniia pisatelei o nem," in his "Neizvestnye i maloizvestnye materialy o protopope Avvakume," *TOdl* 9 (1952): 404.

[29] E. A. Maimin, "Protopop Avvakum v tvorchestve L. N. Tolstogo," *TOdl* 13 (1957): 504–05.

[30] Maimin, "Protopop Avvakum," 505.

[31] I. Z. Serman, "Protopop Avvakum v tvorchestve N. S. Leskova," *TOdl* 14 (1958): 404–05. On the impact of the Life of Avvakum on the composition of *Soboriane*, see also Valentina Gebel', *N. S. Leskov v tvorcheskoi laboratorii* (Moscow, 1945), 98, 134–36; and V. Iu. Troitskii, "Nekotorye siuzhety i obrazy drevnei literatury u N. Leskova," in A. N. Robinson, ed., *Russkaia literatura na rubezhe dvukh epokh (XVII–nachalo XVIII v.)* (Moscow, 1971), 392–95.

[32] Serman, "Protopop Avvakum," 406.

[33] Cf. Robinson, "Tvorchestvo Avvakuma," 121.

but nevertheless he wrote a language such that every writer ought to study it."[34] Leskov was similarly repelled by what he justifiably perceived as Avvakum's fanaticism.[35]

The attitude of some Russian intellectuals towards Avvakum was vastly different, however. Throughout the latter half of the century Russian radicals expressed sympathy, if not downright admiration, for the Old Believers and their intransigent archpriest.[36] The Soviet scholar A. N. Robinson, who has thoroughly documented the reception of Avvakum by nineteenth-century Russian intellectuals, observes that for Russian radicals like those active in the 1860s and later the Populists, it was the perception of Avvakum as a popular hero and fighter that most captured the imagination.[37] Chernyshevskii made a characteristic comment when he exhorted a fellow exile: "Remember Archpriest Avvakum, who frightened the rats with a skull-cap in his dungeon, he was a man, not kissel [a kind of starchy jelly] with gruel."[38] Similarly, in a discussion of Rakhmetov, the radical literary critic Nikolai Shelgunov (1824–1891) urged: "Remember Avvakum, and you will understand what a whole-hearted, organic nature means . . . iron, really iron."[39] Somewhat later, Vera Figner (1852–1942), a member of the terrorist group the People's Will, favorably compared the courageous willingness to die of her comrade Aleksandr Mikhailov (1855–1884) to that of Avvakum.[40]

One of the most striking instances of a radical's admiration for

[34] Lukonina, "Moe znakomstvo s I. S. Turgenevym," 55–56. Cited in Robinson, "Tvorchestvo Avvakuma," 122.

[35] Cf. Serman, "Protopop Avvakum," 406.

[36] Cf. James Billington, *The Icon and the Axe: An Interpretive History of Russian Culture* (New York, 1970), 392, 402. The terrorist and member of the People's Will Aleksandr Mikhailov even settled among the Old Believers for a time, hoping to discover "revolutionary socialistic ideals" among them. See the entry on Mikhailov in the *Bol'shaia sovetskaia entsiklopediia*, 3d ed. (Moscow, 1970–1978). On the possible psychological kinship of the Old Believers and the nihilists, see Zernov, *The Russian Religious Renaissance*, 32.

[37] Robinson, "Tvorchestvo Avvakuma," 125.

[38] V. Ia. Kokosov, "K vospominaniam o N. G. Chernyshevskom," in *Rasskazy o kariiskoi katorge* (St. Petersburg, 1907), 307. Cited in Robinson, "Tvorchestvo Avvakuma," 126.

[39] N. V. Shelgunov, "Russkie idealy, geroi i tipy," in N. K. Piksanov and O. V. Tsekhnovitser, eds., *Shestidesiatye gody: Materialy po istorii literatury i obshchestvennomu dvizheniu* (Moscow, 1940), 180.

[40] Vera Figner, *Pss*, vol. 5 (Moscow, 1929), 265.

Avvakum was that of Gorky, who singled out for praise among all Russian preachers Avvakum and Tikhon of Zadonsk.[41] For Gorky, Avvakum was preeminently a "fighter" (*boets*), and his Life the "unsurpassed model of the fiery and passionate speech of a fighter."[42] Both Avvakkum and Nikon seemed to him "people of exceptional physical and spiritual strength."[43]

The enthusiasm for Avvakum among Russian radicals, which has persisted into the Soviet period, can to some extent be explained by Avvakum's anti-establishment status, by the tendency to "link ideas about Avvakum with progressive aspirations."[44] According to this interpretation of Avvakum, the archpriest resembles nothing so much as a populist radical, filled with sympathy for the common folk and democratic loathing for ecclesiastical and tsarist hierarchies. Yet this reasoning does not entirely explain the respect enjoyed by Avvakum among Russian radicals. For not only the archpriest's supposed populism, but also his intransigence, his fanaticism—in short, his distinctively Josephite qualities—proved appealing to the early Russian radicals and their ideological descendants. Shelgunov's admiring comment cited above is indicative of this tendency, as is the characteristic assertion by the popular Soviet poet Dem'ian Bednyi (1883–1945): "The illustrious Archpriest Avvakum was tormented like a martyr, the man was put in an earthen hole for long years, but he did not yield . . . A man of steel!"[45] While writers like Leskov and Turgenev attempted to dissociate the man from his writings, Russian radicals were confronted by no such dilemma. These intellectuals, in whose cosmology the Avvakum-like Rakhmetov occupied a sacred place, perceived Avvakum's rigid dogmatism as laudable heroism. This view came to influence not only fictionalized Soviet accounts of his life, but also Soviet critical response to reworkings of his autobiography.

Since its publication in 1861, the popularity of Avvakum's Life and the personality of its author has been expressed in several literary works.

[41] M. Gor'kii, *Lev Tolstoi, A. P. Chekhov, V. G. Korolenko* (Moscow, 1928), 52.

[42] M. Gor'kii, *Ss* 27: 166.

[43] V. A. Desnitskii, "A. M. Gor'kii nizhegorodskikh let," in *Gor'kii na rodine: Sb. vospominanii o zhizni M. Gor'kogo v Nizhnem Novgorode* (Gor'kii, 1937), 201. Cited in Robinson, "Tvorchestvo Avvakuma," 129.

[44] Robinson, "Tvorchestvo Avvakuma," 134.

[45] Dem'ian Bednyi, "My partiia truda i poriadka," *Izvestiia*, 4 January 1931. Cited in Robinson, "Tvorchestvo Avvakuma," 135.

Writers have employed both poetry and prose to re-narrate events so graphically described in the archpriest's autobiography and other, imagined incidents. The works which will be discussed here include Daniil Mordovtsev's historical novel *The Great Schism* (*Velikii raskol*, 1881), the poem "Archpriest Avvakum" ("Protopop Avvakum," 1887) by Dmitrii Merezhkovskii, Maksimilian Voloshin's poem of the same name (1918), Vasilii Fedorov's poem "Avvakum" (1964), and Iurii Nagibin's story "The Fiery Archpriest" ("Ognennyi protopop," 1975).[46] All of these works draw on Avvakum's Life and reflect his perception of himself as a saintly figure.

Daniil Mordovtsev (1830–1905) was a writer and historian of liberal, even mildly radical leanings who spent thirty-odd years as a bureaucrat in Saratov. He was the author of numerous historical novels. *The Great Schism* is the story of several prominent figures of the latter half of the seventeenth century, including Avvakum, his arch-enemy Nikon, and several of Avvakum's followers and admirers.[47] Of the latter, the most attention centers on Boiarynia Feodosiia Morozova (1632–1675), a wealthy Muscovite widow who was willing to endure prison and worse in defense of her faith. In contrast to Avvakum's autobiography, the novel plunges *in medias res* with the condemnation of Avvakum and Nikon in Moscow in the 1660s. This narrative structure enabled Mordovtsev to incorporate passages based on Avvakum's autobiography in conversational form. For example, Avvakum responds to the gratifying curiosity of Morozova and other female upper-class adherents of the Old Belief by describing some of his early experiences in prison and Siberia. Many passages in this section and others are borrowed almost verbatim from the original Life.

Yet in spite of Mordovtsev's literal borrowings from Avvakum's autobiography, the personality of the archpriest acquires a different, mellower cast in *The Great Schism*. While the narrator often describes Avvakum as a fanatic and speaks of his iron will, and while the archpriest certainly expresses the intransigence generally associated with him, he exhibits at the same time none of the crude harshness of his

[46] Another renarration of the story of Avvakum was produced by Mikhail Osorgin in 1938. See "Avvakum," in his *Povest' o nekoei devitse: starinnye rasskazy* (Tallinn, 1938), 34–42. Because it is largely only a dry and impersonal recitation of episodes described in Avvakum's *Life*, I have not discussed it here.

[47] The text of *The Great Schism* (*Velikii raskol*) is found in D. L. Mordovtsev, *Ss*, vols. 12–14 (St. Petersburg, 1901).

historical prototype. In private encounters he often appears gentle, even kindly. In addition, his relationship with his wife, of central importance to his autobiography, is given short shrift in Mordovtsev's novel. Instead, the relationship between Avvakum and Morozova is depicted in a chastely romantic light. Avvakum's interest in the gracious *boiarynia* is made explicit when, in a dream about his aforementioned temptation by one of his parishioners, he imagines the young woman as Morozova. This thematic invention gives the archpriest an entirely different image. Rather than appearing the tough-minded zealot of the original Life, he becomes more approachable, more human. This diffuses his Josephite identity, making him display less a radical single-mindedness than a liberal good nature.

While of interest because of its modified image of Avvakum, *The Great Schism* does not so much adapt the archpriest's autobiography or portray the archpriest himself, as fancifully reconstruct all the events and personalities connected with the schism. For adaptations more exclusively concerned with the events narrated in the Life, one must look to the poems by Merezhkovskii and Voloshin. Both of these works present an integrated account of the career of Avvakum.

In the course of his life Dmitrii Merezhkovskii (1866–1941), the husband of the poet Zinaida Gippius, exhibited interest in a number of different political, literary, and religious movements. In his youth a Populist sympathizer, he later associated with the Symbolists and still later with various offbeat religious movements. After the Revolution of 1917, he became an émigré and vehement anti-Communist. Merezhkovskii is best known for his much-translated Christ and Anti-Christ trilogy, *Julian the Apostate, or the Death of the Gods* (*Smert' bogov* [*Iulian Otstupnik*], 1893), *Leonardo da Vinci, or the Gods Resurgent* (*Voskresshie bogi* [*Leonardo da-Vinchi*], 1896), and *Petr and Alexis, or the Antichrist* (*Antikhrist* [*Petr i Aleksei*], 1902). "Archpriest Avvakum" is an early expression of his interest in religious history and issues.

Because of censorship objections, "Archpriest Avvakum" first appeared in print in 1888 in a slightly bowdlerized form. It was published in its entirety, with authorial revisions, in 1904.[48] The poem is

[48] For details, see A. I. Mazunin, "Tri stikhotvornykh perelozheniia 'Zhitiia' protopopa Avvakuma," *TOdl* 14 (1958): 408. Merezhkovskii's and Voloshin's poems are also discussed by Günther Wytrzens, "Der Protopop Avvakum in der russischen schönen Literatur," *Wiener Slavistisches Jahrbuch* 17 (1972): 310–19.

a first-person narrative divided into eleven sections. With the exception of the last, ostensibly written on the day Avvakum is to be burned at the stake, each section treats a major episode described in the Life: the beating of the archpriest by the military commander Afanasii Pashkov, leader of the expedition to Siberia in which Avvakum took part, for example, or the equally famous and much-cited incident, described below, when Avvakum provided his own brand of encouragement to his long-suffering and temporarily despondent wife.

A major difference between Avvakum's Life and Merezhkovskii's rendering of it involves a sentimentalization of the narrative.[49] In the original Life, for example, Avvakum provides the following terse but evocative account of a conversation with his wife in the course of their Siberian exile:

> The country was barbarous, the natives hostile . . . The poor archpriestess dragged herself along, . . . Once, dragging herself along, she fell, and another person just as weary trudged up into her and right there fell down himself. They were both shouting, but they couldn't stand up. The peasant shouted, "Little mother, my Lady, forgive me!" But the Archpriestess shouted, "Why did you crush me, father?" I came up, and the poor [woman] reproached me, saying, "Will these sufferings go on a long time, Archpriest?" And I said, "Markovna, right up to our very death." And sighing, she answered, "Good enough, Petrovich, then let's be getting on" (78).[50]

In Merezhkovskii's hands, the severe contours of this episode are relieved by traces of affection absent from the original:

> Оба на снегу они лежат,
> И барахтаются в шубах, встать не могут и кричат:
> «Задавил меня ты, батько!»—«Государыня, прости!»
> Что тут делать,—смех и горе! я спешу к ним подойти,
> И бранит меня с улыбкой, и бредет она опять:
> «Протопоп ты горемычный, долго ль нам еще страдать?»

[49] Cf. Wytrzens, "Der Protopop Avvakum," 314, 317.

[50] The text of the Life of Avvakum is found in Gudzii, *Zhitie protopopa Avvakuma*, 53–122. In producing my translations, I relied extensively on Kenneth N. Brostrum's translation of the Life. This is found in Brostrum, *Archpriest Avvakum*, 37–112.

«—Видно, Марковна, до смерти!» Тихо, с ласковым
лицом:
«—Что ж, Петрович, отвечает, с Богом дальше
побредем!»

(They were both lying in the snow, and they floundered in their coats, they couldn't stand up and they shouted: "You crushed me, father!"—"Forgive me, my lady!" What is there to do,—laughter and grief! I rushed to go up to them, and she scolded me with a smile, and dragged herself along again: "You wretched archpriest, do we still have long to suffer?" "Apparently until death, Markovna!" Quietly, with an affectionate face, she answered: "Well then, Petrovich, let's be getting on further with God!") (104).[51]

In a similar vein, Avvakum observes of the holy fool Kirill: "Bednyi drug! Kak za rebenkom, ia ukhazhival za nim" ("Poor friend! I looked after him like a child") (101). Such expressions of tenderness are characteristic of the entire poem—they soften the impact of Avvakum's experiences and the impression made by his personality. The archpriest's final precept is fully in keeping with this gentler image: "Tak vozliubim zhe drug druga,—vot poslednii moi zavet./ Vse v liubvi,—zakon i vera. . .vyshe zapovedi net" ("So let's love one another,—here is my last precept. Everything is in love,—law and faith. . . there is no higher commandment") (107). As the Soviet scholar A. I. Mazunin observes, such a forgiving spirit directly contradicts the worldview of the historical archpriest.[52]

Because of its lack of verisimilitude, "Archpriest Avvakum" finds no favor with Mazunin. In fact, he is vehement in his objections to the work: "The poem of D. S. Merezhkovskii, in which Avvakum is shown only as a humble sufferer and martyr, who reconciled himself to his fate and his enemies, excessively impoverishes and denigrates the image of the archpriest."[53] This confirms his earlier assertion that:

From the Life rich in events and facts Merezhkovskii selects only scenes which show the suffering and humility of the archpriest. Avvakum the fighter, the man of enormous energy and will, does

[51] The text of "Archpriest Avvakum" ("Protopop Avvakum") is found in Dmitrii Sergeevich Merezhkovskii, *Pss*, vol. 14 (Moscow, 1914): 99–107.

[52] Mazunin, "Tri stikhotvornykh perelozheniia," 409.

[53] Mazunin, "Tri stikhotvornykh perelozheniia," 409.

> not interest Merezhkovskii and is alien to him, who celebrated not struggle, but weak will, wasting away, and death.[54]

Mazunin's criticisms of Merezhkovskii's portrayal of Avvakum illustrate the official Soviet interpretation of the archpriest, an interpretation inherited from the nineteenth-century Russian radicals with their admiration of Avvakum's Josephite qualities. To some extent his reservations are valid, for Merezhkovskii's Avvakum does exhibit an uncharacteristic spirit of charity and kindliness. Yet Mazunin exaggerates when he asserts that Merezhkovskii desired only to portray the suffering and humility of his hero. While Merezhkovskii's Avvakum does not possess the indomitable will that was the hallmark of his historical prototype, at the same time the majority of his actions and statements are not motivated by the profound humility typical of the kenotic saints, for example. The humility he does exhibit is simply one expression of the general temperateness of his personality as imagined by Merezhkovskii.

At the very beginning of "Archpriest Avvakum," the archpriest declaims: "Gore vam, Nikoniane! vy glumites' nad Khristom,—/ Utverzhdaete vy tserkov' pytkoi, plakhoi da knutom!" ("Woe to you, Nikonites! you mock Christ,—you affirm the church with torture, the executioner's block, and the knout") (99). This accusation sets the tone for the entire narrative. Nikon and his supporters are portrayed as men of grotesque violence, while Avvakum and his followers often exhibit a pleasing courtesy and tenderness. This is not humility but rather Merezhkovskii's apparent notion of the civilizing effect of true religious commitment. His Avvakum is a kindly old gentleman, in whose mouth the strident statements borrowed from the Life have an incongruous ring. As in *The Great Schism*, saintliness in "Archpriest Avvakum" appears as a kind of sentimental religious devotion alien to the original autobiography.

Merezhkovskii's portrayal of Avvakum is vastly different from the image fostered by Soviet historiography and literature. Equally different, but of another tenor, is Maksimilian Voloshin's narrative poem composed in the wake of the 1917 Revolution. The atmosphere of apocalyptic mysticism that informs some of Voloshin's other poems of this period, like "Holy Rus' " ("Sviataia Rus'," 1917), is also characteristic of "Archpriest Avvakum." The first-person account of Avvakum's life

[54] Mazunin, "Tri stikhotvornykh perelozheniia," 408.

is preceded by an introduction with a celestial setting that stresses the divine intention behind the archpriest's genesis:

> И слышал я:
> Отец рече Сынови:
> —Сотворим человека
> По образу и по подобию огня небеснаго . . . —
> И голос был ко мне:
> «Ти подобает облачиться в человека
> Тлимого,
> Плоть восприять и по земле ходить.
> Поди: вочеловечься
> И опаляй огнем!»

(And I heard: the Father said to the Son: —Let us create a man in the image and likeness of heavenly fire. . . —And a voice came to me: "It behooves you to array yourself as a perishable man, to assume flesh and walk on the earth. Go: become a man and singe with fire!") (51–52).[55]

At the end of the poem, Avvakum's execution is presented in a similarly purposeful light:

> Построен сруб—соломою накладен:
> Корабль мой огненный—
> На роднну мне ехать.

(The framework is built—it is heaped with straw: my fiery ship—[it is time] for me to go to my homeland) (71).

Framed by such expressions of divine involvement, the account of Avvakum's life acquires a patina of numinousness, and his experiences assume symbolic as well as historic significance.

Mazunin scorns this development in Voloshin's poem, asserting that in the process the figure of the archpriest is deprived of "[the spirit of] activity" and "will."[56] This criticism does not prove justified. Though filled with symbolic connotations, Voloshin's Avvakum remains distin-

[55] The text of "Archpriest Avvakum" ("Protopop Avvakum") is found in Maksimilian Voloshin, *Demony glukhonemye*, 2d ed. (Berlin, 1923), 51–72. Voloshin was also the author of a lengthy narrative poem on the life of Serafim of Sarov, "Sviatoi Serafim" (1919), which was published in *Novyi zhurnal* 72 (1963): 10–50.

[56] Mazunin, "Tri stikhotvornykh perelozheniia," 410.

guished by an independence of resolve. What is absent from his portrait, and what undoubtedly rendered it less palatable to the Soviet scholar, is only the insistence on steely hardness of character.

Like Merezhkovskii's, Voloshin's poem is divided into roughly a dozen sections, each of which focuses on an important and spectacular episode in Avvakum's life. Voloshin is even more faithful than Merezhkovskii to the language of the original autobiography.[57] His account of the famous conversation between the archpriest and his wife cited above provides a good example:

Приду—она пеняет:
‹‹Долго-ль муки сей нам будет, протопоп?››
А я ей:
‹‹Марковна, до самой смерти››.
Она ж вздохня ответила:
‹‹Добро, Петрович.
Ин дальше побредем››.

(I came up—she reproached [me]: "Will our sufferings go on a long time, archpriest?" And I [said] to her: "Markovna, until [our] very death." And sighing she answered me: "Good enough, Petrovich, then let's be getting on") (58–59).

Unlike Merezhkovskii, Voloshin does not soften the contours of this episode. Rather, he presents the actions and words of the original Life in a succinct and forceful manner.

Another good example of the method of adaptation employed in "Archpriest Avvakum" is the account of the miraculous nourishment of the archpriest during one of his many prison stays. In Avvakum's autobiography this occurrence is described at enthusiastic length:

On the third day I was voracious, that is, I wanted to eat, and after Vespers there stood before me, whether an angel or a man I didn't know and to this day I don't know, but only that he said a prayer in the darkness, and taking me by the shoulder led me with my chain to the bench and sat me down, and put a spoon in my hands and gave me a small loaf of bread and a little cabbage soup to eat—it was very tasty, very good! And he said to me, "Enough, that will suffice thee for strengthening." And he was gone. The

[57] Cf. Wytrzens, "Der Protopop Avvakum," 315.

doors did not open, but he was gone! It's amazing if it was a man, but what if it was an angel? Then there's nothing to be amazed about, there are no barriers to him anywhere (66).

In Voloshin's poem, the important details of this remarkable visitation are described in briefer, even clipped terms:

Ста предо мной—не вем кто—
Ангел, аль человек,—
И хлеба дал и штец хлебать,
А после сгинул,
И дверь не отворялась.

(There stood before me—I don't know who—an angel, or a man,—and gave [me] some bread and cabbage soup to eat, and afterwards disappeared, and the door did not open) (55).

Here as well much of the original lexicon has been retained, but the style is vastly different. Avvakum's winning garrulousness has been replaced by the measured tones of a confirmed, yet serene mystic.

Neither Merezhkovskii nor Voloshin preserves the aggressive and pragmatic religiosity so characteristic of the original autobiography. Merezhkovskii's Avvakum is gentler than his historical prototype; Voloshin's appears curiously detached. Supremely conscious of his own eternal significance, he is less passionately involved in the quotidian details of his existence. In Voloshin's poem, Avvakum emerges as a stylized persona, an iconic distillation of the earthy fanatic who dominates the autobiography: the hagiographical perspective that is only one feature of the original becomes prominent. Explicitly the agent of divine will, Voloshin's Avvakum has a more saintly aura than the protagonists of the other works discussed thus far.

The impact of Avvakum's writings and personality on turn-of-the-century intellectual circles was not limited to fictional representations of his life. In a discussion of the features of the epic Russian woman, Gorky cites the famous conversation between Avvakum and his wife as an expression of essential Russian feminine qualities of simplicity, lovingness, and self-sacrifice.[58] Elsewhere Gorky draws a comparison between the personalities of the archpriest and Leo Tolstoy, saying that there lived within the great writer "part of the obstinate soul of Arch-

[58] Gor'kii, *Ss* 24: 72.

priest Avvakum."[59] Another Russian writer who evoked comparison with Avvakum was Dostoevsky, about whom an admiring listener commented: "When Dostoevsky read, the listener . . . was entirely in the hypnotic power of this emaciated, plain old man, with the penetrating gaze of his eyes . . . which burned with a mystical fire, probably the same luster which once burned in the eyes of Archpriest Avvakum."[60] Much later, Nadezhda Mandel'stam described in her memoirs the intense interest of her husband, the poet Osip Mandel'stam, in Avvakum's Life. She also spoke of the significance of the Life to her after her husband's arrest and disappearance during the 1930s:

> When I was left alone, I kept on being sustained by O. M.'s words: "Why do you think you ought to be happy?" and also by the words of the Archpriest Avvakum: "How much further do we have to go thus, archpriest?" asked his exhausted wife. "Until the very grave, [priest's] wife," answered her husband, and she stood up and and went on.[61]

The admiration for Avvakum's Life by two such antagonistic personalities as Gorky and Nadezhda Mandel'stam attests to the widespread appeal of his violent experiences and compelling manner of narration.

The writings of Avvakum have retained their popularity in the Soviet Union. Between 1956 and 1962 30,000 copies of his writings were published, as many copies or more than Soviet publishers allotted the majority of pre-nineteenth-century Russian writers.[62] The variety of perceptions of the intransigent archpriest in pre-revolutionary and early post-revolutionary literature has disappeared, however. Instead, interpretation of Avvakum's personality and activities codified by official Soviet historiography has had a decided impact on the contemporary fiction and literary criticism devoted to the archpriest. The appraisal by

[59] A. M. Gor'kii, "Lev Tolstoi," in N. N. Gusev and V. S. Mishin, eds., *L. N. Tolstoi v vospominaniakh sovremennikov*, vol. 2 (Moscow, 1955), 413.

[60] S. A. Vengerov in *Rech'*, 25 April 1915. Cited in A. G. Dostoevskaia, *Vospominaniia* (Moscow, 1971), 353.

[61] Nadezhda Mandel'shtam, *Vospominaniia* (New York, 1970), 61. On Osip Mandel'stam's interest in Avvakum, see *Vospominaniia*, 259; and Nadezhda Mandel'shtam, *Vtoraia kniga* (Paris, 1972), 128.

[62] Cf. Maurice Friedberg, "Literary Output: 1956–1962," in Max Hayward and Edward L. Crowley, eds., *Soviet Literature in the Sixties: An International Symposium* (New York, 1964), 173–76.

the Soviet scholar V. E. Gusev in his introduction to a major edition of Avvakum's writings captures the essence of this point of view:

> [Though] a minister of religion, he was simultaneously flesh of the flesh of the simple people, he was "by birth and by worldview the true son of the peasant milieu; bookish enlightenment gave him a certain additional weapon in the battle for the Old Belief, but did not in essence change his nature." And although Avvakum scarcely recognized clearly the actual social content and meaning of the events that were taking place, however, [because he was] connected by innumerable spiritual threads with the representatives of various strata of Russian society, he was *objectively* [emphasis added] the mouthpiece for popular attitudes, he embodied in all his activity, including literary, the spirit of the anti-feudal movement— the passionate implacability, anger, iron will to battle, uncompromising readiness to stand to the death for his ideals,—all those feelings which boiled in the breast of the people, while still enslaved and ignorant, enmeshed in the chains of feudal oppression and religious prejudices.[63]

In a similar vein, a recent biobibliographical dictionary of Russian writers asserts that Avvakum's personal protest against the cruelty inflicted on him "is objectively joined with the democratic protest of the broad laboring masses" and that in his writings one finds "the bright and strong figure of a fighter for an idea."[64] In its emphases, this interpretation easily derives from the opinions of pre-revolutionary Russian radicals. Again, Avvakum emerges as a Josephite of unconsciously progressive tendencies.

Both Vasilii Fedorov's poem "Avvakum" and Iurii Nagibin's story "The Fiery Archpriest" are in keeping with the standard Soviet view of Avvakum. A longtime Communist Party member, Fedorov (1918–) expresses characteristic attitudes in his work. Official Soviet scholarship speaks approvingly of his appraisal of Avvakum's historical significance.[65] The poem begins with a discussion of the grief and chaos into which the schism plunged Russia. The role played by Avvakum in these

[63] Gudzii, *Zhitie protopopa Avvakuma*, 17. Gusev quotes here from N. M. Nikol'skii, *Istoriia russkoi tserkvi* (Moscow, 1930), 119.

[64] See entry on Avvakum in *Russkie pisateli: biobibliograficheskii slovar'* (Moscow, 1971).

[65] See, for example, I. Denisova, *Za krasotu vremen griadushchikh: Poeziia Vasiliia Fedorova* (Moscow, 1971), 33.

events is described in a manner that underscores his unyielding and forceful nature. He reacts with contempt to the demand that he accede to the wishes of his captors: he spits on them and reviles them. When the tsar himself begs him to submit, Avvakum responds with flashing eyes: "Khudu ne uchi! Bog, on pravdu liubit" ("Do not teach evil! God, he loves the truth") (280).[66] Throughout the poem, this archetypally Josephite stubbornness occupies a prominent position in the characterization of the archpriest.

In contrast to Merezhkovskii's and Voloshin's works, Fedorov's "Avvakum" is not a cohesive adaptation of Avvakum's autobiography. Instead, the poem provides a generalized portrayal of the archpriest's existence and emphasizes less his suffering than his often violent assaults on sin and heresy. Fedorov takes liberties with historical reality in order to describe an imagined encounter between Avvakum and Sten'ka Razin (1630?–1671), the leader of a Cossack uprising in 1670–1671 and the darling of Soviet historians, who perceive the rebellion instigated by him as a progressive reaction against feudal oppression. Razin is discussed in exalted, heroic terms. Yet if Fedorov's Avvakum has a fault, it is his blindness to the most appropriate object of his wrath, namely Russia's princely oppressors. His reaction on learning the identity of the Cossack revolutionary is thus one of uncharacteristic fear, for he considers Razin the devil's agent. The narrator regrets this failure to achieve a union:

Дать стране дорогу
Только им по силе.
Стойте!
Сговоритесь,
Черт вас подери!
Не играйте слепо
Судьбами России.

(It is in their power alone to give the country a path. Stop! Come to an agreement, the devil take you! Do not play blindly with the fate of Russia) (286).

In this wistful lament for what might have been, one senses the assumption that Avvakum and Razin embodied common concerns and social

[66] The text of "Avvakum" is found in V. D. Fedorov, *Ss*, vol. 2 (Moscow, 1975), 276–87.

forces. This interpretation of the schism, which downplays the significance of purely religious issues, is typical of Soviet historiography.

Iurii Nagibin (1920–) is probably best known for his portrayal of contemporary, ordinary Soviet life. He has also written a number of stories about Russian writers and composers. "The Fiery Archpriest" reveals its debt to official Soviet perceptions in its very title, which suggests Avvakum's dynamic and unbending character. The story is set on the day of Avvakum's execution and begins with an example of the archpriest's famed refusal to submit to oppression. Called an unfrocked priest by the *strelets* corporal who comes to lead the Old Believers to their execution, Avvakum immediately objects: "I am an archpriest, and not an unfrocked priest" (161).[67] When the strelets rudely order Avvakum's compatriot Epifanii to get moving, Avvakum demands that he show respect for the monastic rank. Further dispute culminates in his assertion: "Even the great sovereign Aleksei Mikhailovich . . . did not teach me to be silent" (162). This proud intransigence typifies his behavior throughout the story, and wins him the grudging respect of even the strelets. Thus, like Fedorov's poem, Nagibin's story more than retains the archpriest's Josephite character.

Much of "The Fiery Archpriest" consists of rambling recollections of Avvakum's experiences recounted in the third person. Many of these are drawn directly from the Life. Unlike some earlier authors, however, Nagibin does not use Avvakum's original lexicon except in the form of direct quotation, offering instead an interpretive description of events that often relies on either a more contemporary or a more poetic vocabulary. His account of the famous conversation between the archpriest and his wife is a good example:

> And then the long-suffering archpriestess . . . wailed with anger and despair: "How much longer will these sufferings go on, Archpriest?" And the archpriest answered her with perhaps the only words capable of lifting her to her feet: "Markovna, right up to our very death!" And sighing, she said: "All right, Petrovich, then let's be getting on" (165).

Whereas the original Life only implicitly suggests the motives that inspire the words of the couple, Nagibin provides a thorough commen-

[67] The text of "The Fiery Archpriest" ("Ognennyi protopop") is found in *Druzhba narodov*, 1975, no. 4: 161–76. The *streltsy* were members of regular army units of the sixteenth and seventeenth centuries.

tary. This didactic tendency is characteristic of the entire story and extends to an explanation of Avvakum's socio-political significance. The narrator claims that the simple people recognized in the archpriest "an intercessor before the Lord God from the anger of the tsar and the patriarch" (165). Avvakum's affinity with the common people is also suggested in the discussion of the church council at which he was condemned: "It was expected that the luminaries of the Greek Orthodox Church . . . would smash and throw down into the dust the muzhik-like priest" (167). Later the narrator speaks of Avvakum's "direct muzhik-like discourse" (170). Indeed, his writings as well as his actions are perceived as demonstrating his admirably unaffected nature. For example, he recalls the monk Epifanii's assertion that what distinguishes him from earlier Russian writers is the fact that he includes in his autobiography prosaic episodes like one involving the family hen.

The lengthy description of the archpriest's execution that occupies much of "The Fiery Archpriest" constitutes a final, wholly invented paean to his invincible courage. Avvakum refuses to beg for mercy and, unlike Merezhkovskii's protagonist, shows no inclination to modify his harshness towards his oppressors, telling the strelets he should expect no softening of his lot in the hereafter. The narrator presents Avvakum's intransigence as opposition to an unjust power, as a rejection of the slavish, blind obedience demanded by this power. In short, he perceives Avvakum less as a religious dissident than as a social revolutionary, an interpretation based on prevailing Soviet views.

In the writings of Fedorov and Nagibin, Avvakum displays a more aggressive and rigid personality than in the novels and poems by Mordovtsev, Merezhkovskii, and Voloshin. While the earlier works have a closer connection with the language of the original Life, the Soviet pieces depict the psychology of the archpriest in a manner more faithful to Avvakum's preeminently Josephite character. For example, in Nagibin's story the purely fictitious conversation of the archpriest exhibits a plausibly coarse tone lacking in Merezhkovskii's or Mordovtsev's more genteel portrayals.

All of the works discussed here retain the auto-hagiographical bias of the *Life of the Archpriest Avvakum, Written by Himself*: they all implicitly praise Avvakum for his distinctive brand of piety and reveal nothing but scorn for his opponents. Once again, however, the difference lies in what the various authors perceive as admirable about the archpriest. Merezhkovskii, Mordovtsev, and Voloshin give greater prominence to his faith, Fedorov and Nagibin to the ruthlessness and harsh courage which he employs in the defense of that faith. It is the Soviet writers who thus more fully capture the Josephite essence of Avvakum's personality.

THE CONTINUED Soviet mining of Avvakum's Life as a subject for poetic or fictional treatment bears witness to the enthusiasm still generated by Josephite values. Such enthusiasm embraces a wide variety of literary possibilities. The severe and intransigent faith lauded by Josephite hagiographers (and auto-hagiographers) finds an admiring reception not only in purportedly historical representations, but also in "modern" characters who display Josephite qualities. On one level, the Avvakum of the archpriest's own account and the populist zealot of official Soviet interpretation, as well as steely progressives like Rakhmetov and Pavel Vlasov, are but two sides of the same typological coin. The latter echo the former, much as Dostoevsky's kenotic heroes display associations with their saintly models. In this context, Chernyshevskii's and Gorky's strong approval of Avvakum should not be forgotten, for radical approbation of Josephite attitudes was often firmly grounded in the Old Russian literary and hagiographical tradition.

The literary admiration of Josephite character traits by pre-revolutionary Russian radicals and conformist Soviet writers has led to the secularization of traditional saintliness in the cause of a sanctified social purpose. While Soviet scholars concur with Avvakum in considering him a laudable figure, their reasons often diverge. In the eyes of the former, much of the archpriest's praiseworthiness derives from his social rather than religious significance. In the case of Avvakum's radical literary confreres, this shift in emphasis is made completely explicit: these sober paragons exhibit a religious fervor in their devotion to purely secular aims. The persistence of the Josephite type in modern Russian culture thus lies, not in a commitment to any specific faith, but in the ways in which that faith reveals itself. In contrast to the kenotic, the hallmark of Josephite behavior remains not a precise spiritual philosophy, but the external manifestations of an unyielding dogmatism.

CHAPTER SIX

Anti-Hagiography: Tolstoy's Assault on Orthodoxy

> But the usual attributes of places of the administration of justice were the same: the mirror, the icon—emblem of hypocrisy—and the portrait of the sovereign—emblem of servility.
>
> Leo Tolstoy, ***Resurrection***

OF THE MANY approaches to hagiography adopted by Russian writers, one of the most complex and effective was that of Leo Tolstoy. Unlike many of his contemporaries, Tolstoy could not dissociate hagiography from its ecclesiastical context, could not divorce literature from religious ideology. When he rejected Orthodoxy, he also rejected many of its literary productions. In doing so, he appears to have made a distinction between official and popular hagiography, just as he distinguished between institutionalized and popular Christianity, condemning the one and applauding the other. In two of his later works, "The Posthumous Notes of the Elder Fedor Kuzmich" ("Posmertnye zapiski startsa Fedora Kuzmicha," 1905) and "Father Sergii" ("Otets Sergii," 1890–1898), he implies a scathing criticism of official hagiography and of various aspects of Orthodoxy. These two stories represent Tolstoy's final resolution of a lifelong uncertainty about the authenticity of saints and their followers and the literature devoted to them. As such, they occupy an important place among modern Russian works influenced by hagiography.

Tolstoy's Religious Ambivalence

Like many of his peers, Tolstoy was exposed at an early age to hagiography and the popular devotion to saints, holy men, and the miraculous. This was at least partially due to the presence throughout his childhood of his aunt Aleksandra Osten-Saken at his home, Yasnaya Polyana. Aleksandra Osten-Saken was in her later years deeply religious: she lived a simple life of service and charity and eventually died at Optina Pustyn'. In his unfinished memoirs begun in 1903, Tolstoy gives a thumbnail sketch of his aunt's existence: "Her favorite occupations were readings of saints' Lives and conversations with wanderers, holy fools, monks, and nuns, some of whom always lived in our home, while some would only visit my aunt."[1]

Such childhood impressions had an impact on Tolstoy's fictional writings long before he became preoccupied with the proper expression of religious commitment. One of Aleksandra's frequent visitors was a lay nun who in her youth had wandered about Russia disguised as the holy fool Ivanushka. She undoubtedly provided the model for the young monk Ivanushka, also a woman in disguise, who appears in *War and Peace* (*Voina i mir*, 1869) in the episode of the visit of "God's folk" to Princess Mariia Bolkonskaia at Bald Hills. Ivanushka is accompanied by the garrulous old pilgrim Pelageia, who enthusiastically describes for her upper-class audience a wonderworking icon of the Mother of God. The old woman is particularly impressed by the icon's ability to weep tears of holy oil and is upset when Pierre and Prince Andrei react sceptically to this display of credulity.

This brief episode is symptomatic of the ambivalence regarding religion in general and Orthodoxy in particular characteristic of Tolstoy's earlier works, from *Childhood* to *Anna Karenina* (1877). A respect for the simple religious devotion of the common people on the part of some, generally female, members of the educated elite is matched by an intolerance among other upper-class characters of the mystical, miraculous, and ritualistic side of Orthodoxy. As was seen earlier, such ambivalence also expresses itself in the episode in *Childhood* involving the wanderer and holy fool Grisha. Nikolai Irtenev's father, and initially Nikolai himself, scoff at Grisha's eccentric habits and pretensions to mystical intuition. Yet like Princess Mariia, both Nikolai's mother and eventually Nikolai himself admire the holy man's naive religiosity.

These ambiguities were not resolved in *Childhood*. A resolution of the conflict between yearning for faith and distaste for ritual was deferred for decades. How terrible a problem this could be is very clearly illustrated in *Anna Karenina*, in Konstantin Levin's wedding preparations. Levin must take communion so he may marry within the Church, and he wrestles with the conflicting feelings evoked by the enforced involve-

[1] L. N. Tolstoi, *Pss*, 90 vols. (Moscow, 1928–1958), 34: 363.

ment in Orthodox ritual. Untouched or even irritated by the ceremonies in which he must participate, he nonetheless senses that some part of the truth is at stake here, and he reacts with mixed emotions to the old priest who gives him communion:

> he was left with a vague recollection that what the kind, nice old man had said to him was not at all as stupid as it had seemed to him at first, and that there was something here that needed to be clarified. "Of course, not now," thought Levin, "but sometime later." Even more than before, Levin now felt that there was something vague and unclean in his soul, and that with regard to religion he was in the same position that he saw so clearly and disliked in others.[2]

In the thirty-odd years after the writing of *Anna Karenina*, the search for spiritual clarity came to occupy first place in Tolstoy's creative activity, and the vagueness from which Levin suffered was largely overcome by the author. Tolstoy's ambivalence was resolved by the decisive separation of faith and ritual; after a brief dalliance with Orthodoxy in the late 1870s, he proceeded to condemn the official Church, linking ritual to hypocrisy and evil. "What is a church?" asks Beelzebub in the reworking of a legend, "The Destruction of Hell and Its Restoration" ("Razrushenie ada i vosstanovlenie ego," 1903), and one of his servant devils responds: "A church is what you have when people lie and, feeling that they're not being believed, always say, calling God to witness: 'By God, what I say is true.' "[3] And in his diary Tolstoy concluded: "Orthodoxy and Christianity have in common only the name. If ecclesiastics [*tserkovniki*] are Christians, then I am not a Christian, and vice versa."[4] How pernicious and corrupt Tolstoy came to consider the representatives and rituals of the Church is amply illustrated in *Resurrection* (*Voskresenie*, 1899) (the novel whose proceeds he used to finance the emigration to Canada of the Dukhobors, members of a Christian sect persecuted by the tsarist government). One of the most damning passages concerns a service conducted for a group of prisoners. The episode provides an excellent example of Tolstoy's well known satirical use of the device of *ostranenie*. From the priest's clothing to the

[2] *Pss* 19: 8.

[3] *Pss* 34: 103.

[4] Diary entry 3 August 1890, *Pss* 51: 71.

biblical text selected for the reading, every aspect of the service is subjected to merciless criticism.[5] Not even the sacrament of the Eucharist is exempt from mockery:

> The essence of the service consisted in the assumption that the small pieces of bread cut by the priest and placed in the wine, with certain manipulations and prayers, are transformed into the body and blood of God. . . . The principal act occurred when the priest, having taken a napkin with both hands, rhythmically and slowly waved it over the saucer and the golden cup. This was the very moment when from the bread and wine were made flesh and blood, and therefore this part of the service was surrounded with particular solemnity.[6]

The priest here is perceived as ridiculous at best, a hypocritical participant in a meaningless ritual at worst. Moreover, attention is implicitly drawn to the false status of the Church as the handmaiden of the state. This evil comes under explicit attack in "The Divine and the Human" ("Bozheskoe i chelovecheskoe," 1906), in which a priest attempts unsuccessfully to offer his services to the revolutionary Anatolii Svetlogub immediately before his execution. "Merciful Lord," he begins, but Svetlogub will not allow him to continue, and the narrator comments: "He almost said an unkind word to the priest who was participating in what was being done to him and was speaking about mercy."[7] As is well-known, Tolstoy's outspoken opposition to the Church and growing influence eventually led to his excommunication in 1901.

A logical component of Tolstoy's interest in exposing Orthodoxy's moral bankruptcy was a critical examination of hagiography. He was undoubtedly familiar with numerous saints' Lives. His library at Yasnaya Polyana included both the *Prolog* and the *Reading Menaea*.[8] More important than the mere fact of possession, in *A Confession* (*Ispoved'*,

[5] The term *ostranenie* (literally, making strange) was first used by the Formalist critic Viktor Shklovskii to describe the device of presenting a scene from an alienated perspective. Shklovskii alludes to this episode in "Paralleli u Tolstogo," in his *Khod konia: Sbornik statei* (Moscow, 1923), 118.

[6] *Pss* 32: 135.

[7] *Pss* 42: 211.

[8] On the precise editions of the *Reading Menaea* and the *Prolog* consulted by Tolstoy, see Tolstoi, *Pss* 23: 534.

1882) Tolstoy asserts that in the course of his search for faith the Lives of holy men became his favorite readings:

> I listened to the conversation of an illiterate peasant wanderer about God, faith, life, and salvation, and the knowledge of faith was disclosed to me. I became close to the people, listening to their opinions about life and faith, and I understood the truth more and more. The same thing happened to me on reading the *Reading Menaea* and the *Prolog*; it became my favorite reading. Excluding the miracles and regarding them as fables expressing thoughts, this reading opened to me life's meaning. There were the Lives of Macarius the Great, of the prince Ioasaf (the story of Buddha), there were the discourses of John Chrysostom, the discourses about the traveller in the well, the monk who found gold, and Peter the publican. There were the stories of the martyrs, all announcing one thing, that death does not exclude life; and there were the stories of the ignorant, stupid men who knew nothing about the teaching of the Church, but were saved.[9]

In a similar vein the narrator of the unfinished story "Notes of a Madman" ("Zapiski sumashedshego," 1884) observes of his spiritual regeneration: "From that time I began to read the holy scripture. The Bible was incomprehensible to me, seductive, while the Gospel moved me. But most of all I read the Lives of the saints. And this reading comforted me, offering examples which seemed more and more possible for imitation."[10] In her diary, Tolstoy's wife Sof'ia confirms this impression, noting that her husband called the Lives of the saints "our real Russian poetry."[11]

At the same time, however, Tolstoy also objected vehemently to the implications of some hagiographical works, to the notion of a network of saints capable of accomplishing astonishing miracles. While in *What is Art?* (*Chto takoe iskusstvo?*, 1898) he approved of the early Christianity that "recognized as good works of art only legends, saints' Lives, ser-

[9] *Pss* 23: 52. Tolstoy translated a few such Lives into modern Russian for popular consumption. For discussion of these, see Al'bert Opul'skii, *Zhitiia sviatykh v tvorchestve pisatelei XIX veka* (East Lansing, Mich., 1986), 92–93, 100.

[10] *Pss* 26: 473.

[11] *Dnevniki Sof'i Andreevny Tolstoi. 1860–1891*, M. and S. Sabashnikov, ed. (1928), 34. Cited in E. A. Maimin, "Protopop Avvakum v tvorchestve L. N. Tolstogo," *TOdl* 13 (1957): 503.

mons, prayers, and hymns that evoked in people love of Christ, tender emotion [*umilenie*] at His life, desire to follow His example, renunciation of worldly life, humility, and the love of people," he condemned ecclesiastical Christianity for "having established a heavenly hierarchy similar to the pagan mythology, the worship of it, of Christ, of the Mother of God, of angels, of apostles, of saints, and of martyrs, and not only of these divinities but also of their images."[12] Tolstoy objected to art devoted to this "heavenly hierarchy" because he considered it divisive, intended to provoke hostility toward adherents of other religions.[13]

Implicit in Tolstoy's comments about official Christianity, saints, and art is an acute awareness of Church painting, music, and literature as propaganda. This follows logically from his theory, developed in *What is Art?*, of the didactic capacity of art. Tolstoy recognized the tremendous popularity of hagiographical literature among the peasants; his own adaptations of hagiographical tales for didactic purposes testify to this. To the extent, then, that hagiographical works propagated ecclesiastical thought, they could only be inimical to Tolstoy. While there were some exceptions, many Lives or parts of Lives must have been objectionable to him. In the passage cited above, for example, he says that he disregarded the miracles described in the Lives he singles out. In this context, Georges Florovsky's observation about Tolstoy's approach to religious literature is apropos: "He would read the lives of the saints, the writings of the fathers and masters of spirituality; but, again, he was selective, omitting miracles and whatever pertained to dogma. Christianity was not his actual starting point."[14]

This observation is borne out by the fact that even when Tolstoy professed admiration for some saints recognized by the Orthodox or Catholic Church, he attempted to isolate their virtue from their adherence to an ecclesiastical organization:

> All these good people—like both Francises, of Assisi and of Lobes, our Tikhon of Zadonsk, Thomas à Kempis, and others, were good people, in spite of the fact that they served a cause hostile to Christianity [the Church], and they would have been even better and

[12] *Pss* 30: 69–70.

[13] *Pss* 30: 157.

[14] "Three Masters: The Quest for Religion in Nineteenth- Century Russian Literature," *Comparative Literature Studies* 3 (1966): 134.

> more worthy if they had not fallen under the sway of the delusion which they served.[15]

In using hagiography in his own writings, Tolstoy pursued various approaches. Earlier it was seen how, like his contemporary Leskov, he adapted hagiographical tales that confirmed (or could be altered to confirm) his own anti-ecclesiastical conception of Christianity. In "Three Old Men" this purpose is achieved simply by emphasizing the latent implications of the original tale, which exalts naive faith over formal religiosity. In "Two Brothers and Gold" the plot and the status of the characters are changed so as to eliminate any positive references to monasticism; the narrative focuses exclusively on the superiority of unassuming good works to ostentatious material charity. In the unfinished play based on the folk variant of the legend of Aggei, the *pan*'s moral regeneration also leads to a devotion to good works; here Tolstoy accomplished his intention by combining different versions of the original story to produce a plot most congenial to his own moral view.

Stories like these and Tolstoy's own comments on his reading of saints' Lives suggest that he believed that some hagiographical works possessed redeeming features and that some saints were worthy of admiration. Two types of holy men, however—the virtuous ruler and the saintly monk—, rarely evoked anything but scepticism and scorn. The former was unpalatable as the embodiment of an inhumane state, the latter as the proponent of an unproductive Orthodoxy. In "The Posthumous Notes of the Elder Fedor Kuzmich" and "Father Sergii" Tolstoy "exposes" myths of the pious ruler and the self-denying monk. Unlike his adaptations of hagiographical tales, which take place in a chronological limbo, these two stories have a nineteenth-century setting, and their criticism of contemporary society and religious life is much more direct. At the same time, however, both "The Posthumous Notes of the Elder Fedor Kuzmich" and "Father Sergii," but especially the latter, make significant statements about longstanding assumptions of hagiography.

Fedor Kuzmich and the Saintly Prince

As early as 1890, Tolstoy thought of writing about Fedor Kuzmich, the wandering holy man rumored to be Alexander I. While he considered

[15] This observation is made in *The Kingdom of God is Within You* (*Tsarstvo bozhie vnutri vas*, 1890–1893), *Pss* 28: 56.

him to be an obvious impostor who purposely surrounded himself with an atmosphere of secrecy, he thought that the legend of Alexander's transformation itself possessed a certain beauty.[16] In late 1905 he finally began "The Posthumous Notes of the Elder Fedor Kuzmich." The story was never finished, however, and it appeared in print only posthumously in 1912.[17]

The legend of Fedor Kuzmich has been said to exhibit "the features of the saint-prince cult."[18] The belief that the wanderer was in reality Alexander I has found adherents even in this century.[19] As the historian Michael Florinsky points out, the legend is in keeping with the mystery that surrounded the "enigmatic tsar" during his lifetime.[20] According to the legend, Alexander did not really die at Taganrog in 1825. Instead, resolving to atone for the patricide with which his reign began, the tsar arranged his own disappearance. A common soldier was buried in his place; he himself secretly vanished and adopted the guise of the itinerant hermit Fedor Kuzmich. The latter first attracted attention in 1836. Flogged and exiled because he did not own a passport, he died in Siberia in 1864. After his death he was popularly venerated as a saint.[21]

The veneration extended to Alexander in the guise of Fedor Kuzmich was not without precedent in his lifetime. As noted, the image of the saintly prince often exerted a powerful appeal for the Russian cultural consciousness. Michael Cherniavsky has chronicled the rediscovery in the course of the Napoleonic wars, largely on the part of the gentry, of the image of the saintly ruler.[22] In 1814 this culminated in the joint

[16] See M. S. Sukhotin's account of his conversation with Tolstoy about Fedor Kuzmich in "Tolstoi v poslednee desiatiletie svoei zhizni po zapisiam v dnevnike M. S. Sukhotina," in *Literaturnoe nasledstvo*, vol. 69, no. 2 (Moscow, 1961): 148. See also Tolstoy's letter of 2 September 1907 to Grand Duke Nikolai Mikhailovich in *Pss* 77: 185.

[17] *Pss* 36: 588–89.

[18] Michael Cherniavsky, *Tsar and People: Studies in Russian Myths* (New Haven, 1961), 147.

[19] For the most detailed account of the controversy, see Lev Liubimov, *Taina imperatora Aleksandra I* (Paris, 1938). Folk stories reminiscent of the legend of Fedor Kuzmich were told about Vladimir Lenin after his death. See Nina Tumarkin, *Lenin Lives!: The Lenin Cult in Soviet Russia* (Cambridge, Mass., 1983), 198–99.

[20] Michael T. Florinsky, *Russia: A History and an Interpretation*, 2 vols. (New York, 1953), 2: 650.

[21] In his *Istoriia kanonizatsii sviatykh v russkoi tserkvi* (Moscow, 1894), E. E. Golubinskii includes Fedor in his list of "revered deceased [ascetics]" ("*pochitaemye usopshie [podvizhniki]*") (343).

[22] Cherniavsky, *Tsar and People*, 128–36, especially.

decision by the Senate, the State Council, and the Holy Synod to give Alexander the new title, "The Blessed" (*Blagoslovennyi*). As Cherniavsky observes, "for the nineteenth century, Aleksandr Blagoslovennyi was an equivalent for what, in earlier centuries, would have been St. Alexander."[23] While to some extent this action constituted nothing more than deliberate myth-making, it also represented a sincere, nearly reverential admiration for the charismatic tsar. It has been claimed that Alexander enjoyed a greater popularity than any tsar since Aleksei Mikhailovich, the seventeenth-century ruler given the sobriquet "the quietest one" (*tishaishii*).[24] Tolstoy captures this attitude in the description in *War and Peace* of Nikolai Rostov's enthusiasm for Alexander, which, the writer hastens to observe, is typical of the Russian soldiers. "My God! How happy I would be if he ordered me to throw myself into the fire right now," thinks Nikolai.[25] When he sees Alexander again, his reaction is described in terms eminently applicable to the image of a saintly prince:

> As he approached everything became brighter, more joyful, more significant, and more festive around him. Closer and closer to Rostov moved that sun shedding beams of mild and majestic light around itself, and here he already felt himself enveloped in those beams, he heard his voice—that affectionate, calm, majestic, and yet so simple voice.[26]

"The Posthumous Notes of the Elder Fedor Kuzmich" represents a conscious debunking both of the notion that there was anything particularly remarkable about Alexander prior to his flight from office and of the idea that Fedor Kuzmich was a saint. An indictment of the viciousness of imperial life based on details culled from memoirs and historical accounts, the story also demonstrates that the attainment of virtue demands a constant struggle.[27] Fedor Kuzmich emerges not as a noble ruler turned serene saint, but as a complex personality whose moral

[23] Cherniavsky, *Tsar and People*, 135.

[24] Allen McConnell, *Tsar Alexander I: Paternalistic Reformer* (New York, 1970), 186.

[25] *Pss* 9: 302.

[26] *Pss* 9: 311.

[27] On Tolstoy's sources, see *Pss* 36: 585. Tolstoy's most extensively used source was N. K. Shil'der, *Imperator Aleksandr Pervyi, ego zhizn' i tsarstvovanie*, 4 vols. (St. Petersburg, 1897–1898).

strivings are evocative more of Tolstoy himself than of the often two-dimensional hermits of hagiographical legends.

In his reminiscences about his birth, Tolstoy's Alexander mentions that he was given his name at the wish of his grandmother, Catherine the Great, as an augury that he should be as great a person as Alexander the Great and as saintly as Alexander Nevskii. The mention of the Novgorodian hero points explicitly to the role played by the image of the saintly prince in the spontaneous as well as intentional propaganda surrounding the person of Alexander I. The reality was very different from the image, however, as the sometime ruler observes early in his notes:

> In Taganrog I lived in the same state of folly in which I had lived all these last twenty-four years. I, the greatest criminal, the murderer of my father, the murderer of hundreds of thousands of people in wars of which I was the cause, a vile debauchee, a villain, believed what was said about me, considered myself the savior of Europe, the benefactor of mankind, an exceptional perfection, un heureux hasard, as I said to Madame de Staël. I considered myself such, but God did not abandon me completely, and the vigilant voice of my conscience gnawed at me unceasingly (60–61).[28]

This bitter self-condemnation is a significant departure from the traditional image of the saintly prince. Most striking is the denunciation of military achievement. While the victories of medieval princes like Alexander Nevskii and Dmitrii Donskoi were sources of hagiographical glory, Alexander I's accomplishments in the Napoleonic wars are perceived as nothing more than mass murder. Thus martial prowess, one primary attribute of many saintly princes, is denied Alexander, and, even more importantly, its general validity is implicitly questioned. Deprived of his claims to military greatness, Tolstoy's hero is not permitted any other virtues either. "Vile debauchee" and the other terms of opprobrium which he heaps upon himself are not expressions of the modesty topos, for nothing in Fedor's recollections of his imperial self serves to contradict this unflattering self-appraisal. "The Notes" are unfinished, and hence little is learned about Alexander's adult life except for the days immediately preceding his pretended death, but what little is described is wrapped in an atmosphere of falsity and pride.

[28] The text of "The Posthumous Notes of the Elder Fedor Kuzmich" ("Posmertnye zapiski startsa Fedora Kuzmicha") is found in *Pss* 36: 59–74.

Even as a child Alexander manifests an exaggerated sense of self-importance, forcing his playmate Sasha Golitsyn, the future ober-procurator of the Holy Synod, to ask his forgiveness for having accidentally pushed him. Fedor observes, "It was impressed upon us . . . that all people are equal and that we must remember this. But I knew that those who spoke thus did not believe this" (72).

Given the depravity of Alexander's existence as tsar, his decision secretly to abandon his throne comes not as a logical culmination to a virtuous life, but as a radical break with his past. Like many Tolstoyan characters, Alexander realizes that he has been preoccupied with externals, that his real concern should be the nurturing of his soul. Significantly, this is accompanied by a loss of interest in the good opinion of those around him: "And all my former desires to renounce the throne, which were then [motivated] by the desire to show off, to astonish, to grieve people, to show them my greatness of soul, now returned, but they returned with new force and with complete sincerity, no longer for people, but for myself, for my soul" (64).

From a Tolstoyan point of view, Alexander's moral instincts are correct when he seeks to abandon his throne unbeknownst to anyone. Yet, just as Alexander's life as tsar does not conform to the stereotype of a saintly prince, so too does his existence as the wanderer Fedor Kuzmich not prove entirely free from lapses in virtue. There is a continuity between Alexander's two lives symbolically expressed by the intense dislike he feels, as tsar, for Louis XVIII of France, and, as a simple hermit, for his constant visitor Nikanor Ivanovich. "Nikanor Ivanovich is a great temptation for me" (69), observes Fedor. Exposure to the object of his enmity evokes in him a gloom which he dishonestly attributes to poor health. Thus, although those around him ascribe to him numerous powers and virtues, the old man has not yet attained the serenity he seeks. "Their notion about my insight is very oppressive to me. Everything that I say in opposition they ascribe to my humility" (69), he says. As in the case of Alexander belittling his greatness, this is not an instance of false modesty. Moreover, in dismissing any imputations of saintly insight on his part, Fedor is expressing a typically Tolstoyan anti-mystical bias.

The true state of Fedor's soul is revealed in his dreams. As he himself notes, "when one is awake it is possible to deceive oneself, but a dream gives a true appraisal of the degree [of virtue] which you have attained" (68). In one of his dreams, a strange woman presses close against him and instead of being afraid of her or of sin, Fedor worries only that his wife will see. In another, he greedily hoards some pieces of candy, refusing to share them with a little boy. The message is clear to the point of heavy-handedness; however he appears to others, Fedor's inner being is far from saintly.

Even in their unfinished state, "The Notes" provide an illuminating contrast to a conventional hagiographical legend. On the one hand, the saintly prince so dear to Orthodoxy, heroic in battle and virtuous at home, is roundly rejected. It seems unlikely that the late Tolstoy would have found any of the medieval saintly princes more deserving of admiration than Alexander I. On the other hand, while "The Notes" attest to Fedor's sincerity in trying to live virtuously, they also demonstrate that he has by no means achieved saintliness. More than anything else, "The Notes" call into question the notion of total and instantaneous moral transformation often reflected in Orthodox hagiography. Instead, their picture of moral striving free from mysticism and the miraculous is more in keeping with Tolstoy's own conception of the path to goodness.

Father Sergii and the Saintly Monk

The "Posthumous Notes" present a distinctly Tolstoyan alternative to the traditional Orthodox view of the ruler and wandering holy man. "Father Sergii" also seeks to offer a corrective to Orthodox views. In it, monasticism, one of the cherished institutions of Orthodoxy, comes under attack. Throughout "Father Sergii," brilliant psychological analysis of vanity and its dangers accompanies a scathing exposure of the pitfalls of the monastic life. Yet this assault appears in a story which owes a large debt to the hagiographical tradition. Both the structure and meaning of "Father Sergii" should be analyzed against the backdrop of hagiography.[29]

As has been pointed out, most notably by Rostislav Pletnev, portions of Father Sergii's story are extremely reminiscent of the legend of the Phoenician hermit Iakov the Faster, found in both the *Reading Menaea* and the *Prolog*.[30] Both Sergii and Iakov resist the blandishments

[29] An earlier version of this section of this chapter appeared in "Hagiographical Motifs in Tolstoy's 'Father Sergius,' " *South Atlantic Review* 47 (1982): 63–80.

[30] The legend of Iakov is found under March 4 in the *Reading Menaea* and December 27 in the *Prolog*. It lacks sections on the childhood and youth of the saint, and begins

of a sinful woman through self-inflicted pain, achieve great fame, and perform miracles, only to succumb to sexual temptation because of an excess of pride. Yet "Father Sergii" is not a reworking of a hagiographical legend like, for example, Leskov's "Beauteous Aza" or Tolstoy's own "Two Brothers and Gold,"—"Father Sergii" deals, not with the world of the early Christian desert fathers, but with nineteenth-century Russia. In it a young man, upon discovering that his fiancée has been the mistress of Nicholas I, abandons a promising military career to become a monk, only to find true spiritual fulfillment after he leaves the monastic life in shame.[31] The implications of this story are broader than those of the more straightforward reworkings: the subject of "Father Sergii" is less a specific hagiographical legend than hagiography itself—in particular, the type of hagiography devoted to monastic saints. In this context, it seems no accident that Tolstoy's protagonist bears the name of Russia's most beloved saint, Sergii of Radonezh.

Examination of "Father Sergii" reveals adaptations of many hagiographical topoi. Idiosyncratic as Sergii's ultimate path to salvation may be, until he yields to sexual temptation he both behaves like and is considered a saint. Yet there is a significant difference between Tolstoy's handling of topoi and that of the traditional hagiographer. For traditional hagiography, topoi normally not only supply guidelines for behavior, but also serve as spiritual markers. A saintly action is assumed to stem from a saintly motive. In the case of Father Sergii, however, this assumption does not prove justified. Instead, an ever-widening gap

---

with his temptation by the harlot. As far as I can ascertain, Iakov is identical with the sixth-century Syrian James the Hermit who is honored by the Catholic Church on January 28. Pletnev's comparison between Iakov and Sergii is outlined in "'Otets Sergii' i Chet'i Minei," *Novyi zhurnal* 40 (1955): 118–131. A version of this article also appeared in German in *Zeitschrift für slavische Philologie* 10 (1933): 106–25. More recent discussions of this parallel are found in E. Kupreianova, "Motivy narodnogo eposa i drevnei literatury v proizvedeniiakh L. N. Tolstogo," *Russkaia literatura*, 1963, no. 2: 163–68; Dietrich Gerhardt, "Tolstoj, Irtenev und Otec Sergius," *Die Welt der Slaven* 18 (1973): 121–52; Julia Alissandratos, "Leo Tolstoy's 'Father Sergius' and the Russian Hagiographical Tradition," *Cyrillomethodianum* 8–9 (Thessaloniki, 1984–1985): 149–63; and Opul'skii, *Zhitiia sviatykh*, 117–20. Pletnev argues that "Father Sergii" is not anti-Orthodox. My analysis of the story, which in some ways coincides with that of Alissandratos (see especially 156–62), does not support this interpretation.

[31] It is interesting to note that one of the famous nineteenth-century Russian mystics, Ignatii Brianchaninov, was an officer in the engineers before he became a monk and was for a long time opposed by Nicholas himself in his desire to abandon his secular career.

between motive and behavior becomes evident in the course of the story.

The youth of Stepan Kasatskii, later Father Sergii, would seem to have much in common with that of a typical saint. Of noble birth, he is well-endowed with physical, moral, and intellectual charms. His behavior as a young cadet is generally exemplary; "he did not drink or lead a dissolute life, and he was remarkably upright"(5).[32] He is generous and seemingly unpreoccupied with material gain; when he joins a regiment, he gives half his fortune to his sister because the remainder is more than adequate for his support. His capacity for learning is also tremendous, and he excels at anything to which he chooses to devote himself, whether that be mathematics, French, chess, or riding.

Nor is the young man devoid of religious inclination. When he decides to make a complete break with his former life and enter a monastery, his sister errs in assuming that he is inspired solely by a prideful desire to show his contempt for an uncongenial world. As the narrator points out, mingled with his "feeling of pride and his desire for ascendancy" is a "truly religious feeling," a "childlike faith" (11) which has never been destroyed. The notion of a faith which goes back almost to the cradle is another aspect of the topos of precocious piety. In conjunction with his capacity for astounding intellectual achievement and his propensity for the righteous life, the suggestion that Kasatskii has been a believer since childhood completes the picture of an aspiring monastic saint. This picture is subtly undermined, however, in a number of ways. Although Kasatskii generally behaves in a laudable fashion, his quick temper leads him to violent excesses. Nor is he sexually chaste. Even more importantly, his search for self-perfection is marred precisely by that pride and desire to shine sensed by his sister. Indeed, it is Kasatskii's inordinate desire for recognition that ultimately paves the way for his downfall. Although the prince exhibits some characteristics typical of a saint even before he becomes a monk, he carries at the same time the seeds of his own destruction within him. His moral situation resembles that of the young Tolstoy himself as described in *A Confession*:

> The beginning of everything was, it goes without saying, [the search for] moral perfection, but soon it was replaced by [the search for] perfection in general, i.e. by the desire to be better not before oneself or before God, but by the desire to be better before

[32] The text of "Father Sergii" ("Otets Sergii") is found in *Pss* 21: 5–46.

people. And very soon this striving to be better before people was replaced by the desire to be stronger than other people, i.e. more glorious, more important, richer than others.[33]

When Kasatskii decides to enter a monastery, his mother tries to dissuade him, presumably because she feels it would be a waste of his talents. This conflict resembles that of numerous saints and holy men, including Feodosii of the Kievan Cave Monastery and Paisii Velichkovskii (who is mentioned in "Father Sergii"); Feodosii's mother repeatedly thwarted his desires, even using physical violence to do so, while Paisii was forced secretly to leave Kiev (and his mother) in order to become a monk. Kasatskii's gift of his entire estate to his sister at this time, mentioned at the very beginning of the story, and the donation of the rest of his fortune to the monastery he enters should be noted, for they also constitute conventional gestures. In an earlier era, for example, Anthony of Egypt, to whom explicit reference is also made in "Father Sergii," gave away all his property and sold his possessions for the benefit of the poor, retaining only a small sum for his sister's support. He later decided that even this must be relinquished and placed his sister in a convent. That the narrator of "Father Sergii" draws attention to Kasatskii's gifts provides yet another link between the young man and the typical saint of hagiography.

The monastic existence of Kasatskii (now Sergii) follows a pattern common to Russian monastic saints: he lives in a coenobitic community for several years before embarking on the life of a hermit. During this stage he is forced to confront the conflict, familiar to hagiography, between obedience and the search for spiritual perfection. Wary of furthering his career (like many an exemplary monk), he would like to refuse to be sent to a prestigious monastery near St. Petersburg. Yet he obediently accedes to the wishes of his elder, who has instructed him that he "must not decline if he is appointed to a higher post" (13–14). The elder's manner here resembles that of the bishop of Sergii of Radonezh, who, when the latter expressed reluctance to become an abbot, rebuked him with the observation that he had learned all the virtues except obedience. Any similarity between the two monks ends here, however. In seeking to avoid monastic honors, Sergii of Radonezh is motivated by genuine humility, while Tolstoy's Sergii is striving to resist temptation; unlike the former, he is secretly ridden by ambition.

[33] *Pss* 23: 4.

Nor does he possess a true sense of humility, but is instead guided by far different feelings. As has been noted, he simply transfers his keen spirit of competition to the monastic sphere.[34] His pride has survived intact his becoming a monk. While the encounter between Sergii of Radonezh and his bishop enhances the impression of the former's saintliness, the analogous episode in "Father Sergii" points to Sergii's growing hypocrisy.

In his new monastery, Sergii's acute sense of his own superiority, aggravated by his violent temper, gives rise to an unpleasant but revealing incident. Angered by what he perceives as the excessive worldliness of his abbot, Sergii exclaims: "Your Reverence, I left the world to save myself from temptation . . . why then do you subject me to it here, during prayers and in the house of God?" (16). Superficially, this question may reflect a pious sentiment, but it also directly contradicts the principle of obedience and, what is worse, betrays excessive pride. Recognizing his error, Sergii asks for guidance from his elder, who recommends that he become a hermit in another monastic community.

In Sergii's life as a hermit, he, like many other hermits, is besieged above all by doubt and lust. As the narrator emphasizes, the two are related, for Sergii is most susceptible to lust when he suffers religious doubts. This struggle leads the aspiring saint to both his greatest victory over the flesh and his most ignominious defeat, in the episodes involving the divorcée Makovkina and the merchant's daughter Mariia.

Immediately before Makovkina's unexpected nocturnal visit, Sergii is tormented by lustful thoughts; he remembers vividly the shoulders of a widow who had once been his mistress. This detail reflects another topos: in the *Historia lausiaca* (Palladius' fifth-century history of the Palestinian monks, which was much read by Russian monks), a monk struggling with temptation is so susceptible to the memory of a girl he once saw that the devil chooses hers as the form in which to approach him. Similarly, Mary of Egypt is tormented in her desert solitude by memories of her life as a harlot.

When Makovkina appears at his door, Sergii at first wonders whether it is true that, as he has read in various Lives, the devil sometimes assumes the form of a woman; Iakov the Faster, who was mentioned earlier, also wonders briefly if his visitor is the devil in disguise. Makov-

[34] T.G.S. Cain, *Tolstoy* (New York, 1977), 147.

kina answers Sergii's unspoken question with the words, "But I am not the devil" (21). Yet when Sergii later succumbs to Mariia's charms, she does not deny his (spoken) accusation that she is the devil, and instead responds enigmatically, "Well, perhaps, never mind" (36). Symbolically, she does constitute a devil for Sergii, much as Stepanida represents a devil for Irtenev in another story by Tolstoy, "The Devil" ("D'iavol," 1889).

Unlike Mariia, Makovkina does not triumph over Sergii, however. He brings about his victory largely through an act of self-inflicted violence: he chops off his forefinger. The pain distracts him from all lustful thoughts and permits him not only to regain his self-control, but also to exert a beneficial influence on Makovkina. She is sufficiently impressed by his action to reevaluate her own existence and a year later enters a convent; this is also true of the harlot who harasses Iakov.

This episode is particularly revealing if contrasted with its possible models. In the story of Iakov, the hermit distracts himself by placing his hand in the fire while conversing with the woman. As was noted in the preceding chapter, a similar occurrence is described in the autobiography of Archpriest Avvakum. Greatly tempted by one of his parishioners while hearing her confession, Avvakum lights three candles and thrusts his hand into the flames, keeping it there while he speaks with the young woman.[35] In his confrontation with Makovkina, Sergii attempts to emulate Iakov, and possibly Avvakum, thinking to himself: "I will go, but as did that father who laid one hand on the fornicatrix, but put the other on the brazier" (25). As his hut contains no brazier, he sticks his hand into the lamp flame, but cannot endure the pain.[36] Instead, he chops off his finger. Victory is thus his for the moment, but Sergii's failure to emulate precisely previous ascetics suggests a lack of moral stamina and points towards his later inability to resist temptation.

After the incident with Makovkina, Sergii's fame increases, as does his apparent virtue. His ascetic practices gradually become more pronounced and eventually he eats only rye bread; the detail lavished on his diet is in keeping with the hagiographical tradition. When his fame reaches its zenith, however, he does not maintain such austere habits.

[35] There is evidence in Tolstoy's published notes to indicate that he was familiar with Avvakum's autobiography. Cf. *Pss* 48: 402, 410–11, 524.

[36] There is a similar episode in "The Devil" ("D'iavol," 1889–1890).

Several years after the episode with Makovkina, Sergii performs his first cure. The manner in which this comes about recalls many saints' Lives. When asked to lay hands on the head of a sick boy, Sergii is initially reluctant because he fears such an action would be morally presumptuous. Remembering the parable of the righteous judge, however, he agrees to pray for the child and consoles himself with the logic dear to saints throughout history, that if a miracle occurs he will merely be the instrument of God's will. Anthony of Egypt expresses the same thought when he tells those for whom he prays "to know that healing belongs neither to him nor to men at all, but only to God."[37] Such thinking enables the saint to preserve a commitment to humility.

Yet naturally others interpret miracles in a different way, attributing them not only to God, but also to the saint who performs them. Thus, as the years pass and Sergii heals more people, other monks come to live nearby and soon a church is built, as well as a hostelry to accommodate his numerous visitors. Eventually Sergii is almost completely deprived of solitude. Unlike Iakov, he does not fear vanity and take himself off to a cave; convinced by church authorities that it would be wrong to turn away those who wish to see him, he gradually subordinates his entire existence to the demands of his visitors. As with many renowned Russian monks, Sergii does not seek the community, the community comes to him. Unlike his saintly precursors, however, Sergii is corrupted in the process.

On the day that Sergii meets Mariia, he celebrates vespers in the nearby church. During the service he feels faint and nearly falls, but insists on continuing, thinking to himself: "that is the way saints do" (30). With gratification he overhears people commenting on his fortitude: "A saint! An angel of God!" (30). Both Sergii and his observers are correct in their appraisal of his external actions. In his apparent refusal to yield to physical weakness, Sergii is indeed behaving like a saint. Sergii of Radonezh, for example, was distinguished in old age by his strength of purpose: "He performed many unfathomable miracles, and reached an advanced age, never failing from his place at divine service; the older his body grew, the stronger grew his fervor, in no way weakened by age."[38] Unfortunately, however, the ostentatious religious

[37] Athanasius, "Vita Antonii," in Jacques Paul Migne, ed., *Patrologia Graeca*, 161 vols. (Paris, 1857–1889), vol. 26, Chapter 56, Column 925b. The translation is mine.

[38] "The Life, Acts, and Miracles of our Reverend and Holy Father Abbot Sergius," in

devotion of Tolstoy's Sergii is purely external, as his complacent awareness of his own praiseworthiness indicates.

An incident after the church service exposes Sergii's less than saintly motives even more clearly. Because he is obviously exhausted, one of the other monks attempts to disperse the crowd of visitors. In a self-consciously virtuous gesture, however, Sergii allows the people to approach. Speaking to them, he is touched by the faintness of his voice—in other words, he is impressed by his own sanctimoniousness. The physical strain is too much for him, but he insists that the crowd not be turned away and, secure in the knowledge that "the crowd would be driven away anyway, . . . he sen[ds] his attendant to speak in order to produce an impression" (32). This observation lays bare the self-serving nature of Sergii's motives; the desire to make an impression, to gain worldly recognition, lies at the root of his actions, as it always has. With justification Sergii himself wonders how much he does for God, how much for people.

The depth of Sergii's corruption is revealed by the ease with which the sensual and weak-minded Mariia seduces him. Before she even comes to his cell, Sergii is curious about her physical charms. In a sense, he is ripe for a fall. This is underscored by the contrast between the languid ploys of Mariia and the more elaborate yet unsuccessful efforts of the much more attractive Makovkina. Sergii is simply no longer capable of resisting temptation; his career as a monk has led, not to spiritual perfection, but to moral corruption and sanctimonious hypocrisy.

A seemingly trivial bit of narrative detail lends support to this interpretation. Sitting outside his cell before Mariia's visit, Sergii is approached by a sparrow, but the bird quickly flies away, "frightened of something" (34). This incident represents a direct contravention of the hagiographical topos which stresses the close rapport between saintly men and dumb creatures.[39] The classic example of this phenomenon is the life of Francis of Assisi, but Russian hagiography boasts its own characteristic incidents; the hermit Pavel of Obnora, who spent many years living in a suitable tree trunk in northern Russia, was found

Medieval Russia's Epics, Chronicles, and Tales, trans. and ed. Serge A. Zenkovsky (New York, 1963), 235.

[39] Such a rapport is intended to recall Adam before the Fall. Cf. Derwas J. Chitty, *The Desert a City: An Introduction to the Study of Egyptian and Palestinian Monasticism under the Christian Empire* (Oxford, 1966), 16.

feeding birds perched on his head and shoulders, while Sergii of Radonezh had a long-standing friendship with a bear.[40] That the opposite occurs in "Father Sergii" is significant. Nature, it seems, cannot be deceived by Sergii, although men may be. The artificiality of Sergii's existence is highlighted by this symbolic exposure, which serves as a prelude to the more explicit unmasking of his true character in the scene with Mariia.

Although Sergii's career ends ignominiously, before he is seduced he is regarded as a saint, and his external behavior does reveal parallels with the Lives of many illustrious Byzantine and Russian monks. As has been seen, this similarity is achieved largely through the adaptation of hagiographical topoi. The difference is that "Father Sergii" often retains only the superficial form of a topos, while substituting a content that represents a radical departure from accepted hagiographical norms. Thus, while medieval hagiographers assume a complete correspondence between motive and action, Tolstoy does not: Sergii's motives for ostensibly virtuous actions are often tainted by selfish concerns. This mixed psychology was alien to many medieval writers, who tended to interpret motives in black and white terms; for example, Iakov is completely virtuous until he succumbs to pride, after which he quickly falls from grace. Tolstoy's hero, however, is always the subject of conflicting desires, even when he appears most saintlike.

The major stumbling block to Sergii's quest for sainthood is that he desires perfection not as an end in itself, but as a means to acquire recognition. Moreover, this weakness in his character leads him into a vicious circle; the more effective his efforts are and the more recognition he achieves, the greater becomes the gap between his saintlike behavior and his increasingly corrupt motives. In a sense, it would have been better for Sergii's soul if he had not successfully resisted Makovkina.

Sergii is clearly not a saint. Indeed, he becomes less and less saintly as time goes by. The use of hagiographical topoi in discussing him might therefore seem inappropriate in a way that their use in characterizing Father Zosima in *The Brothers Karamazov*, for example, does not. The situation is complicated by the fact that often topoi are introduced into "Father Sergii" only to be undermined; their validity as barometers of the soul is constantly called into question. This apparent contradic-

[40] Without referring to Sergii by name, Zosima mentions this episode from his Life in *The Brothers Karamazov*.

tion is resolved and the function of this technique clarified, however, when one sees that Tolstoy's story is not an imitation but rather a critique of a saint's life which aims at an exposé of monasticism.

In "Father Sergii" a hagiographical form is endowed with an antihagiographical content; it is the tale of a sinner told in images traditionally associated with a saint. This technique demonstrates the limitations of hagiography as a narrative form which may overlook internal developments. If one were acquainted only with the external details of Sergii's life before his encounter with Mariia, he would indeed appear to be a saint. By including analysis of the inner processes of Sergii's mind, however, Tolstoy demonstrates that behavior and intent are not necessarily synonymous. In this highly effective fashion he attacks the institution of monasticism from within, as it were.

Hostility towards monasticism is implicit at many points in "Father Sergii." In describing the early stages of Sergii's career as a monk, for example, the narrator suggests that only the practice of obedience towards his elder enables Sergii to bear the tedium of the church services, the irritant of continual visitors, and the moral shortcomings of the other monks. Such observations contribute to a negative evaluation of monastic life, as does the description of the aforementioned abbot, who radiates a gross sensuality and a most unspiritual opportunism. His unsavory portrait is complemented by the addition of a sycophantic sacristan. Much later, after Sergii has achieved fame, one of the most telling details is his realization that because he attracts visitors and donors to the monastery, the monastic authorities arrange things so that he can be "most useful" (28). In other words, they are inspired by the crassest sort of ambition and greed. The authorities cloak their true motives in the guise of Christian charity, however, telling Sergii that he is necessary to people and that, according to the principle of Christian love, he should not avoid people who wish to consult him. Once again, the logic that in a saint's Life would seem pure and unselfish here smacks of sanctimonious cant.

Nor are those who flock to monasteries exempt from criticism. The well-to-do visitors to the metropolitan monastery where Sergii clashes with the abbot seem to lack genuine religious feeling—especially the women, who are interested only in the physical appearance of the monks. Later, Sergii perceives many of the pilgrims who come to visit him as representatives of a "common, most irreligious, cold, conventional type" (31), hardly an accolade. He is disgusted by the number of drunken old soldiers who visit monasteries only in the hope of being given food and by the peasants who come with practical questions about business and family matters. The visitors seem in general to be selfish people with concerns that have little or nothing to do with religion.

Much of this hostility toward monasticism undoubtedly stems from Tolstoy's general and increasing suspicion of ecclesiastical practices and Orthodox theology. It is entirely logical that the man who believed that "of all the godless ideas and words there is no idea or word that is more godless than that of a Church" should be antagonistic towards Orthodox monasticism.[41] The very concept of the contemplative, eremitic life was alien to Tolstoy, who wrote: "there is no calm for him who lives for worldly aims among people, or for him who lives for a spiritual aim alone. Calm occurs only when a person lives for the service of God among people."[42] He also objected to what he perceived as monasticism's dependence on the labor of others, its exploitation of slavery.[43] In their study of "Father Sergii," Harry Walsh and Paul Alessi have documented Tolstoy's distaste for the institution of monasticism, which the writer once described as "spiritual sybaritism."[44] Elsewhere he commented that:

> Some men, seeing in the lessons of Christ a teaching about the salvation of the soul for the sake of a crudely conceived eternal life, have withdrawn from the world, taking pains only about what they should do for themselves, how they should perfect themselves in solitude—which would be ridiculous were it not pitiable. . . . Truth is only in that teaching which points out an activity, a life, which satisfies the needs of the soul, and which is at the same time a constant activity for the good of others.[45]

Moreover, as has been noted, Tolstoy was also sceptical of miracles, and he frowned on the conception of sanctity as detrimental to the ideal of the complete equality of men under religion.[46] This would have made

[41] "Church and State" ("Tserkov' i gosudarstvo," 1902), *Pss* 23: 477.

[42] Diary entry 17 July 1898, *Pss* 53: 204.

[43] Diary entry 28 February 1890, *Pss* 51: 23.

[44] "The *Apophthegmata Patrum* and Tolstoy's *Father Sergius*," *Comparative Literature Studies* 19 (1982): 1–10. Tolstoy's observation was inspired by his visit to Optina Pustyn'.

[45] Cited in George Rapall Noyes, *Tolstoy* (New York, 1918), 250.

[46] Cf., for example, "What is Religion?" ("Chto takoe religiia?" 1901–1902), *Pss* 35: 167–69.

the institution of elders like Sergii, who in nineteenth-century Russia often acquired the status of living saints, especially abhorrent to him.

Tolstoy's antagonism towards monasticism also had a personal basis. On several occasions before writing "Father Sergii," the author visited Optina Pustyn' and the elder Amvrosii.[47] Amvrosii, who is described in "Father Sergii" as the elder of Sergii's first abbot, was the most recent representative of the revitalized monastic tradition initiated by Paisii Velichkovskii.[48] As has been seen, he was much respected by numerous Russian intellectuals, most notably Dostoevsky. Even during the period when Tolstoy dallied briefly with Orthodoxy, however, he found Amvrosii unimpressive at best.[49] In their memoirs, several of his children mention the negative reaction their father had to Optina Pustyn' and its famous elder.[50] Of the monks at Optina Tolstoy commented: "What I saw in Kiev [at the Kievan Cave Monastery] is confirmed—the young novices are holy, God is with them, but the elders are not, the devil is with them."[51] He was also repelled by Amvrosii's visitors. While others were touched by the elder's willingness to discuss the most mundane problems with the peasants, Tolstoy was irritated by the very mention of such concerns in a religious context.[52] Undoubtedly such impressions colored his treatment of both Sergii and his visitors.[53]

[47] Tolstoy's first visit to the monastery took place in 1877, but his most well known visit occurred in 1881. On this occasion, the writer attempted to travel incognito in peasant garb, but the ruse did not succeed.

[48] The suggestion that Amvrosii was the elder of Sergii's first abbot does not seem chronologically likely; Sergii became a monk during the reign of Nicholas I, while Amvrosii did not become an important figure until after the death of his predecessor Makarii in 1861.

[49] An account of Tolstoy's visits to the monastery in 1877 and 1881 is provided in Henri Troyat's biography (*Tolstoy*, trans. Nancy Amphoux [New York, 1967], 464, 496–99).

[50] See Sergei Tolstoy, *Tolstoy Remembered by His Son*, trans. Moura Budberg (New York, 1962), 50; Ilya Tolstoy, *Tolstoy, My Father: Reminiscences*, trans. Ann Dunnigan (Chicago, 1971), 116–17; Alexandra Tolstoy, *Tolstoy: A Life of My Father*, trans. Elizabeth Hapgood (New York, 1973), 221–22, 241–42.

[51] Diary entry 27 February 1890, *Pss* 51: 23.

[52] In an article on visits to Optina by Russian writers ("Optina Pustyn' i palomnichestvo v nee russkikh pisatelei," *Istoricheskii vestnik* 122 [1910]: 327–39), D. P. Bogdanov fondly describes how on one occasion Amvrosii gave detailed advice about the care of turkeys to a peasant woman. It is noteworthy that Bogdanov does not discuss Tolstoy's visits.

[53] One of Tolstoy's visits to Optina Pustyn' took place in 1890, shortly before he

One need not know hagiography to sense Tolstoy's antagonism in "Father Sergii" towards Orthodox monasticism or to grasp the fact that monastic recognition contributes to Sergii's pride and moral corruption. The awareness of the hagiographical subtext of the story, however, does facilitate an appreciation of the full extent of Tolstoy's criticism. "Father Sergii" is not simply the tale of a "bad" monk. Because it demonstrates that an apparently virtuous monk may really be corrupt, it constitutes a more generalized and thus more devastating attack on the monastic way. Thus it casts doubt on the moral integrity of real monks, Amvrosii, for example. The use of hagiographical topoi makes Tolstoy's revelation that beneath the veneer of saintlike gestures may lurk a radically different story all the more damning. "Father Sergii" is not only an exposure of Sergii's personal failings, but also an examination of the entire monastic system, particularly the institution of elders. The monastic way emerges as false; because monastic virtue inevitably draws attention to itself, it leads to living for men, not God. Monasticism culminates, not in a display of virtue, but in virtue on display.

Tolstoy's attack on hagiography does not cease with Sergii's fall. Instead, the ending of "Father Sergii" deviates radically from the traditional hagiographical model in general and the legend of Iakov the Faster in particular. Tolstoy thus rejects the Orthodox conception of salvation and portrays his own version of the good life.

In the legend of Iakov, the monk compounds his sin of fornication by murdering the object of his lust and throwing her body into a river.[54] When he confesses his sins to the brothers at a nearby monastery, they urge him not to despair, but to repent. A sympathetic hermit he meets in the desert also provides encouragement, drawing a parallel with the apostle Peter, who denied Jesus, but later went on to achieve great glory. After Iakov has repented for ten years in a cave, God returns his gift of wonderworking and restores him to his former position. The implication is that Iakov has learned his lesson and hence deserves the rewards of virtue. This is in keeping with the Orthodox tradition expressed by Dostoevsky, for example, that no matter how much one

began work on "Father Sergii." In her reminiscences of her father, Alexandra suggests that this visit probably gave him much material for his story (305). It seems likely that the impressions gained on his earlier visits also played a role in the composition of the story.

[54] At one time Tolstoy also considered having Sergii murder Mariia. Cf. Pletnev, " 'Otets Sergii' i Chet'i Minei," 127.

has sinned, it is still possible to find salvation within the context of the Church.

Father Sergii's end and the lesson to be drawn from it are far different from that described in the Life of Iakov or any other Orthodox saint. What Sergii discovers after leaving the monastery reflects a Tolstoyan conception of virtue. Any hope that Sergii (now once more Kasatskii) still has at this point is embodied in his childhood acquaintance Pashenka. Fortune has not smiled on Pashenka; she has borne the burden of a terrible marriage, the death of her only son, and financial destitution. Kasatskii also remembers that she is ill-equipped to deal with life, being "not exactly stupid, but insipid, insignificant, and pitiful" (37). Yet Pashenka somehow seems to represent his "salvation" (38) and, when an angel instructs Kasatskii in a dream to visit her, he joyfully sets out to do so.

The conditions of Pashenka's life have not greatly improved since Kasatskii last saw her. Yet she is the mainstay of her family, both financially and emotionally. In this she is guided by an instinctive goodness of which she herself is unaware. Instead, she blames herself for her problems: "I've lived a very vile, bad life, and now God is punishing me, and it serves me right. And I live so badly, so badly!" (41). In response to Kasatskii's questioning, she also berates herself for poor religious habits, mentioning her failure to attend church regularly and her tendency to pray mechanically. This detail implicitly underscores the fact that genuine religious feeling is not linked to an observance of the forms of religion.

Kasatskii is impressed by Pashenka's combination of goodness and unaffected humility, and believes that he now understands the significance of his dream: "Pashenka is exactly what I should have been, and what I was not. I lived for people, on the pretext of living for God; and she lives for God, imagining that she lives for people" (44). Kasatskii's realization calls to mind a similar concern expressed by Prince Dmitrii Nekhliudov's inner voice in *Resurrection*: "are you acting as you are acting truly before your conscience, or are you doing this for the sake of people, in order to take pride in yourself before them?"[55] Virtue, Kasatskii reasons, manifests itself in disinterested actions for others. Essential to true virtue is the lack of expectation of reward or praise. As

[55] *Pss* 32: 202.

Kasatskii has so painfully learned, the praise of men can only corrupt. Acting on his newfound knowledge, he sets about creating a life in which he will neither seek nor gain praise.

The fiction of Tolstoy's later years is filled with characters who share Pashenka's self-effacing nature. In the unfinished story, "Mother" ("Mat'," 1891), the narrator describes the tutor Petr Nikiforovich as possessing "the meekness and humility of unconscious Christianity," adding that "he was certain that he could not endure the teaching of Christianity, but meanwhile his entire life was one of selflessness."[56] Petr Nikiforovich's philosophy consists primarily in a belief in active love, in the necessity for serving and improving life. To fulfill his dream of taking as little as possible from others and giving as much as possible of himself, he observes a strict asceticism in regard to clothing and food. He does this not for his own sake, but for others.

The novel *Resurrection* also abounds in characters who live virtuously without even a hint of self-righteousness. The political prisoner Simonson, for example, lives according to an elaborate set of self-established rules that govern every aspect of his behavior. An eccentric, his integrity is nonetheless irreproachable. Characteristically, however, the narrator observes that at the same time Simonson was "extremely shy with people and modest."[57] It is Simonson who exerts a profound influence on the former prostitute Katiusha Maslova. Moreover, Maslova herself comes to embody the same sort of unconscious goodness as does Pashenka. "What a good woman you are," exclaims Nekhliudov, and smiling pitifully through her tears, Katiusha responds: "I, good?"[58]

The goodness embodied in these and other characters in Tolstoy's later fiction has much in common with the kenotic ideal discussed in earlier chapters. A pervasive humility accompanied by a strong tendency towards radical self-abnegation—to the point of eccentricity—is especially characteristic. In fact, in considering the problem of overcoming vanity, Tolstoy came to the same conclusion of many Russian saints: "in order to conquer a concern for human glory, it is necessary to concern oneself with ill fame—you cannot escape holy foolishness [*iurodstvo*]."[59] In a similar vein, he observed:

[56] *Pss* 29: 252–53.
[57] *Pss* 32: 370.
[58] *Pss* 32: 433.
[59] Diary entry 6 August 1890, *Pss* 51: 72.

> It often came into my head, and I have written, that holy foolishness (in Christ), i.e., the intentional representation of oneself as worse than you are, is the highest characteristic of virtue. Now I see that it is not only the highest characteristic, but is the essential first (or rather, second) condition for every good life. As soon as a person frees himself somewhat from the sins of lust, then immediately he deviates and falls into the worse pit of human glory. And just as for training oneself to continence there is a way and methods, . . . thus it is for the struggle with love of fame. And one of the first exercises is . . . not to take advantage of an incident of good glory . . . And this is holy foolishness. It is holy foolishness to pretend to be depraved intentionally . . . not to destroy the bad opinion that has been established and to rejoice in it, as an emancipation from the greatest temptation and the attraction to a true life of fulfilling God, is natural and proper.—This theme must be elaborated in Sergii.[60]

It is ironic that in combatting one model of hagiographic virtue, the author should find inspiration in another. Where his vision of humility departs most noticeably from traditional kenoticism is in its rejection of the need for any link to formal Christianity.

Whether intentionally or not, however, "Father Sergii" demonstrates that total humility is not possible for everyone. The inherent problem with the virtue of the story's end is that it is based not only on the lack of desire for recognition, but on the lack of recognition itself and on ignorance of one's own virtue. Pashenka is truly convinced of her own worthlessness and also receives no appreciation from her family. It is impossible for Kasatskii to duplicate this. Although he develops a technique of leaving a place before people can express their gratitude, there is something artificial about this behavior, for, unlike Pashenka, Kasatskii knows when his actions are laudable. On one occasion, for example, he is especially pleased because he has "scorned the opinion of people. . . . the less significance the opinion of people had, the more strongly God was felt" (46). Is this self-consciousness really so different from what is described earlier in the story?

Kasatskii's grasp and practice of true virtue at the end of "Father Sergii" are not made completely plausible. As one critic has observed, Tolstoy intended Pashenka to "unselve" Sergii, to disarm his powerful

[60] Diary entry 29 May 1893, *Pss* 52: 81–82.

ego, but the attempt did not succeed.[61] The sometime monk remains far too self-aware to acquire Pashenka's brand of humility. He also retains his imposing and impressive personality, and avoidance of recognition is not the same as failure to achieve it. Thus, while the first part of "Father Sergii" constitutes a devastating critique of hagiography and the monastic way of life, the second part is unconvincing as a fable of Tolstoyan Christianity; Kasatskii is no more capable of eradicating his self-consciousness and living "simply" than either Levin of *Anna Karenina* or Olenin of *The Cossacks* (*Kazaki*, 1863) before him.

Leskov's observation that "the *Prolog* is rubbish, but in that rubbish there are pictures such as you couldn't make up" has been mentioned before.[62] To a certain extent, his statement epitomizes the attitude of many of his contemporaries to hagiographical material; above all, saints' Lives provided a wonderful mine of plots, situations, and characters. In "Father Sergii," Tolstoy moves beyond this view of the potential uses of hagiography. As an exploration of the hagiographical personality and the monastic life, "Father Sergii" represents an important commentary on Orthodox conceptions of goodness and is one of Tolstoy's most effective anti-ecclesiastical works. As a corrective to the prevailing assumptions of official hagiography, it is unmatched in nineteenth-century Russian literature. At the same time, however, it demonstrates once again the persistent appeal of kenotic features for the Russian spiritual imagination.

[61] John Bayley, "*King Lear* and *Father Sergius*: A Parallel," *Forum for Modern Language Studies* 4 (1968): 68.

[62] N. S. Leskov, *Ss*, vol. 11 (Moscow, 1958), 362.

CONCLUSION

> Russian literature was born from the "Western injection" and began as an imitation of Western literature; but it became a great world literature, and more than just a literature of modern Christian thinking, only when it ceased to be either Western or Eastern. The more clearly its Christian root was revealed, the more it became simply Russian.
>
> In some mysterious way . . . Russia's primitive Christian Orthodox inspiration turned out to be the soul, the conscience, the profundity of this upper-class Western culture. More than that, what Eastern Orthodoxy alone revealed, sensed, and perceived in the world, in man, and in life became the source of new depths and discoveries in Russian literature.
>
> Alexander Schmemann,
> *The Historical Road of Eastern Orthodoxy*

FROM THE seventeenth century on, Russian literature became increasingly secularized. In terms of attention from the literate public, chronicles tended to yield to histories, sermons to essays, hymns to poetry, and legends and tales to novels and stories. Purely religious literature assumed a subordinate position in regard to the dominant literary trends of the eighteenth and nineteenth centuries. As the preceding chapters have shown, however, one should never overemphasize the gap between medieval and modern Russian culture. There were many bridges between the old and new Russia, not the least of which was the large number of Orthodox saints and the multifarious literature devoted to them.

Within the literary corpus of Old Russia, saints' Lives and other hagiographical works occupied a central position not unlike that of the novel in later Russian literature.[1] As a genre, hagiography afforded monastic authors the opportunity to develop a wide range of narrative

[1] The nineteenth-century philologist Fedor Buslaev drew such a comparison. See Al'bert Opul'skii, *Zhitiia sviatykh v tvorchestve russkikh pisatelei XIX veka* (East Lansing, Mich., 1986), 22.

and didactic motifs. For lay believers, saints' Lives often provided exciting entertainment as well as moral edification. For this reason, perhaps, from their first composition or translation into Church Slavonic up to the present day such literature has consistently intrigued the Russians. The nineteenth-century revival of interest in the medieval period intensified and regenerated this enthusiasm. Equally important given the flight from a traditionally Orthodox conception of culture, is the fact that in the nineteenth century some educated readers conspicuously detached their fondness for hagiographical literature from Orthodox devotion. The appreciation of saints' Lives thus did not necessarily imply a commitment to Orthodoxy. This secularization in turn greatly increased the range of applications of saints' Lives to contemporary literature. Severed from its specific religious moorings, hagiography became a prominent vehicle for the expression of a variety of moral, social, political, and other concerns by writers espousing a diverse set of beliefs.

Why did hagiography prove so attractive to nineteenth-century Russian writers? On the one hand, the answer lies in Leskov's famous comment about the virtues of *Prolog* rubbish. This deliberately provocative assertion points to one longstanding source of appeal of literature devoted to saints—its often unquestionable narrative liveliness. The saints' Lives that acquired the greatest popularity among the Russian common people—like those of the martyr George, Alexis, the Man of God, Mary of Egypt, Nicholas the Wonderworker, Sergii of Radonezh, and the holy fool Vasilii of Moscow—were from one point of view simply exciting stories. Episodes like Alexis abandoning his home and his bride on their wedding night, George slaying the dragon, or Vasilii daring to castigate even the tsar all responded to a love of the spectacular characteristic of unsophisticated readers and listeners. Nor were Russian writers immune to the charms and narrative potential of a gripping plot. From chronicle tales like that of Vasil'ko blinded by jealous fellow princes to legends of the extravagantly repentant harlot Mary of Egypt, poets and novelists throughout the century generally chose to rework those hagiographical works marked by narrative drama.

It would be a mistake, however, to follow Leskov in reducing nineteenth-century Russian literary interest in saints' Lives to a delighted recognition of a treasure-trove of plots. Rather, the core of much hagiography, the nature and signs of sanctity, was itself of burning interest to many members of the educated elite. Radicals and nationalists alike exhibited a predilection for regarding Russia and its culture, those they admired, or their personal credos in a sanctified light. Konstantin Aksakov's comparison of the course of Russian history with a saint's Life, Nikolai Ogarev's poem about Kondratii Ryleev, which epitomized the worshipful devotion granted the Decembrists by subsequent generations of would-be reformers, the dubbing of Dobroliubov as "Saint Nikolai" by his youthful admirers, or the exalted and thinly disguised representation of their own cherished beliefs by writers from Aleksandr Odoevskii to Maxim Gorky—all such displays of histrionic enthusiasm and earnest exaggeration testified to a desire, often uncontaminated by irony, to portray contemporary concerns and historical figures in as venerable a manner as possible.

For authors who wished to portray their subjects in a positive light, hagiography provided a mode of representation and filled a need for readily accessible terms of reference through which to express their own conception of laudable behavior. Believing that they had discovered the contours of sanctity, many Russian intellectuals found in hagiography both corroboration and analogues for their beliefs. Often the perusal of hagiographical literature helped make precise their definition of virtue. Thus, for many Russian thinkers and writers, hagiography was far from a dry legacy of an irrelevant medieval past. Instead, it was a vital, complementary response to immediate concerns. Alexander Herzen's effusions to his future wife regarding the *Reading Menaea*; the exhortations of Fedor Dostoevsky's character Zosima concerning the salutary effects of reading the Lives of Mary of Egypt and Alexis, the Man of God; Gorky's praise of Archpriest Avvakum's personality and language; as well as the many other expressions of approval of hagiographical literature noted in the preceding chapters—all these reveal an appreciation, albeit often idiosyncratic, of hagiography that exceeded the purely historical. Leskov's claim suggests that hagiography represented the raw material from which writers could construct their own moral edifices. While this suggestion has a certain validity, it is also true that for many writers, including Leskov, hagiography provided spiritual models worthy of description or emulation.

As this study has shown, there were three significant approaches in the exploitation of literature devoted to saints: the revision of existing Lives and hagiographical episodes; the creation of new "Lives" through the use of essentially traditional traits and devices; and the antagonistic adaptation of hagiographical conventions in a manner calculated to cast doubt on the ethical validity of saints' Lives. Of these approaches, the most complex was the third, and it is thoroughly developed only in certain stories by Leo Tolstoy. The step-by-step exposure of hagiography's underpinnings demanded a subtle attention to detail and a ruthless grasp of psychology of which few writers were capable. Of course, Tolstoy's desire to heap scorn on everything ecclesiastical was unusually virulent. Presumably most nineteenth-century Russian writers did not want to attack hagiography in such a thoroughgoing fashion. As challenges to the hagiographical tradition, "Father Sergii" and "The Posthumous Notes of the Elder Fedor Kuzmich" are virtually unique. Nonetheless, they comprise an important part of the Russian intellectual response to hagiography, precisely because they are so intimately concerned with the very nature of saints' Lives.

More common than critiques were reworkings of material on saints and princes and productions of what may be called neo-hagiography. The straightforward adaptations of hagiography discussed in this study include: poems (produced largely in the 1820s) devoted to episodes from the lives of saintly princes, whose authors were either Decembrist poets or their sympathizers; the reworkings of legends and tales (written primarily in the 1880s), many of which express a vision of Christianity at times inconsonant with official Orthodoxy; and the various literary versions of the Life of Archpriest Avvakum (composed from the 1880s to the 1970s) that reflect diverse interpretations of the Old Believer's personality and activities. All of these works share a dependence, to one extent or another, on a particular, readily recognizable source or sources. Some of these works do in fact reflect Leskov's dictum regarding the *Prolog*, while others derive not only their subject matter, but also their moral slant from an original source. A major difference between the Decembrist poetry and the other reworkings, however, is that the former often relied on the modified form of hagiography exemplified by Nikolai Karamzin's *History of the Russian State* and thus acquired their hagiographical perspective on the early Russian princes in a mediated fashion.

Another shared feature of many reworkings discussed in this study is their tendentiousness. Very rarely does an author appear to have been motivated by purely aesthetic considerations in revising hagiographical material. Most authors were not simply interested in updating the legends and tales from a linguistic and stylistic point of view. Especially in the nineteenth century, Russian writers selected hagiographical figures and episodes in large part because of their suitability as vehicles for the expression of contemporary concerns. The Decembrist poems of the 1820s and the stories of the 1880s produced by writers like Tolstoy, Leskov, and Vsevolod Garshin differ markedly in their thematic focus, but each group of works reflects a common desire to represent in literary form an ethical scheme—in one instance a program geared largely towards the production of public virtue, in the other of private goodness. A similar purposefulness informs other, isolated reworkings, although it may take forms less pronouncedly ethical; perhaps the best example is Aleksei K. Tolstoy's poem "John Damascene," which is primarily concerned with questions involving the integrity and independence of the artist. Regarding the various poems and stories devoted to Avvakum, while they are not programmatic in nature, some of them exhibit a different sort of tendentiousness, the effort to portray the archpriest in a socially progressive light.

Russian authors' intentions in reworking hagiography were often unabashedly didactic, regardless of whether their focus was primarily civic or private. From Ryleev, with his approving quotation of Julian Niemcewicz's remarks on inculcating a love of homeland through literary representations of laudable historical incidents, to Boris Almazov, who anticipated Leo Tolstoy in producing reworkings explicitly "for the people," to Leskov, with his list of *Prolog* entries containing material suitable for artistic reproduction, Russian writers used saints' Lives in order to edify. As twentieth-century examples like that of Vasilii Fedorov's poem "Avvakum" demonstrate, this tendency has persisted. The reigning purpose of adaptations of hagiography has always conformed, *mutatis mutandis*, to Father Zosima's sentiments about the beneficial impact on simple peasant auditors of certain stories from the New Testament and the Lives of the saints. The urge to reform, to effect social or moral change, lies at the base of many reworkings of hagiographical material.

As mentioned above, however, it would be rash to assume that Russian writers only exploited plots, remaining untouched by other features of their sources. Many writers were influenced in their conception of virtue by the qualities of saintly figures found in the medieval hagiographical repertoire. The Decembrists, for example, often idealized the same virtues ascribed to early Russian princes by the medieval chroniclers, while many writers who borrowed legends from the *Reading Menaea* or the *Prolog* continued to promulgate that self-effacing, untutored spirituality exhibited by some of the saintly personalities described in these compilations. Finally, many modern literary versions of Avvakum's Life approve of the same traits the archpriest clearly admired in himself.

Yet while works like the Decembrist poems devoted to medieval princes or the numerous adaptations from the *Prolog* and the *Menaea* do indeed reflect a traditional conception of virtue, the impact of hagiographical spirituality on modern Russian literature is most evident in the sphere of neo-hagiography, in nineteenth- and twentieth-century works with a contemporary setting whose protagonists resemble saints in their personalities or actions. The examples of neo-hagiography discussed in this study not only exploit the formal elements of hagiography such as familiar topoi, but also give new life to traits which had long been attractive to the Russian spiritual imagination (traits still in evidence in the nineteenth century in monastic elders like Amvrosii of Optina Pustyn'). These two features, the formal and the psychological, often complement one another. In both hagiography and neo-hagiography, for example, the topos of wretched attire is generally associated with particular spiritual characteristics. This is true not only of a medieval work like the Life of Feodosii of the Kievan Cave Monastery, but also of a modern novel like *The Idiot*.

My analysis of Russian neo-hagiography points to three major saintly types who influenced nineteenth- and twentieth-century Russian authors. Two of these types, the kenotic monk and the holy fool, often exhibit overlapping characteristics which derive from exaggerated humility. This kind of spiritual personality appears most commonly in novels and stories by either convinced adherents of Orthodoxy, like Dostoevsky (or, in this century, Alexander Solzhenitsyn), or writers like Leskov who embraced a moral philosophy with strong Christian overtones. Such characters occur undisguised, as, for example, Dostoevsky's Tikhon or Zosima or Leskov's Pamva, or in a transmuted form, as Dostoevsky's Prince Myshkin, Leskov's Golovan, or Uspenskii's Avdot'ia. In the latter instances, the characters are neither monks nor traditional holy fools, but display the behavior and spiritual qualities characteristic of these types.

Kenotic personalities do not occur as positive figures in works by radical, ostensibly atheistic writers. Instead, these writers grant their heroes Josephite virtues, qualities like intransigence and severity, which within the Josephite monastic tradition possess a positive connotation. In works by writers like Gorky and Nikolai Chernyshevskii, these traits are transferred, with a similarly approbatory interpretation, to Russian radicals of the latter half of the nineteenth and early twentieth century. Characters like Gorky's Pavel Vlasov and Chernyshevskii's Rakhmetov may be seen as secularized Josephites, in whom a fanatical devotion to a rigid conception of Orthodoxy has been replaced by an equally passionate and inflexible vision of social progress.

In comparison to adaptations of legends and tales or critiques of saints' Lives, neo-hagiography proved to be a major part of the Russian literary scene. Unlike revisions of hagiographical literature, neo-hagiography did not become so quickly and firmly entrenched in a didactic mold. Nor did it suffer from the aura of esotericism or antiquarianism which characterizes some reworkings. In contrast to works like "Father Sergii" or "The Posthumous Notes of the Elder Fedor Kuzmich," on the other hand, it dealt with a wide range of themes of more general interest. With its contemporary setting and characters and its thematic richness, neo-hagiography attracted a broader audience than the other kinds of use of hagiographical material, in this way exposing the Russian reading public to traditional and conventionalized types of personalities. Some of the most famous Russian novels, like *The Brothers Karamazov* or Boris Pasternak's *Doctor Zhivago*, exhibit signs of the neo-hagiographical approach. Simultaneously, the traits associated with the Josephite type of saintly monk were canonized by official Soviet literature and reoccur to some extent in numerous undistinguished works, whose authors perhaps unconsciously reiterate a centuries-old conception of virtue. Through both literary classics and pedestrian potboilers, hagiography continues to influence the tastes of twentieth-century readers.

The remarkable number of authors who have participated in the modern exploitation of hagiography and the great variety of works they produced assure this field of literary endeavor a significant position in the history of Russian literature. Moreover, the wide range of adaptations of hagiographical writings, critiques of saints' Lives, and productions of neo-hagiography suggests interesting conclusions regarding the nature of Russian literature and culture. Most obviously, the viability of medieval forms as vehicles for modern concerns is amply illustrated by this kind of literature, in which contemporary religious, political, and social questions all find expression. Simultaneously, the modern

Russian works that make use of hagiography confirm a literary as well as a spiritual continuity between medieval and modern Russian literature and culture. The religious traditions and forms embraced by the newly Christianized Russians in the eleventh century remained of critical cultural value to both their Orthodox and secularized descendants.

This study has concentrated on nineteenth-century Russian literary works. As the occasional examples drawn from Soviet literature indicate, however, the interest in and use of hagiography did not cease with the Revolution of 1917. Indeed, within the larger cultural sphere, hagiographical techniques assumed prominence in propagandistic posters and pamphlets of the post-revolutionary years and, in ways that persist to some extent to the present day, in the cult of Vladimir Lenin.[2] "Earlier there were the relics of Sergius of Radonezh and Serafim of Sarov; now they want to replace these with the relics of Vladimir Ilich," complained an outraged Leon Trotsky.[3] In transmogrified form, hagiography continues to thrive at the very heart of official Soviet culture. At the same time, the Orthodox pantheon of saints still commands tremendous respect among true believers: religious centers like the Holy Trinity Monastery founded by Sergii of Radonezh attract countless visitors, some simply curious, others devout, just as in Tolstoy's day. Even holy fools have not disappeared from the Russian scene. In a work written in the early 1960s the popular writer Viktor Nekrasov provides a description of one such fool that calls to mind other, similarly negative accounts of earlier centuries.[4] Most important for the examination of hagiography's impact on modern Russian literature is the revival of interest in the Orthodox heritage among Soviet intellectuals of the past three decades. Such interest may stem from renewed faith, as in the case of Solzhenitsyn. It may be divorced from such commitment, as in the fictional case of Iurii Karlinskii, the cynical defense lawyer in Andrei Siniavskii's satire "The Trial Begins" ("Sud idet,"

[2] On the Lenin cult, see especially Nina Tumarkin, *Lenin Lives!: The Lenin Cult in Soviet Russia* (Cambridge, Mass., 1983). On hagiography and early Soviet propaganda, see Tumarkin, 69, 86.

[3] Nikolai Vol'skii [N. Valentinov], *Novaia ekonomicheskaia politika i krizis partii posle smerti Lenina: gody raboty v VSNX vo vremia NEP; vospominaniia* (Stanford, Cal., 1971), 90–92. Cited in Tumarkin, *Lenin Lives!*, 174–75.

[4] Victor Nekrasov, "On Both Sides of the Ocean," in Patricia Blake and Max Hayward, eds., *Half-way to the Moon: New Writing from Russia* (Garden City, N.Y., 1965), 198–99.

1960): about Karlinskii's livingroom the narrator observes: "There was even a real icon here. Not in the front corner [the traditional Orthodox position], but in a cultivated location—above the radio set, next to a Japanese engraving."[5] Whatever their precise impetus, these familiar cultural developments suggest that the powerful symbiosis between hagiography and modern Russian literature has not yet come to an end.

[5] Andrei Siniavskii [Abram Terts], "Sud idet," in *Fantasticheskii mir Abrama Tertsa* (New York, 1967), 249.

INDEX